Photo by Doris Heyden, 1963

DONALD CORDRY (1907–1978) was an artist, designer, and well-known investigator in the ethnography of Mexican Indians. He brought to this book an extensive knowledge of art history in general and the Pre- and Post-Conquest Mexican codices in particular as well as a background in cultural anthropology. He was the author, with Dorothy Cordry, of *Mexican Indian Costumes* (University of Texas Press, 1968).

CORDRY, Donald Bush. Mexican masks. Texas, 1980. 280p ill maps bibl index 79-22254. 39.95 ISBN 0-292-75050-1. CIP

A truly fine and needed book—well made and rich in information about the significance and function of masks throughout Mexico. Cordry, a thorough researcher, writes with ease about the symbols used in the masks and their relation to Mexico's European and Indian traditions. Masks and mask-makers of recent times as well as masks made in pre-Hispanic years are included. The photographs clearly indicate the workmanship and the materials from which the masks have been fabricated. Each photograph is accompanied by detailed data that facilitate comparisons. Highly recommended for all academic libraries, for the book touches on basic psychological characteristics related to the use of masks and deals with the specifics of masks used throughout the history of Mexcio.

MEXICAN MASKS

by DONALD CORDRY University of Texas Press   Austin and London

LIBRARY OF CONGRESS
CATALOGING IN PUBLICATION DATA

Cordry, Donald Bush.
  Mexican masks.

  Bibliography: p.
  Includes index.
    1. Indians of Mexico—Masks.   2. Masks
—Mexico.   I. Title.
F1219.3.M4C67   731'.75'0972   79-22254
ISBN 0-292-75050-1

Facing title page
1. Possible Devil mask, dance unknown. This
extraordinary mask, carved from a single piece
of hardwood, probably dates from the mid-
nineteenth century. The concept of duality is
indicated by the two faces, with three eyes and
two mouths. Also shown in Fig. 206*b*. Photograph by Carlos López Campos. *Jaleaca, Guerrero; 42 cm.; hardwood, paint.* II.B.D.

FOR DOROTHY
WITH LOVE

The Mexican mask-makers reveal the same plastic vigor which is to be found in African and Oceanic sculpture. Their masks are equally important and comparatively unknown.

(Miguel Covarrubias,
in MEXICAN FOLKWAYS, 5, no. 3
[1929]: 116)

CONTENTS

DONALD CORDRY (1907-1978)

Foreword by Peter T. Furst

TRANSFORMATION was a dominant theme in traditional Mesoamerican thought. It remains so to this day—just below the surface here, overtly there, or deeply buried as a kind of pan–Native American ideological substratum, to which Indian Mexico belongs no less than do the native peoples of the Northwest Coast or Amazonia. From his first venture on horseback into the sierras around Taxco, Guerrero, in 1931, Donald Cordry was fascinated with this fundamental concept, as manifested in Pre-Columbian art and iconography, in sacred myths and folktales, and especially in the carved and painted dance masks he found in Nahuatl-speaking villages that were then—as indeed many still are—far from the mainstream of Mexican national life. In part brought about by an early friendship formed on that initial visit with a very old traditional painter of *retablos*, one of the last of his sacred craft, who also introduced him to masks in their cultural context, his interest in masks became the lifelong passion that has now, nearly fifty years later, culminated in this important work, whose manuscript and splendid photography he completed just before his death in Cuernavaca, Morelos, on August 30, 1978. As these pages demonstrate, from the start their author had the informed vision to perceive in many of these Mexican masks not only the overt Spanish Catholic inspiration, but more distant ancestry in the sacred transformational pageantry of Pre-Hispanic native civilization and, earlier still, the masked dances and propitiatory magic of the shaman as transformer and mediator between the complementary and interdependent worlds of gods, ancestors, animals, plants, and man.

Donald Cordry came to Mexico in the summer of 1931 as one of a small group of artists from Minneapolis. Among them was Dorothy Mann, with whom he had a casual acquaintance as a fellow art student and who five years later, in New York City, became his wife and lifelong collaborator. Mexico now draws millions of tourists every year, and there are paved roads almost everywhere, patrolled by emergency road service crews provided free by the Ministry of Tour-

2. Rastrero mask, Tecuani Dance. The Rastrero (Tracker) and his Dog hunt and kill the Tigre in the Tecuani (Wild Beast) Dance, as well as in the related Tlacololero Dance. The use of possum fur and the painted white-rimmed eyeglasses make this Rastrero very distinctive. *El Potrerillo, Guerrero (Nahua); 40.6 cm., including beard; leather, paint, possum fur.* I.A.C.

ism and flanked by government-owned gas stations open twenty-four hours a day 365 days a year. Every town has tourist accommodations, and jet aircraft connect all regions with the capital. It was very different in the early 1930's, when one could not even drive all the way to Mexico City from the U.S. border, and when Taxco, whose beautiful mountainous setting, picturesque colonial architecture, benign climate, and comfortable accommodations now attract visitors by the thousands each year, had only a small colony of expatriate artists and writers, and one actual hotel. On the hill overlooking the old silver-mining town, where the Hotel Rancho Taxco-Victoria now stands, the artists from the Twin Cities found a spartan little *casa de huespedes* (guest house) operated by a Swedish lady, and it was from here that Donald Cordry, a tall young man of singular physical beauty, set out for the first time on foot and horseback to remote mountain hamlets, few of whose inhabitants could speak or understand anything but their own dialect of Nahuatl, the language of the Aztecs. What they *could* understand and appreciate, however, was their young visitor's interest in and respect for their crafts and their traditions. Donald Cordry had fallen in love at first sight with Indian Mexico, and that love communicated itself across the barriers of language and culture.

Though he often said much later on that he lived "only for beauty," this is not quite accurate. He certainly did love beautiful things and surrounded himself with them (Dorothy herself, by the way, was very attractive as a young woman and now, in her seventies, still retains much of that beauty in combination with intellectual vitality). As a talented and often inspired designer and craftsman Donald was for many years the creator of elegant forms in silver, gold, copper, tin, and other materials that found a ready market inside and outside Mexico (Helena Rubinstein was an early client of his workshop) and that today, three decades later, are still copied by some Mexican craftsmen. But he lived at least as much for information as for esthetics—first-hand wherever possible, from the mask carvers themselves or their descendants and fellow villagers; from the gifted women whom he persuaded to part with their finest embroideries and weavings for his own collections and for museums; from native religious practitioners and traditional storytellers; toward the end of his life, when he was no longer able to travel into the mountains himself, from itinerant Indian traders and merchants in masks and folk art who made his beautiful house (designed by himself) a regular stop; from professional friends with field experience among native peoples; and from his own constantly growing library whose hundreds of books and out-of-print pamphlets on every facet of Mesoamerican art, archaeology, ethnohistory, and ethnology, on the Puebloan cultures of the Southwest, on the peoples and arts of the Arctic, the Northwest Coast, and other Native American societies, made it one of the most comprehensive private research libraries anywhere. (He loved his books, but he was also generous to a fault in lending even rare and valuable editions, and when he had duplicates he often made presents of them to special friends. My own library has been so enriched with several hard-to-find early Mexican ethnographies.)

Donald held no advanced academic degree, but he was one of the few Meso-american scholars who could truthfully claim not only to own but to have read all twelves volumes of Fray Bernardino de Sahagún's monumental sixteenth-century *Florentine Codex*, along with most other published Early Colonial writings on Aztec and other native Mesoamerican religion and ritual, including those of Durán, Motolinía, Torquemada, and Las Casas. There were no boundaries to his intellectual curiosity, no academic straitjacket, no favorite "model" or theoretical bias to confine his inquisitive mind to any one discipline, culture, era, or explanation of cultural facts in his quest for information. Ethnographic, mythological, folkloric, ethnohistoric, and technical documentation was the hallmark of his whole long career as an eclectic collector of "beauty," and it is this, not just the objects themselves (however outstanding their esthetic and technical merit) that gives his collections of masks and indigenous costumes— many now owned by major museums—their special value. In this book, of course, the essential documentation of the illustrated works of art is considerably enriched by broad comparative analysis and discussion, based on his extensive ethnographic knowledge within and beyond the boundaries of Mexico.

Donald Cordry's autodidactic career as a careful and scholarly ethnographer of the arts and crafts of Indian Mexico might be less remarkable had it been the fruit of a particularly stimulating early home environment with deeply understanding parental inspiration and encouragement. This was not the case, however. Quite on his own, Donald developed an insatiable hunger for literature, especially of the documentary kind. As a teenager he painted theatrical scenery during summer vacations and spent his earnings on books and, eventually, on tools, paints, and materials with which to create a world of miniature theater uniquely his own. He enrolled in the Minneapolis Institute of Art, where, for four years or so, he was ever the nonconformist, but where he also absorbed technical proficiency in a large variety of materials. With his parents' basement as studio-workshop-theater, he experimented with different forms and techniques of puppetry. In his early twenties, he carved many extraordinary wooden marionettes and hand puppets with which he gave much-admired public performances in and around the Twin Cities until 1934. His puppets came to the attention of Paul McPharlin, Blanding Sloan, Martin Stevens, and Tony Sarg for their individuality, outstanding design, and mechanical excellence. Donald was never one to rest on his laurels, devouring every book and journal dealing with puppetry, and every review, description, and even the briefest notice of other puppet shows, to see what he might learn from them. He became an enthusiastic collector of modern and antique puppets from around the world, especially the remarkable shadow play puppets of Indonesia, China, and Southern Asia, where shadow plays performed with flat, translucent, articulated puppets have long been a major cultural tradition. At his death his collection still included some fine Javanese shadow puppets acquired more than fifty years earlier.

He never lost that intense early fascination with puppetry, for in 1951, shortly before a bout with the painful *Herpes zoster* virus (for which medicine still has no answer) left him with half his face paralyzed, he again began carving large marionettes that are real works of art and with which he hoped to give performances for Mexican children in Cuernavaca. It was a dream not to be fulfilled, for in 1953 he suffered a massive stroke that left him confined with one side of his body paralyzed for over eighteen months and from which—though he did not allow it to hinder research, writing, and even more research in the field, to the very end of his life—he never fully recovered. Fortunately, some of his consummate knowledge of the history, art, and technology of puppetry is preserved in the extensive correspondence between him and Paul McPharlin, now housed in the Detroit Institute of Arts. His own puppets, some of which are in private collections and in one European museum, have been published in various puppetry journals. There is obviously a direct relationship between this early and, indeed, lifelong interest in puppetry and his fascination with Mexican masks and the articulated *maromeros* (see Fig. 110) and other puppetlike components of Mexican religious pageantry.

In 1934, with Mexico as a permanent home still a remote dream, Donald Cordry felt the need to broaden his experience. Putting his own creations away, he moved to New York, where by then Dorothy Mann was also living and working as an artist. He was immediately hired as puppet designer and puppeteer by Tony Sarg, traveling with that famous company, teaching its summer workshop, and making all the marionettes for its productions. But he had not forgotten his first exposure to the transformational masks of Guerrero, and began to look through the museums and libraries of the city for Mexican masks and whatever might have been written about their history and meaning. He found almost nothing. He thought perhaps George Heye's growing collection of American Indian art and artifacts might include masks from Mexico or that Heye might be able to give him information. Instead, Heye suggested that Donald return to Mexico to collect dance masks and other arts and crafts for the Heye Foundation (now the Museum of the American Indian), a commission he enthusiastically accepted, although the proffered stipend was modest even by the standards of the 1930's. For six months, in 1935, Donald scoured the mountains of Michoacán and Guerrero on foot and horseback, laying the foundation for the Museum's extensive collections of Mexican ethnographica. He returned to New York, Tony Sarg, and, eventually, Dorothy Mann, more taken with Indian Mexico than ever. In 1936 he and Dorothy were married. There was little money, but Mexico remained for both a powerful magnet.

In 1937, the Cordrys set out for an extensive ethnographic collecting trip to the rugged Huichol territory in the Sierra Madre Occidental in Jalisco and Nayarit, an expedition on foot and horseback under the auspices of the Heye Foundation in New York and the National Museum of Anthropology and History in Mexico City that was to last nearly six months. When I began my own studies of Huichol religion, ritual, and art in the mid-1960's, the Huichols were still relatively isolated and their traditions largely unmodified by modernization. Some of their most important rituals, particularly the long pilgrimage undertaken in the dry season by small groups of the most devout Huichols to collect the divine peyote cactus in the high desert of north-central Mexico, some three hundred miles to the east, were still essentially unknown to the outside world, except for a brief second-hand account published by the Norwegian ethnographer Carl Lumholtz at the turn of the century. But there were several airstrips located on high mesas amid the steep Huichol mountains, and, though unpaved, these permitted relatively easy access to the Indian country, the flight from Tepic in small (and not always very trustworthy) planes taking little more than an hour. In the Cordrys' day, as in the earlier time of Lumholtz, Konrad Theodor Preuss, Leon Diguet, and, in 1934–1935, Robert M. Zingg, there was only one way to travel in and out of Huichol country—on foot or horseback, along steep mountain trails, up and down the nearly perpendicular sides of deep canyons and across streams whose velocity and depth in the rainy season sometimes interrupted all communication for months at a time. Under the best of conditions, the trip from Tepic, the capital of the small West Mexican state of Nayarit, into the Huichol country took five or six days, on horses that had to be purchased from traders living on the western slopes of the sierra. There is a chronic shortage of food in the sierra, especially in the weeks before the harvest, but the year 1937 was a particularly hard one for the Indians, who were then as now, in the majority, subsistence maize farmers who plant their small milpas with the traditional *koa*, or digging stick. It was a difficult time also for the ethnographer-collectors, and the Cordrys often spent considerable time in search of food for themselves and for their horses. They had found that money had little utility for the Indians in their own environment; instead, having first observed what Huichols came down from the sierra to Tepic to buy, they took the tiny ceramic beads favored by women and men for their superbly crafted bead necklaces, wristbands, and ear ornaments, needles and thread, colored cotton yarn for embroidery (another craft at which Huichol women excelled, then as now), mirrors, coffee, and a few other staples to exchange for Huichol arts and crafts. In terms of collecting, photographing, and recording ethnographic data, those six months were an enormously rich experience for the Cordrys, one from which Mexican ethnography still benefits. Donald's Huichol photographs (he was even then a photographer of thoroughly professional accomplishment) of Huichol life are of inestimable value, not only directly for Huichol studies over time, but for comparative ethnography as well. They provide valuable pictorial evidence of extraordinary cultural stability from the time of Lumholtz, who studied the culture and collected its art and artifacts for the American Museum of Natural History in the last decade of the nineteenth century, to the present. Somewhat unexpectedly, they have also been of use in the interpretation of Mixtec symbolism. One of the Huichol rites in which the Cordrys were participant observers, and which Donald recorded on film, was the ceremony of the Drum and the First Fruits, which the Huichols call Tatéi Néirra, meaning the celebration or fiesta of Our Mother (the Drum). In this ritual, young children up to the age of five, magically protected by the colored thread crosses that have become known (erroneously) as "god's eyes," and metaphorically transformed into birds, are wafted into the sky on the sound of the shaman's drum on a celestial journey to Wirikúta, the sacred land of the peyote in the high desert of San Luis Potosí, in north-central Mexico. The symbol of this magical journey, which introduces the children to the tradition of the peyote pilgrimage, is a cord of ixtle (sisal) fiber, to which is attached a row of small cotton balls representing the clouds. These, in turn, are manifestations of the Rain Mothers of the four directions, and in another Huichol ritual are also represented by popcorn. A strikingly similar "sky rope," also festooned with cotton, is depicted in two Pre-Hispanic Mixtec codices, Codex Vienna and Codex Zouche-Nuttall, where the same rope represents the path traveled between sky and earth by the culture hero 9 Wind and a pair of divine ancestors, respectively. Lumholtz also observed the sisal string with its cotton puffs, but the unmistakable analogy between this sacred Huichol symbol, still employed today, and its Mixtec counterpart of six or seven centuries ago was recognized only recently by comparison of Donald Cordry's photograph of the ceremony, published in 1968 in the Cordrys' monumental study *Mexican Indian Costumes*, with the Pre-Conquest pictorial manuscripts.

The Cordrys also made it to the neighboring Cora country, but their most extensive collections were of embroidered Huichol men's and women's costumes, long belts of undyed brown and white wool representing serpents (worn only by men but probably derived from the serpent belts that characterize Pre-Hispanic Mother Goddesses), beadwork, thread crosses, votive gourds decorated with wool yarn, wax images of animals and people, glass and ceramic bead work, disks of soft stone with painted or incised images of deities and other sacred beings, effigies of supernaturals, shaman's chairs and their miniature counterparts made for the gods, deer snares, home-made violins, guitars and drums, reed flutes, hunting bows and arrows and bows used to make magical music with which to "charm" deer and other game, and a hundred other items from the material and sacred inventory of Huichol culture. It was an important collection in and of itself, and it was to set the standard for much of Donald's collecting activities among Mexican Indians. What he did not find—because they did not exist—were Huichol dance masks comparable to those he had previously collected in Guerrero and Michoacán, with the single exception of a somewhat crude, unpainted wooden mask representing Great-Grandmother Nakawé, the fundamental old Huichol earth goddess, some of whose magical activities as creator-transformer in Huichol origin mythology Donald recognized as strikingly similar to those of the Puebloan Spider Grandmother. More recently I did find one more supernatural being represented by a single mask—the divine Deer whom the Huichols address as Elder Brother. His likeness was actually the dried facial skin of a real deer, with the antlers still attached and the empty eye sockets serving as eyeholes for the wearer. (Donald Cordry collected one such mask, which he kept for himself and treasured for many years.) That this was indeed a real mask, to be worn and not just suspended by a string in some sacred locale, was evident from the cotton gauze pads sewn to the inside to protect the wearer's forehead and nose from being chafed. I was told, however, that this type of mask is very rare indeed; and, in fact, Huichols rely almost exclusively on face painting (see Fig. 108) as a mark of transformation into divine ancestors or gods. As Donald Cordry notes in these pages, the flat wooden Huichol masks gaudily painted with symbols resembling those used in sacred face painting on the peyote pilgrimage are made strictly for the tourist trade and are never employed in the native setting. In any event, masks as vehicles of transformation were found to be so rare in Huichol ritual as to effectively exclude that most traditional of indigenous societies in Mexico from the Mesoamerican masking complex—unless, of course, one sees face painting as simply a fugitive or ephemeral version of the more permanent masks that can be and are used over and over, sometimes for many generations.

But with or without removable masks, as Donald Cordry recognized, the concept of transformation runs through and even dominates all of Huichol belief and ritual. Cordry was particularly interested in an origin tradition which links the Dog Wife motif, shared by a number of North Mexican peoples with semi-nomadic Desert Culture antecedents, with the story of the destruction of a previous world by water, and which also illuminates the functional interrelationship of the facial mask and the outer garment with transformation. Because it exemplifies both the traditional concept of transformation by means of assuming or discarding another's outer garment or likeness and the qualitative equivalence of humans and animals, it is worth recounting in some detail:

In ancient times a man, whom my informant called Watákame, Clearer of Fields, went into the brush to clear land for planting. He cut down many trees and made them ready for burning. When he returned the following morning, all the trees had been put back in their place, standing upright, with their foliage intact. He thought to himself, "Some animals must be doing this thing. All my work for nothing." Again he cut many trees and piled them up for burning. The following day it was the same: all his work had gone for nothing and the trees were again standing upright. Angry and frustrated, he once more felled trees and cut brush. On the third morning he found everything as it had been before. This time he asked Great-Grandmother Nakawé, the old goddess of the earth, who was playing these tricks on him. She replied, "There is no use to go on, because everything will be covered with water." She told him to cut down a wild fig tree and make a watertight box from its trunk. Then she gave him five kernels of maize—blue, white, yellow, red, and multicolored—five beans, and five seeds of different species of squash. For his companion Nakawé gave him a small black female dog with a white spot on its throat. When the waters rose, she sealed Watákame, the dog, and the seeds inside the box, seated herself on top, and poled and paddled to the four sacred cardinal points, south, north, east, and west. In each of the four directions they found the ancient people singing and dancing to hold back the waters, but to no avail. From the Nanáwata and other doomed peoples they learned the dance of the yarn balls and other ancient dances that are still performed on the reed flute and the drum made from the hunting bow and a hollow gourd. When dry land reappeared, Nakawé fashioned images of plants and animals which she brought to life with her staff, her magical weaving, and her songs. She found a rock shelter for Watákame and his dog and told him to clear new land for the seeds she had given him. He was sad because all his fellow Héwi people had drowned and he had no one but the little dog as companion and no woman to make his tortillas and *atole* (maize gruel) and bear his children. Nakawé said that when he had cleared land he could make people come out of his fingers, but he continued to be sad.

In the morning Watákame emerged from his cave to clear land with his stone hatchet. The little dog would run a little way with him and return to the shelter. When he came home hot, tired, and hungry, thinking that there would be nothing for him to eat, the little dog greeted him joyously, jumping up and down, and leading him into the cave. Awaiting him by the fire was a stack of hot tortillas and a bowl of *atole*. "How can this be?" he wondered. "I have no wife to make these things for me. There is only this little dog." But he ate his fill and went to sleep. The following day he again found tortillas and *atole* waiting for him, and again the next. That night he asked Nakawé, who appeared as a little old white-haired woman carrying her staff of bamboo root, how this could be when he was alone and there was no woman to make these things for him. She said, "Tomorrow leave as though you were going to the field, but really hide behind a tree and see what happens." The next morning he hid behind the tree and watched as the little dog barked a few times and disappeared into the cave. A few moments later he was surprised to see a young woman, black of skin, emerge with a container to fetch water from the nearby stream. He watched until she had gone from sight and again asked Nakawé, "How can this be? There is only a dog in there." The old goddess told him to enter the cave and see what he could find. Inside, beside the hearth, he found the skin of the dog, whose animal owner was nowhere to be seen. On Nakawé's instructions, he put the skin in the fire, and, as he did so, he heard plaintive cries from the river, "Ah, no, you are burning me, you are burning me!" Quickly he took the white *nixtamal* water in which maize had been soaking in lime and threw it over the burning woman, who came running to try and save her discarded skin. The lime water made her lighter, which is why Indians have skin neither black nor white but of a color somewhere in between.

Her old skin consumed by the fire, Dog Woman was unable to return to her animal form. She remained human and bore him many children. Thus she became the divine female ancestor of the Huichol people.

The Huichol tradition is obviously related to the widespread "Swan Maiden" motif, shared as myth or popular folktale by many people throughout the world. The linkage of the motif, invariably involving marriage to some animal or bird transformed into human shape through the loss of its fur or feather cloak, to the universal deluge, however, seems to be characteristically American Indian, occurring in both North and South America; in South American mythology, for example, a pair of male culture heroes, sole human survivors of the Flood, marry a pair of Parrot Girls whose feathers they steal and destroy or hide to prevent their return to their original bird shape. More to the point, the Huichols are at least in part the descendants of the northern desert-dwellers collectively known as Chichimeca, loosely meaning "Lineage of the Dog," and it was the interesting and entirely plausible suggestion of the Mexican ethnohistorian Wigberto Jiménez Moreno that it is their common tradition of the dog as female ancestor that gave the Chichimecs—to whom the Aztecs, too, traced their origin—their name. An interesting question that always intrigued Donald Cordry is whether any of the dog masks used in ritual dances in both Mexico and Guatemala ultimately bear some relationship to the Pre-Hispanic dog-as-ancestor tradition.

The absence of masks in the otherwise highly developed mythological and ritual transformation complex among the Huichols hardly mattered, of course, in the face of the wealth of other symbolic arts for which the Huichols are justly famed, particularly in woven and embroidered textiles (the colorful yarn paintings are a more recent development, mainly in response to the growing market for native arts and crafts inside and outside Mexico). In fact, Donald's determination to publish, before it was too late, a major study of the traditional costumes of the principal Mexican Indian populations, including their history, cultural context, technology, and symbolism, first took shape while photographing Huichol women at their backstrap looms and learning something of the magical power of the loom, its parts, and the symbolic designs produced with them—indeed, the whole complex relationship of weaving and weaving tools to female and agricultural fertility—in the Huichol belief system.

Following the Huichol field experience, Donald Cordry added the Southwest Museum in Los Angeles, with its extensive collections of American Indian art and ethnographica, to the list of major U.S. institutions with which he had a working relationship. He and Dorothy collaborated on two important monographs based on their field work in Puebla and Chiapas in 1939 and 1940, *Costumes and Textiles of the Aztec Indians of the Cuetzalan Region, Puebla, Mexico,* and *Costumes and Weaving of the Zoque Indians of Chiapas, Mexico,* published in 1940 and 1941 as Southwest Museum Papers 14 and 15.

In 1941 the Cordrys went to Oaxaca on the occasion of the great Indian State Fair that drew tens of thousands of indigenous people from all over that most Indian of states in the Mexican federal republic. Largely because of its numerous different indigenous groups and the considerable survival of traditional beliefs and arts and crafts among them, the Cordrys decided to settle in Oaxaca, and there, in 1942, Donald founded the workshop that produced, first in Oaxaca and later in Mexico City and Cuernavaca, for almost twelve years and with never more than a handful of native craftsmen to help him, Donald's creative designs in jewelry, screens, lamps, furniture, silver and other metalware, statuary, mirrors, featherwork, and all sorts of elegant articles, many of them noteworthy for the unexpected ways in which he managed to combine the old and the new and traditional crafts with modern forms and materials. Donald was a prolific and resourceful designer and craftsman, but essentially the workshop was always a means to an end, the end being the financing of innumerable forays into the remote hinterlands to collect and record ethnographic data. Over the years, the Cordrys spent time with more than a third of Mexico's seventy or so surviving indigenous populations, including the Seris and Mayos in the north; Huichols and Coras in Jalisco and Nayarit; Tarascans in Michoacán; Mazahuas and Otomís in the state of Mexico; Huastecs, Tepehuas, and Totonacs in Veracruz; Mazatecs, Cuicatecs, Chinantecs, Zapotecs, Mixes, Mixtecs, Triques, Tlapanecs, and Amuzgos in Oaxaca and neighboring Guerrero; Zoques in Chiapas, as well as Tzotzils and other Maya-speakers; and speakers of Nahua dialects in different parts of the country, including the mountains of Guerrero and the Sierra de Puebla.

In 1944, the workshop was moved to Mixcoac, in Mexico City, a move in part necessitated by the market: Oaxaca lacked many needed materials, and sales were mainly in the capital. But the real impetus was access to the archival and anthropological literature in the Mexican capital, as well as the extensive museum collections and the intellectual stimulation of contact with other scholars and aficionados of Mexican prehistory, art, and ethnology. A close friendship also developed between Donald and Miguel Covarrubias that was to last until the latter's death in 1957. Covarrubias was a major influence on Donald Cordry, who was greatly impressed by the Mexican painter's understanding of his nation's prehistory and art and his almost intuitive insistence, in the face of strenuous opposition from some U.S. archaeologists, that the Olmecs belonged in the first millennium B.C. as Mesoamerica's "mother civilization" rather than being, as some then still thought, a late aberration of Maya civilization. Covarrubias, in turn, was at least equally impressed by Cordry's scholarly enthusiasm and determination to preserve on film, on paper, and in museum collections as much as possible of the arts and crafts of Indian Mexico before it was too late. Covarrubias was to use many of Donald's superb Mexican Indian photographs in his *Mexico South* (1947), as was Frances Toor in *Treasury of Mexican Folkways* (1947), which also reproduced Huichol and Zoque folktales recorded by Donald during his travels in the Sierra Madre Occidental and Chiapas. The high altitude of the Mexican capital was increasingly hard for Donald, however, and in 1949 the Cordrys made their final move, this time to Tlaltenango, then a largely rural community surrounded by milpas and orchards but since absorbed as a barrio into the rapidly expanding city of Cuernavaca, an hour by car over a ten-thousand-foot pass south of the capital.

Donald was only forty-five when, in 1953, he suffered the stroke that closed the workshop forever and that, for too long, removed him from active research and photography in the field. But, mainly by sheer willpower, he bounced back from semiparalysis, and by the mid-1950's was already beginning to organize the hundreds of black and white and color photographs and the text for what was to become a classic in modern ethnographic scholarship, the Cordrys' *Mexican Indian Costumes*, published by the University of Texas Press in 1968. Not only the rich ethnographic, ethnohistorical, and technical documentation in that book but especially Donald's superb pictorial ethnography, much of it depicting customs and costumes that have since become rare—if they have not disappeared altogether—earned high praise; Covarrubias in his Foreword contrasted it favorably with the purely artistic *tours de force* of so many photographic essays on Mexico that emphasize the picturesque, on the one hand, and the purely scientific, on the other:

> *Donald Cordry's photographs do not belong to any of these categories; rather they partake of the best qualities of all of them. In a strictly photographic sense they rank with the best work of the modern photographers who have turned their cameras on the Mexican scene, for they are striking, dramatic, and always beautiful pictures. They possess, in addition, a direct human appeal that derives from the uncomplicated honesty of Cordry's approach. To a surprising degree they succeed in capturing the serenity, mystery, and monumental plasticity of his subjects. But more than this, they constitute an invaluable portrait of remote and little-known peoples who prefer their ancient modes and manners to a modern world about which they know little and care less, and against which their only defense is a stubborn refusal to abandon their antique ways of life.*

The work received instant acclaim, and shortly after its publication Donald was honored by the Mexican government with the Sahagún Medal, a coveted recognition awarded by the Instituto Nacional de Antropología e Historia and the Museo Nacional de Antropología for the most distinguished contributions to Mexican scholarship. Donald Cordry, ex-puppeteer and craftsman, self-taught ethnographer of indigenous *traje* and masks, thus joined the company of North American and European expatriate scholars who made Mexico home and who have made, or are making, lasting contributions to Mesoamerican anthropology and ethnohistory. Paul Kirchhoff and Roberto J. Weitlaner (whom everyone called "Papa" and who, just before his death in the ninth decade of a long and productive career that took him from engineering into ethnography, was still planning forays on horseback into remote Indian communities in Oaxaca and Guerrero), come to mind here, as well as the latter's daughter Irmgard Weitlaner Johnson, Howard Barlow, Gutierre Tibón, Isabel Kelly, Barbro Dahlgren de Jordan, Bodil Christensen, Doris Heyden, Nigel Davies, Thelma Sullivan, and others of past and present accomplishments.

With the exception of a three-month-long study and collecting trip to the Cuna Indians of Panama and Colombia in 1969 and one long mask expedition to Guerrero in 1975, from the 1950's on, ill health and lack of travel funds largely confined Donald to his Cuernavaca home. It was an inspiring confinement, to be sure, for the whole world (or so it seemed to the visitor) was represented within its walls—in his books and his eclectic collection, which ranged from Thai and Indonesian puppets to Cuna shaman's paraphernalia, Australian aborigine bark paintings, Eskimo ivories, North American Indian baskets, Navaho blankets, Indian and Chinese Buddhas, Spanish colonial *santos*, West African and Oceanic ancestor figures, antique Talavera tiles, paintings and graphics by modern Mexican artists, seashells, Oriental furniture, as well as his own designs, and, of course, the constantly growing mask collection so brilliantly represented in this book, whose completion Donald knew all too well was a matter of increasing urgency and his consuming passion in the last years and weeks of his life. The collection of *molas* and other Cuna arts and crafts, as well as shaman's curing chants and oral traditions (many, incidentally, from the same informant who worked with the noted Swedish ethnographer Baron Erland Nordenskiöld in the 1930's) constitutes the major unfinished work of Donald Cordry's career—that, and a unique, well-documented collection of wooden dolls which Mexican Indian fathers used to carve for their children before plastic toys flooded even the remotest regions and which Donald collected in the 1930's and 1940's. Both these studies Dorothy Cordry, who participated in all of Donald's field research, hopes to complete for eventual publication.

"The first time I ever saw Donald was at a picnic of artists and art students in Minneapolis in 1928," she recalled recently. "While everyone else at the picnic was gathered in groups either talking or eating, I noticed Donald by himself over near the woods, turning over a log and studying what was underneath. He then put it back the way he found it and went on to look under the next."

He was like that all his life, always his own person, always turning over one more log to see what was underneath, never content with just the surface. But he was also very much driven by the thought that the beautiful things that were so exciting to him and that he was trying to make known, and the traditions that lay behind them, were all going to disappear soon and that if he did not make some contribution to preserving them they would all be lost and forgotten.

Donald Cordry has more than made that contribution.

PREFACE AND ACKNOWLEDGMENTS

MASKS were my first interest in Mexico. As an investigator during the summer of 1931, I made forays by horse into the mountains of Guerrero and discovered the marvelous masks there. Later I was asked by Dr. George G. Heye of the Heye Foundation Museum of the American Indian to make a long trip to investigate and collect masks in Michoacán and Guerrero. I am indebted to the late Dr. Heye for this experience during six months in 1935 and for subsequent study, research, and employment in the Museum in New York.

Until I began this book, my work with masks was intermittent over the years due to my work in other areas of Mexican Indian ethnology. The field work for these other studies did allow me to become familiar with the masks of the Yaquis and Mayos in Sonora; the Huichols of Nayarit; the Nahuas and other groups of Guerrero; the Tarascans of Michoacán; the Nahuas of the Cuetzalan area of Puebla; some of the Indian groups of Oaxaca; the Zoque Indians of Chiapas, as well as the Chiapanecs of Chiapa de Corzo, Chiapas; and the *santeros* (sculptors of church figures and masks) of Tlaxcala, who produce the extraordinary Carnival and Holy Week masks of that state.

Because of the richness of the Mexican folk art heritage, it is impossible to cover the entire country in any depth in one lifetime. This means that there are great gaps of whole states where I have not personally been able to investigate. Friends, who are mentioned below, have provided great assistance in helping me gather this missing information, since I can no longer travel extensively and each day brings the further disappearance of all things indigenous.

I should hasten to add that not all of the romance and glamour of the Indian Mexico has fled. In some ways, it is even more accessible now than before, because it is now possible to reach by road many indigenous areas that previously could be reached only by horseback. Then, too, in the thirties and forties, small planes were not commonly available. There still remain large areas in Mexico that are relatively unknown. There is one large section in Guerrero, for example, where Tlapanec and Popoloca languages are spoken and where people still live in tiny mountain settlements called *cuadrillas*. While these *cuadrillas* do not have electricity or even a marketplace, they have produced some of Mexico's finest mask-makers, such as José Rodríguez.

Generally, however, the heyday of the mask in Mexico is over. Fewer masks are being made, and these are often of far less impressive quality than formerly. Many masks are now made not for the Indians' use but to sell commercially. As Mexico becomes more modernized and its people more culturally homogenized, the deep significance that the mask formerly had will recede. Consequently, my quest has been to preserve and record Mexican masks, their significance, and their links to their Pre-Columbian ancestors.

ACKNOWLEDGMENTS

Because of the diversity of Mexico, its people, and its accomplishments in all of the plastic arts, a project of this magnitude depends upon the efforts and the interest of a great number of people. In particular, I would like to thank my good friend Larry Walsh for his editorial services in organizing this material and in providing continuity within the text; his interest and labors were an invaluable aid.

Likewise, I thank Thelma D. Sullivan, the Classical Nahuatl scholar, with her great knowledge of the Mexican codices, and Doris Heyden with her archaeological and ethnological knowledge, both of whom gave freely of their time in reviewing this manuscript.

Other scholars to whom I extend my gratitude are Dr. Isabel Kelly; Dr. Fernando Horcasitas; Professor Alfonso Medellín Zemil and Professor García Williams, both of Jalapa; Dr. Peter Furst, for his continued interest in my project; Dr. Donald B. Goodall; Julie Jones of the Museum of Primitive Art; Dr. Junius Bird; Dr. María Teresa Sepúlveda of the National Museum of Anthropology of Mexico; Miss Caroline Czitrom, archaeologist; and Dr. Magali Carrera, art historian.

I also extend my thanks to Sra. María Teresa Pomar, Director of the Museo Nacional de Artes e Industrias Populares del INI, who not only lent masks for my study but provided assistance with my survey of forty-six contemporary mask-makers. I am indebted to Dr. Ruth Lechuga, Eduardo Dagash, Lucina Cárdenas, and Marta Turok for their written accounts, photographs, and information, which have added much to this book. For similar services, I also wish to thank Anita Jones, Marcos Ortiz, Walter "Chip" Morris, Toni Beatty, Dr. Enrique Campos Chávez of Chilapa, Tom Lee, and the late Guillermo Echaniz and his wife for their help in obtaining rare reference materials.

My old friends—the late Miguel Covarrubias, Malu Cebrera de Block, Mitchell Wilder, Paul Pérez, Cayuqui Estage, and Janet Esser—have brought invaluable enthusiasm regarding both masks and a book about them. Dr. Max Saltzman has generously given his services in chemical analysis of materials. In particular, I would like to thank Marilyn Olen for her untiring assistance with translations and typing. While it is impossible to list all of the people who have aided me in this study, I would like to extend special thanks to Cuauhtemoc and his people for making this book possible.

Last and most important, I would like to express my gratitude to my wife, Dorothy, for her patient help in so many areas of this mask project, which has occupied us for all of ten years. She alone gave me the support and courage to complete this book.

Donald Cordry
Cuernavaca, Mexico, 1978

Publisher's Note

The manuscript of *Mexican Masks* was completed by Donald Cordry shortly before his death on August 30, 1978. In publishing the book, the Press has received invaluable help from the author's wife, Dorothy Mann Cordry, who took on the responsibility for checking copy and proofs, securing permissions, and answering innumerable questions. Her contribution to the book has been substantial, and we are grateful.

Note on the Illustrations

All illustrations, including color photographs, black and white photographs, and line drawings, are numbered in one sequence and referred to in the text as Figures.

The following information, or as much of it as is available, is given at the end of the caption for most photographs that show masks or other art objects: place of origin or use (with name of Indian group in some cases); measurement (always height unless otherwise specified); materials used; and a coded reference to the Mask Classification System described below.

Except where otherwise indicated, photographs are by Donald Cordry and masks are from the Cordry collection.

Where a photograph shows more than one mask, the individual masks are referred to by letters, moving from left to right and from the top row to the bottom row, as in the following examples:

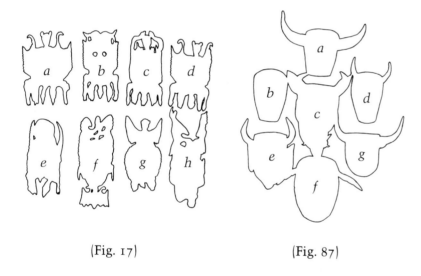

(Fig. 17)   (Fig. 87)

MASK CLASSIFICATION SYSTEM

In order to facilitate comparisons and understanding of Mexican masks, the figure captions include coded references to the following classification system.

I. Anthropomorphic
   A. Realistic
   B. Disproportionate or exaggerated
   C. Single human
   D. One or more humans with additional human elements

II. Anthropomorphic with zoomorphic elements
   A. Realistic
   B. Disproportionate or exaggerated
   C. Single human with some animal elements
   D. More than one human with animal elements

III. Anthropomorphic with phytomorphic elements
   A. Realistic
   B. Disproportionate or exaggerated
   C. Single human with plant elements
   D. More than one human with plant elements

IV. Zoomorphic
   A. Realistic
   B. Disproportionate or exaggerated
   C. Single animal
   D. One or more animals with additional animal elements

V. Zoomorphic with anthropomorphic elements
   A. Realistic
   B. Disproportionate or exaggerated
   C. Single animal with human elements
   D. More than one animal with human elements

VI. Zoomorphic with phytomorphic elements
   A. Realistic
   B. Disproportionate or exaggerated
   C. Single animal with plant elements
   D. More than one animal with plant elements

VII. Anthropomorphic with zoomorphic and phytomorphic elements
   A. Realistic
   B. Disproportionate or exaggerated
   C. Single human with animal and plant elements
   D. More than one human with animal and plant elements

The descriptive classification of each mask is noted in abbreviated form. For example, I.A.C. indicates an anthropomorphic mask (I) of a single human (C) executed in a realistic style (A).

NOTE: "Realistic" and "disproportionate or exaggerated" are relative and somewhat subjective terms, for few, if any, masks can be said to be absolutely accurate in their rendering of real life. The classification of masks as to being realistic or not, then, is a matter of the degree of their departure from reality in comparison to other masks. In a few cases, it has been difficult to judge to which of these categories a mask belongs. However, it should be remembered that this classification of masks exists only as a guide, an aid for comparison, and should not be taken as a definite, absolute judgment.

MEXICAN MASKS

INTRODUCTION: MASKS—FACES OF MEXICO

While we are alive, we cannot escape from masks or names. We are inseparable from our fictions—our features. We are condemned to invent a mask for ourselves and afterward to discover that the mask is our true face.

(Octavio Paz 1970, p. 11)

ON A PURELY PHYSICAL LEVEL, masks are made to hide the real faces of their wearers and to substitute artificial faces drawn from tradition and from the imaginations of mask-makers. However, the act of covering the face is far more profound than a simple disguise, for the face itself has a far greater significance than one's features. While Mexico, like other cultures, has long equated the human face with personality and the "persona" in the Jungian sense, Mexican Indian groups have taken this symbolic process one step further: they directly relate the face to the soul.

In commenting about the significance of the face in Pre-Hispanic Mexico, Miguel León-Portilla states that while the heart "symbolized the source of dynamism in human will," the ancient Nahua peoples believed that "Beyond doubt, 'face' referred to that which most intimately characterized the intrinsic nature of each individual" (León-Portilla 1963, pp. 113–115). On a secular level, this concept of the face is equivalent to the European idea of the ego or the persona. However, such secular terms as *ego* and *persona* misrepresent the world-concept of these Indian cultures, for theirs was a world where nothing was or could be separated from spiritual aspects.

That such spiritual concepts survive among present-day Indians is shown by Alain Ichon in his study of the religion of the Totonacs of the Sierra (1973, pp. 175–176). The Totonacs believe that each individual has two souls, one of which (the *Li-katsin*) resides in the head, the other (the *Lista'kna*) primarily in the heart (although it is also said to be located at the top of the head at times). The only difference between the soul-locations of the Totonacs and the ego-locations given by León-Portilla seems to be semantic, with "soul-locations" more accurately describing actual Indian beliefs in my opinion.

For these Indians, then, covering the face with a mask is the equivalent of temporarily removing the identity and the soul (*alma*) of the mask wearer from the everyday world. But masks do more than just hide one's features: they substitute a "new" face (i.e., new ego, persona, and soul). Therefore, Mexican masks

3. Corcoví masks. In the foreground (*a*) is a fine old Tarascan mask from Michoacán, termed a Corcoví, which was collected in 1935. In the background (*b*) is a more recently carved Corcoví of much less interesting design. The first mask is boldly conceived and relies on drawing and painting for its striking exaggeration, with the exception of the long, carved nose. While this mask is akin to the concept of "primitive" or modern art, the other is carved and painted in a conventional manner with the realistic forms of a human face. Narrow eye slits are above the eyes of both masks. In mask *a*, a free-hanging piece of fur is used to unrealistically suggest hair. *Michoacán (Tarascan); (a) 24 cm., not including hair; (b) 26 cm.; wood, paint, animal fur (a).* (a) I.B.C. (b) I.A.C.

(which are used throughout the country in ritual dances) must be understood as an agent of a profound, mystical transformation in which their wearers become someone or something else.

In ancient times in Mexico, these new faces given by masks were not arbitrary, unconnected fantasies but sprang from the hard life that the Indians led in trying to obtain sustenance and other basic necessities from unyielding nature. Nature was very cruel, a terrible dualistic god: the giver and destroyer of life. At this time, man was both the hunter and the hunted, the killer and the victim. In order to control nature, he discovered the mask as a magical means of covering his own soul and transforming it by assuming the identity of a god powerful enough to control nature and the elements and to make things fertile and prolific, so that his life would be a little easier.

This was the meaning in the beginning, when the ceremonial wearing of a mask was a profound and frightening thing and elevated the wearer to a degree higher than the common man. Now, after so many centuries, only a vague superstitious mystery remains. Even today we hear of venerated masks, such as a certain "Tigre" in a chest in Guerrero. When the chest is opened, it is said that the Tigre actually moves his eyes, blinks, and looks at the persons present.

In regard to contemporary Totonac dance groups (including the Voladores, Negritos, Huahuas, and Moros y Cristianos), Isabel Kelly notes: "Each group reveres a mask, which is believed to take vengeance on a dancer if one of the group fails to observe certain tabus—for example, that of avoiding women before an official dance performance" (1953, p. 175). The fact that some masks are believed to be spiritual entities may also account for the preservation of some of the very old masks, such as the Centurion helmet masks dating from the eighteenth or nineteenth century shown in Fig. 98.

From within the carved images of Mexican masks, two distinctly separate faces look out upon us. The first is a European face that reflects the pageantry and processions, the morality plays, and the history of Spanish Mexico. The other face is much older. It is an Indian face that has somehow survived the centuries of acculturation and religious repression. Much of its symbolism and magical richness has been forgotten, but to the older Indians it still retains to a large degree its mystery.

Thus, the masks of Mexico are a record of its peoples, cultures, religions, and history. Only recently, with the advent of better communications, new roads, television, and more schools, have we been able to see the tremendous power of the past that has remained in isolated areas—traditions, customs, and rituals of another, older world. People have preserved their traditions and beliefs against the greatest odds, hardships, and anguish. Despite the encroachment of foreign cultures and religions, indigenous peoples still can be found in remote areas living and believing in much the same way as their ancestors did in ancient times.

But a new "conqueror," modern technology, is rapidly affecting indigenous cultures which have held out against military conquest and missionary zeal.

4. Metal mask of Xipe-Totec. A flayed person is shown. Xipe-Totec was the god of vegetation. Courtesy of the Museo Nacional de Antropología, INAH, SEP, Mexico City. *Western Coast of Mexico; metal.* I.A.C.

5. Stone mask. Although not readily discernible, there is a snake (or possibly two snakes) running around the head, a motif found in many contemporary masks of various materials. Courtesy of The Metropolitan Museum of Art, The Michael C. Rockefeller Memorial Collection of Primitive Art, Bequest of Nelson A. Rockefeller, 1979. *Area of Mezcala, Guerrero; 14 cm.; stone.* II.A.C.

6. Devil mask, dance unknown. Nothing is known about this mask, which was found in the Lagunilla market in Mexico City. The face is half red and half green, with a pink European baby devil on the nose. The gold scorpion painted on the cheek (at left) is symbolic of evil. This mask shows considerable age and has been repainted many times. At one time it had four wooden tusks, only two of which now remain. *Area unknown (possibly Guerrero); height: 18 cm.; depth at nose: 17 cm.; wood, paint.* I.A.D.

Roads are being cut through the jungles and the jagged mountains; small planes are connecting previously isolated settlements with modern cities. A door is being opened, through which we often discover the miraculous survival of ancient ways of life and belief, but through which also flow the influences which must inevitably bring change.

It is at this historical juncture that this book comes into existence. In part, the book exists because the door has been opened, for when I first came to Mexico, people were very reluctant to show their masks or even to answer questions about them. More importantly, this book exists to preserve a record of the ancient customs, beliefs, and symbolism which the opening of the door threatens to destroy.

With such widespread change and with the glamor of new things, everyone but the most conservative elders has come to want change and to feel ashamed of backward customs. Young people leaving the small *ranchos* and going to large towns to look for work soon find that their old beliefs are ridiculed. These factors will undoubtedly transform masks from a meaningful part of people's lives to a simple folk art made primarily for sale. This change is already a fact in some areas that appear remote but in which masked dances no longer take place and all the old masks have been sold. Yet, because of the prices that these old masks have brought, a new home industry has developed, and Indian youth with no sculpting antecedents are carving masks instead of tending the fields.

This new art form, for all of its fine and different qualities, lacks the significance of the old art of mask-making, which was part of the religious life of the community and was a means of social control—one of the main functions of the mask during the nineteenth and early twentieth centuries in Mexico. Today, many of these religious and social functions, which still existed until quite recently, have been replaced by purely entertainment functions or have faded away completely.

Masks then are links to Mexico's past. Over the last forty years, my wife and I have traveled, often on horseback, pursuing this link and trying to document it before it disappears. We have more than once found old masks whose meaning had been forgotten by all but the oldest villagers and have seen fantastic examples of the craftsmanship of mask-makers who are no longer working. We have recorded descriptions of dances which now exist only in the memories of those who once performed them long ago. We have collected masks, some of which were rotting in native houses, while others were kept carefully tucked away in wooden chests, elaborately wrapped in silk, out of danger but also out of use. And we have been told about the symbolism of masks and ceremonies, symbolism which remains only vaguely in the minds of elderly Indians. It is hoped that this book is a faithful record of the brilliant art of Mexican masks. It is also meant to serve as a tribute to the thousands of able Mexican mask-makers, who in large part remain unknown.

In closing this introduction, it is important to address briefly the overall approach of this book. During the years I have spent in preparing this study, many people have expressed the hope that it would be a catalog of Mexican masks, listing all the villages which have made masks, the chronology of each mask style within each village, the name of each mask-maker, etc. While the desire for such ethnographic data is understandable, it fails to take into account the basic realities of obtaining such information. There are literally thousands of small, extremely remote villages that once produced masks. Most of the mask-makers themselves were part-time craftsmen, small farmers who tilled the soil, planted, and harvested, and only rarely do the very old remember their names as mask-makers, much less when they made particular masks. Often I have gone to a village that once produced large numbers of beautiful, distinct masks, only to find out that no one remembered how the masks were used or even whether they were made in that village.

While it is true that intensive field investigations on a village-by-village basis can still obtain some ethnographic information, my use of such an approach would have resulted in a book that concentrated on a few villages or areas rather than on Mexican masks as a whole. As this book is the first serious treatment concentrating on Mexican masks as a unique art form, I felt that it should seek to define some of the broad aspects of the mask in Mexico: the visual language of its symbols, its artistic achievements, its social and religious uses, the craftsmanship involved in its making. Thus I hope that, by making people more aware of the richness and complexity of the Mexican mask culture, this work will engender further studies of this uniquely beautiful art form before it is too late.

7. Pastorela Dance masks. A group of fine old Michoacán masks with a white Hermit mask in the center. *Cherán, Michoacán, 1935 (Tarascan). (a)* II.B.C. *(b)* I.A.C. *(c)* IV.B.C.

8 9

10

8. Characters and dances unknown. These expressive, rather naïve masks were collected by the late scholar Miguel Covarrubias in the early 1920's. Although Mexican masks were little known at that time, Covarrubias felt that they deserved a place in the best of the world's museums. These two are rather famous, having been exhibited in an Exposición de Arte Mexicano (American Federation of Arts) and reproduced in *Mexican Folkways*, vol. 5, no. 3 (1929), p. 141. *(a) Cuanajo, Michoacán (Tarascan); (b) Santa María, Michoacán (Tarascan); (a) 39 cm.; (b) 50 cm.; wood, paint.* I.A.C.

9. Chameleon masks, Devil Dance. The chameleon stands for good luck and is said to be the King of the Animals, as no animal will eat it. It is an uncommon mask subject. Both of these have great charm and originality, with their multiple horns and the pochote spines (see Fig. 246) about the face. I know of no use for these masks save an Animal Dance that today would be termed a Devil Dance. Property of the University of Arizona. *Tlanipatlán, Guerrero (Nahua); (a) 32 cm., including horns; (b) 33 cm., including horns; wood, paint, pochote spines.* VI.A.C.

10. Vaquero (Cowboy) mask, Vaquero Dance. False beards were mentioned in chronicles of Pre-Columbian times, and the codices contain illustrations of them as well. This large mask appears to have a frankly false beard, but whether this is a hangover from an older tradition or simply the mask-maker's style or fancy is not known. The center section of the beard and chin is movable. *Ixcateopán, Guerrero (Nahua); 48.2 cm.; wood (zompantle), paint.* I.B.C.

11   **12**

In a historical analysis of an art form, it is normally desirable, if not altogether mandatory, to establish some type of chronology for the works of art either on a general basis or for the individual pieces. In the case of Mexican masks, however, it is impossible to date the vast majority of masks with any reasonable accuracy beyond such vague terms as "old," "used," "very old," etc. While I realize that such descriptive terms are somewhat unsatisfactory because of their imprecision, the reader should be forewarned that, except in those rare cases where supplemental documentation exists, any attempt to date a mask (even as to the century) becomes an extremely questionable estimate. In addition, many of these estimates come from mask vendors and informants who have a vested interest in overestimating the age of the mask to make it more valuable to the buyer.

In large part, the inability to date Mexican masks stems from a temporal ambiguity in Mexican culture, an ambiguity that is one of its essential characteristics and charms. It is not uncommon to find Pre-Conquest ideas and beliefs existing side by side with modern ones without apparent conflict or the need to eliminate one or the other. Many times, this cultural accommodation has permitted us to see a past that existed before the Spanish came, but this type of acculturation is by no means consistent or linear throughout the whole of Mexico or even throughout any single Indian group. The "past" that exists in

11. Character and dance unknown. This crude but expressive mask was probably made by a nonprofessional for his own use. The beard is fashioned out of dark fur and home-grown cotton; these suitable materials make a very distinctive mask. Property of the University of Arizona. *Possibly state of Puebla; 25 cm.; wood, paint, animal fur, cotton.* I.A.C.

12. Character and dance unknown. This very old and worn mask was probably made for the carver's own use. The grey, white, and red paint has now practically disappeared, and a large crack has been carefully mended with metal strips and nails. The carving is very expressive, especially when the mask is seen in motion. *A ranch near Teloloápan, Guerrero; 21.6 cm.; wood, paint (oil), fox fur.* I.A.C.

13. Remnant of a fine old wooden mask. *San Martín Pachivia, Guerrero.* I.A.C.

14. Devil mask. This fine Bull or Cow Devil was probably made before 1920 and has been repainted many times. The exaggerated open mouth contains a movable tongue, while the ears are of heavy leather. The tusks are of carved wood, as is the snake-head nose. *Guerrero (Nahua); height: 46 cm.; width of horns: 43 cm.; wood, paint, leather, goat horns.* IV.B.D.

any one village depends on the strength and completeness of oral traditions, the remoteness of the village, and the ardor of individual priests, government officials, and teachers. Thus, a mask-maker in one village may easily produce a mask of a type that has not been produced in other areas of the state for a great many years.

One of the more common methods of dating art work is to use stylistic trends as criteria. However, as pointed out in the section on "Style and Cultural Traditions" in Chapter 1, the cultural diversity and complexity of Mexico, the high degree of individuality permitted mask-makers, and a large number of other variables preclude the identification of traditional styles in any but the most general terms, far too vague to base any estimate of a mask's age upon.

Nor does direct examination of the masks provide any conclusive information. Judging the relative age of a mask on the basis of wear factors is extremely difficult even for the most experienced of experts, as masks were usually worn only once a year during the principal fiesta of the village and carefully preserved for the remainder of the year. Consequently, a well-cared-for mask could have had long use without showing any appreciable wear. On the other hand, as most masks are made of wood, termites and moisture can "age" them very rapidly, so that even the most recent ones may appear to be quite old. In fact because of the severity of both termites and adverse climate in Mexico, it is surprising that any of the very old masks have survived, and I must admit to being highly dubious about the claims put forth for some masks which supposedly date from the seventeenth and eighteenth centuries. Another factor that complicates the dating of masks is the fact that many masks are repainted every few years, thus eliminating a large number of the signs that show age. This is not to say that the trained observer cannot identify an authentic, "used" mask, but extrapolations beyond this point are highly questionable.

Another problem in the task of establishing a chronology for masks is the rapid social change occurring in Mexico. In the vast majority of cases, it is impossible to determine whether a particular mask was made or used in a certain village, much less when it was made or by whom. There is also very little recorded information available, in part because the mask-makers were often itinerant craftsmen whose activities did not merit mention in town records.

In order not to mislead the reader and to avoid implying any historical pattern that cannot be substantiated by the evidence available, I have not included any estimates of the ages of masks in this text, other than those supported by outside documentation. (It should be noted that the problems in dating Mexican masks are very similar to those for African masks, which are also not dated as a standard practice for much the same reasons as listed above.) I have used the term *contemporary* to refer to those masks which either were still being used in dances or were being kept in the small villages until I obtained or photographed them. I would say that they represent a time period roughly equivalent to 1850 to the present, as I doubt that the older, Colonial masks could have survived Mexico's climate and insects without special protection.

PART I: THE MASK

If, as Ortega says, every work of art, or at least every iconic work of art, is a windowframe—the aesthetic form—, with behind it a garden—the content of human experience to which the form refers us—, then the non-objective painting or the sculpture of the extreme modernist is all window. There is no garden. . . .

In contrast, the work of primitive art . . . does have behind it a garden, a wonderfully and complexly designed garden. Only, we cannot see it . . . because it is a garden we have never visited, a work of reshaping the natural world into a system of ideas and feelings that is unknown to us. So slight are the indications given by the object as to this garden that we may not even suspect that it is there.

(Robert Redfield, in Redfield, Herskovits, and Ekholm 1959, pp. 20–21)

15. Mask for Diablo Macho Dance (June 5). A detail from Fig. 17, this mask was made forty or more years ago by José Rodríguez. The frogs held in the mouth may relate to the Aztec ceremonies in which live frogs and serpents were swallowed during the feast of Atamalqualiztli (see Fig. 133). *Cuadrilla Santa Anita, Guerrero (Tlapanec or Popoloca); 38 cm.; wood (palo amargo), paint (oil).* II.A.C.

1. The Mask as Art

MEXICAN ETHNIC ART is a whole art which combines religious, social, and esthetic elements, unlike the more secular, fragmented art of European civilization. Consequently, it is impossible to consider the esthetics of modern Mexican masks in isolation without distorting the understanding of these works of art as integrated phenomena. This chapter, then, should be read in conjunction with Part III, which traces the religious and symbolic underpinning of these masks and places them within their social context.

However, the very complexity of the cultural information embodied within Mexican masks presents a dilemma for the person making initial contact with this art form. Is the appreciation of Mexican masks dependent upon the viewer's knowledge of artistic conventions, symbolism, religious practices, etc., or does such knowledge dilute the masks' impact and prevent the viewer from seeing them as they actually are?

In addressing a similar question in regard to Tlingit masks, Andrew H. Whiteford concludes: "It must be recognized that different kinds of experiences in 'appreciation' have equal validity regardless of their diversity, and almost all such experiences combine esthetic, emotional and cognitive responses. . . . The person likely to derive the greatest enjoyment from an art exhibition is one who possesses ethnological/historical background information and also training in esthetics, but who is able to shift from one to the other and, better yet, to turn it all off on certain occasions as he views the materials on display" (Whiteford 1972, p. 9). The following discussion of the mask as art seeks only to augment the reader's understanding and appreciation of Mexican masks.

Before launching into any detailed discussion of form, style, and design, it is important to touch briefly upon the relationship of Mexican masks to Art. In the past, Mexican masks were often labeled "primitive art" or "folk art," the choice of terms depending more on the cultural background of the viewer than on the art itself. Unfortunately, these labels have more often tended to obscure our view of that art than to clarify it.

16. Probably for Dance of the Marquez. This superlative late-eighteenth- or nineteenth-century mask was carefully hidden and protected in the home of an old Indian, who owned three or more of the original set. He decided to sell one or more of these old masks after seeing a television program about a Mexican painter who collected masks. Eventually, this still sweet-smelling mask was bought by an Iguala mask vendor. The carving of the high-browed head suggests Church carving and its elements of "Old Master" knowledge of the human form. (Compare the execution of this mask with the more stylized Dwarves from La Parota and Barbones from Ostotitlán seen in Figs. 188 and 32, respectively.) The Dance of the Marquez was in fashion around the turn of the century; it is not known which character this mask represents. The very narrow eye slits beneath the eyes are a characteristic feature of very old masks. It would be interesting for a young investigator to trace the history of this beautiful cedar carving. *Coatepec Costales, Guerrero; 47 cm.; wood (cedar), paint.* I.A.C.

In the past, the concept of "primitive art" was particularly ethnocentric and biased, leading to such statements as "All primitive art is marked by a singular indifference to realism" and "When the superiority of man and the nobility of his form become recognized, primitive art is at an end" (Runes and Schrickel 1946, p. 806). Further, there was a large controversy as to whether "primitive art" was the result of inferior mental capabilities on the part of "primitive man," or was produced by normal human beings in "inferior, primitive" societies. The underlying premise of this entire concept was that when these individuals and/or their societies "grew up," they would inevitably and logically come to recognize and emulate the superiority of "Western" civilization and its art as the culmination of creative endeavor.

Fortunately in recent years, we have grown past this type of rigid cultural imperialism to realize that there are many different ways of approaching and organizing reality, each with its own merits, and that technology is not the only yardstick for evaluating worth or value. Within this light, it would seem that the old-fashioned, outmoded views of "primitive art" should be relegated to the intellectual junk pile and forgotten about as quickly as possible, if it were not for the fact that the connotations of its inferiority and lack of sophistication still linger, even in the minds of many people who have come to appreciate such art. Therefore, I feel that, to some degree, it is still necessary to dispel the artificial barriers erected by those labels, so that the beauty of Mexican masks, which are essentially a realistic art form, can be more clearly seen and their achievements more easily celebrated.

In his great pioneering work *Primitive Art*, Franz Boas deals with the question of "primitive art" versus "high art" as follows: "The emotions may be stimulated not by the form alone, but also by close associations that exist between the form and ideas held by the people. In other words, when the forms convey a meaning, because they recall past experiences or because they act as symbols, a new element is added to the enjoyment. The form and its meaning combine to elevate the mind above the indifferent emotional state of every-day life. Beautiful sculpture or painting, a musical composition, dramatic art, a pantomime, may so affect us. This is no less true of primitive art than of our own" (Boas 1955, p. 12). Thus, Boas concludes that while different cultures assign different meanings to forms, the process of art is the same and the art of one culture is by no means intrinsically or structurally superior to that of another.

A further consideration that is germane to the examination of Mexican masks as art is the division between arts and crafts. Formerly, the term *art* was primarily reserved for painting, sculpture, etc., i.e., the traditional art forms of European civilization. Crafts were considered to be utilitarian items which were not regarded as seriously as "art." In accord with this ethnocentric dictum, masks were most often relegated to the non-art category of crafts. In an attempt to remove the cultural bias of such terms without dispensing with them all together, Whiteford notes that "the art historian Douglas Fraser made a clear distinction between art and crafts: only 'objects of paramount importance,' gener-

17. Masks for Diablo Macho Dance (June 5). Eight masks from a set of twenty-five made by itinerant woodcarver/goatherder José Rodríguez (see Fig. 149) and discovered in 1975 in the Comisaría of the *cuadrilla* of Santa Anita, Guerrero, where they had hung for many years. Used in a dance to petition for rain, they all have powerful water symbols such as snakes, toads, lizards, and especially bats. The outstanding workmanship shows Rodríguez's skill and his knowledge of Nahua symbolism. The masks are carved of a hardwood commonly called *palo amargo*. None of the projecting elements (animal parts, etc.) are separate pieces applied to the mask; each mask is carved of a single piece. The mask at lower left (*e*) is said to have been used by the leader of the Diablo Macho Dance. At lower right (*h*) is a mask with the same Asiatic features of high cheekbones and slanted eyes as the mask in Fig. 38, whose early carver may have influenced Rodríguez. Masks *g* and *h* property of the University of Arizona. *Cuadrilla Santa Anita, Guerrero (Tlapanec-Popoloca); 35–38 cm.; wood (palo amargo), paint (oil).* II.A.C.

18. Devil mask, Chulanixtle Dance. This truly great carving was done by José Rodríguez with apparent rapidity and great sureness, giving it the quality of a fine sketch. The continuity of all things animal and human and the power of transformation are clearly evident in this superb Devil. *Chultepec, Guerrero (Tlapanec-Popoloca); 37 cm.; wood, paint.* II.B.C.

19. Abuela Teresa (Grandmother Theresa) mask, Tenochtli Dance. I know of no other mask that shows so many years of hard use and at the same time such loving care taken in maintenance. This Grandmother face was reinforced with handmade fiber on the cheeks in four places. Metal strips can be seen beneath the right eye, and the chin is held together with vegetable glue and small nails. The carving of this very old mask shows extraordinary delicacy of expression. In the village in which this mask was used, the Tenochtli Dance (based on the battle between the Spanish and the Indians of Mexico City [Tenochtitlan] at the time of the Conquest) was performed by eight dancers, who took the parts of Hernán Cortés, Rey Cuauhtemoc, Monarco, Pasqual Bailón, Malinche, el Negro, Huiquixtle (who carries a snake), and this Grandmother figure. *San Miguel Oapan, Guerrero (Nahua); 14.5 cm.; wood, paint.* I.A.C.

ally associated with 'high spiritual values' can be regarded as art; secular and utilitarian objects produced by 'slow, repetitive' processes such as weaving, are classified as crafts or 'lesser arts.' He indicates also that, in the main, art is created by men, crafts are produced by women" (Whiteford 1972, p. 9).

Within this expanded definition of both art and crafts, Mexican masks must obviously be recognized as art, for the primary reasons for making masks were spiritual, as is pointed out in length in Part III. These masks were also accorded great importance within their communities, as is evidenced in the great care that was given to protecting them from year to year. Until recently, masks were hidden and not casually displayed to strangers, and some masks were thought to be spiritual entities. Further, mask-making is almost exclusively a male occupation, one that was often undertaken under the influence of hallucinogenic drugs to enable the mask-maker to encounter the spirit world directly. In recent years, however, the distinction between art and crafts has been fading, since the Indians themselves did not make any such distinction and since almost every aspect of Indian life had a definite spiritual component, particularly some of the "crafts" done by women, such as weaving.

While Mexican masks must obviously be considered as art in this anthropological sense, let us turn to the more technical level of art criticism. According to Runes and Schrickel, "'Art' designates any activity that is at once spontaneous and controlled" (1946, p. 801). To apply this definition to Mexican masks, we must answer two questions: (1) Are the masks "controlled," that is, are there sufficient virtuosity and skill in the craft of mask-making to allow the artist complete control over the execution? (2) Are the masks "spontaneous," or are the motifs, designs, and execution so dictated by tradition as to preclude any real spontaneity of expression by the individual artist? These questions, like any others in art, are best answered by the evidence presented by the masks themselves.

Regarding the question of control, let us first look at the masks made by José Rodríguez from the state of Guerrero, which are shown in Figs. 15, 17, 18, 37, 150, 219, 222, 248, and 313. These masks combine animal and human forms, with a smooth fluidity in the transitions from form to form. The figures are precise and realistic, the surfaces are knowingly finished, and the handling of the paint shows a tremendous talent and ability. In Fig. 146, from Juxtlahuaca, Oaxaca, we see a highly realistic mask of a human face that is extremely well carved and painted. The old mask of Abuela Teresa from San Miguel Oapan, Guerrero (Fig. 19) shows extraordinary delicacy of expression. The huge masks from La Parota, Guerrero, shown in Fig. 188 demonstrate a high degree of wood carving skill in their realistic faces, the highly defined details of the beard, and the almost perfect surface finish. In the extraordinary expressiveness of the Angel mask pictured in Fig. 270 we can again see the skill and control of an unknown mask-maker; the long, shapely nose and the delicately carved teeth show exceptional workmanship, which is all the more surprising considering that the mask is quite thin, ranging from 6 to 7 millimeters in thickness.

20. Mermaid mask, Fish Dance (*a*); Three Stages of Man mask, dance unknown (*b*). Each of these carefully worked copper masks from the region of Altamirano, Guerrero, is lined with cloth, which is glued to any surface that might touch the wearer's face. These masks were made around the turn of the century when there were several active copper mines in the state of Guerrero. Mask *a* represents a smiling Mermaid with her dark tail wrapped around her head, the only copper Mermaid of this conception I have seen. Her face is ringed by black hair all around. The triple human face (*b*) is carefully painted, with a large central face, flanked on its right by a cheerful black face with grey hair and beard. The other face is dark red and has somber features, as does the central face. *Region of Altamirano, Guerrero; (a) 30.5 cm.; (b) 30.5 cm.; copper, paint, cloth, glue. (a)* II.A.C. *(b)* I.A.D.

Nor are the skill and control of Mexican mask-makers restricted to wood carving. In Fig. 20, we see two copper masks from the Altamirano region of Guerrero made with the repoussé technique, each fashioned from a single piece of copper with the ears expertly soldered on. Figs. 21 and 154 show extremely rare silver masks from Guerrero attesting to a high level of metalworking craftsmanship. Mastery of leather is shown in the Tlaxcala Carnival masks in Fig. 29 (*a,b,c*) and in the leather masks shown in Figs. 22 and 70.

These are just a few examples to illustrate and attest to the fact that Mexican mask-makers have more than sufficient technical virtuosity to allow complete control over their materials and the treatment of their subjects. In Mexico, as elsewhere, people make masks for many different reasons and purposes, and the quality of amateur masks often leaves much to be desired. However, the art

21. Silver masks for rain-petitioning dance.
These six very rare masks, from an original set of twelve, were probably made between 1890 and 1910. Mask *c*, an old woman, has the date 1902 hammered into the reverse side of the chin. They weigh between .700 kg. and 1.675 kg. They were made in La Parota, Guerrero, at a time when silver mines were active in the area. During the same period many copper masks were fashioned with a similar repoussé technique in Guerrero (Fig. 20), but I have no news of other silver masks being produced since Colonial times. It is interesting to note that these masks were hidden away and preserved, rather than sold piecemeal for their silver. Each of these masks has earrings soldered on when they were originally made, in the forms of flowers (*c*), monkeys (*d*), squash blossoms (*b*), and squash (*a, e, f.*). The beautiful monkey motif earrings seen in mask *d* are causing particular interest, since a good number of similar artifacts have recently been unearthed at the important archaeological site of Xochipala, Guerrero (see Fig. 158). The monkey earrings measure 3.5 cm.

In the top row we see two female figures, one old (*c*), one young (*a*). The remaining masks are male and exhibit large beards. Mask *e* (lower center) has the intricate, separated beard strands seen in the large wooden masks found in the same area (Fig. 188) and in the Barbones masks from the area east of Ostotitlán, Guerrero (Fig. 32). In contrast to the highly sophisticated Greek feeling of these masks are the potent old water symbols of snakes, which curl into the mouths of *d* and *f*. Mask *c* property of Beth Burstein; mask *e* property of the Smithsonian Institution, Washington, D.C. *La Parota (near Campo Morado), Guerrero (Nahua); 43 cm. (average); silver, cloth lining. (a, b, c, e)* I.A.C. *(d, f)* II.A.C.

of any nation cannot be evaluated by examining the work of Sunday painters, and Mexican masks must be judged, at least in terms of virtuosity and control, on the basis of the best work, which more than amply demonstrates the prerequisite skill to fulfill the "control" criterion for the definition of Art.

Moreover, the ability to produce "finely finished surfaces" cannot be considered the sole criterion of technical proficiency in any branch of the arts, as noted by Paul S. Wingert: "Involved in the misconceptions surrounding primitive art is the additional, mistaken belief that smooth, polished surfaces and refinement of detail stamp a work of sculpture as superior to one in which a vigorous and dynamic realization of form is achieved by an equally strong and direct technique which lacks polish and refinement. If, however, rougher style were given an elegance of finish, and smoother style received an abrupt and

22
23
24
25

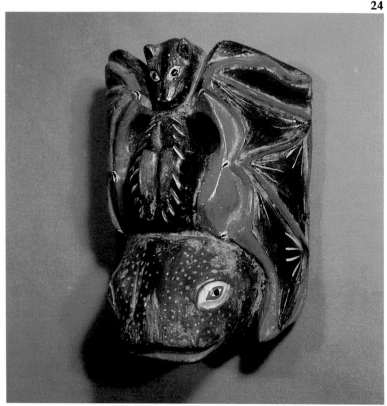

22. Helmet mask, Vaquero Dance (?). This old helmet mask is made of two very thick sections of leather sewn together with leather thongs at the sides. The disproportionately large nose and horns are made of wood. The pointed ears indicate that this was for a Devil character, but the transverse markings on the horns suggest segments of a scorpion, or insect antennae. An unexplained projection of red-painted wood with white circles rises vertically from the forehead. Eye openings between the eyes and the brows are like those found on some very old masks. The Vaquero Dance of the region was also called the Pectoral Dance, but the reason for this is unknown. As this helmet mask is very large, it rested on the dancer's shoulders and chest, perhaps contributing the meaning of the second name. *Area of Axoxuca, Guerrero (Tlapanec); height: 59.7 cm.; width: 61 cm.; leather, paint, wood, ribbons, bells.* II.B.C.

23. Bat mask, Bat Dance or Lord of the Animals Dance. The area of Totozintla, San Francisco, and Tlacozotitlán on the eastern Balsas River produced some of the finest masks in the state of Guerrero. As this area specialized in the Bat Dance, Bat masks were made with infinite variety, from large helmets to small face masks, each highly original. The Totozintla Bat seen here has the extraordinary feature of a jaguar head in both form and coloring. The design has a Colonial Church flavor in the deeply carved, richly embellished outer wing area and the superb polychrome paint over the entire mask. Only the human eyes on the bat wings give any indication that this carving is a mask. I am led to believe by mask study that the mask-makers' idea of symbolism is something we do not comprehend. They often seem to see the bat head as a jaguar, although they do not always paint it as a jaguar (see Fig. 24). *Totozintla, Guerrero (Nahua); height: 35 cm.; width: 36 cm.; wood, paint.* V.A.D.

24. Bat mask, Bat Dance or Lord of the Animals Dance. The bat and the frog have a traditional association thought to derive from their shared ability to jump and their close relationship with water (see p. 203). Property of the University of Arizona. *Totozintla, Guerrero (Nahua); 26 cm.; wood, paint.* IV.A.D.

25. Bat mask, Bat Dance or Lord of the Animals Dance. This superb Bat mask was fashioned with extraordinary artistry and imagina-

tion. I am happy to have been able to preserve for posterity some of these wonderful masks from Totozintla, San Francisco, and Tlacozotitlán that might otherwise have been lost (see also Figs. 230 and 231). Very few Bat masks have been made for some twenty years, and all the old craftsmen are now gone. Collections of the International Folk Art Foundation in the Museum of International Folk Art, Santa Fe, New Mexico. *Totozintla, Guerrero (Nahua); height: 45 cm.; width: 50 cm.; wood, paint, animal teeth.* II.A.C.

26. Deer mask, Tecuani Dance. The individual mask-maker's freedom of expression can be seen in this simple, friendly Deer, with its large, round eyeholes at either side of the head. In sharp contrast to this naïve design is the sophisticated Deer mask from Valle Luz, Guerrero, seen in Fig. 27. *Chilacachapa, Guerrero (Nahua); 27 cm.; wood, paint, deer antlers.* IV.A.C.

27. Deer mask, Tecuani Dance. The conception of this heavy old Deer mask is quite unusual. It has been repainted several times with great care. On a piece of paper pasted to one side of the mask, a poem has been written: "Yo soy como el venadito/que habitó en la sereania./Como yo soy tan mancito,/yo voy de aqua de dia. [I am like the little deer/that lives in the hills./As I am tame,/I come down to drink by day.]" The poem is difficult to read and apparently full of colloquial grammar. *Valle Luz, Guerrero (Nahua and Tlapanec); height: 41 cm.; depth: 34 cm.; wood, paint, deer antlers.* IV.A.C.

26

27

dynamic treatment, the results would be unsuccessful or even incongruous" (Wingert 1962, pp. 9–10). Thus, the apparently "crude" execution of some masks must be attributed to the intended design, rather than to any lack of technical ability.

The second consideration is whether there is opportunity for spontaneity and individual expression in mask-making. This is a more critical concern, for if it can be shown that mask-makers are simply executing traditional motifs, no matter how skillfully, then their work is relegated to that of craftsmen rather than artists. But again, this question is almost instantly resolved once we consider the masks themselves. In Figs. 42, 43, 138, 280, and 282–285, we see a tremendous variety in Moor masks for the Dance of the Moors and Christians, showing both tradition and individual mask-makers' ability. Nor are the differences simply regional, since all but two of these masks were made in the state of Guerrero.

The variety of mask styles begins with the individual mask-maker, and two artists may produce sharply different masks even in the same village, as shown in the Bat masks from Tlacozotitlán (Figs. 230, 231) and Totozintla (Figs. 23–25). In Figs. 7, 60, 139, 155b, 173, 289, and 290, the latitude given individual mask-makers is shown in the different ways they render the Hermit figure of the Pastorela Dance. In fact, the hallmark of Mexican masks is this very spontaneity and individuality—enhanced by the fact that the mask-maker today is generally not restricted by religious or social taboos.

In passing, I should respond to the implication that ethnic art is not realistic, particularly when it comes to depicting the human form. A quick review of the figures listed above shows that one of the predominant characteristics of Mexican masks is realism. Clearly, the mask-makers were accurate observers of both humans and animals. Some masks (such as Figs. 16 and 154) compare favorably to Greek art in their realistic portrayals of human forms. Such realism cannot be attributed only to the European influences of the Spanish and the Church, since ancient Mexico also had a tradition of realistic portrayal of the human figure. In any case, the assumption that another culture's art forms must pass through a Greco-Roman stage of human realism in order to be considered art is extremely ethnocentric and presumes that there is only one correct line of artistic development. As an example of how limited this view is, Covarrubias notes "Ralph Linton tells of a Polynesian sculptor of the Marquesas Islands who, upon seeing a picture of an academic marble nude, asked 'what was the use of making a stone woman that did not feel or smell like a woman'" (Covarrubias 1954, p. 94).

Clearly, Mexican masks deserve to be carefully considered as serious artistic expressions. It is true that the visions of reality embodied in these masks are different than those of European civilization, but in a great many cases it is this difference that gives them their tremendous emotional impact and power, for it provides a fresh view of the basic human condition. These masks allow us to recognize anew elements of our own humanity, unburdened with our cultural clichés and accepted viewpoints. The ability of Mexican masks to profoundly affect viewers from other cultures is a testimony to the high quality of their art.

STYLE AND CULTURAL TRADITIONS

Normally, one of the first considerations of an analysis of an ethnic art is the identification of traditional styles, so that it is possible to group the objects and better judge the unique qualities of each one by comparing it to its peers. This is an extremely difficult process with contemporary Mexican masks, not only because of their characteristic individuality but also because of the complex cultural reality of present-day Mexico.

Because of this cultural complexity, it is important to define the terms and concepts that will be used throughout this chapter. Technically, *style* is defined as "those characteristics of form which are peculiar to a certain work or group of works, and which at the same time distinguish it or them from other works. These characteristic peculiarities must be organic, and thus are recognized as the signs of an expression of a complete work" (Runes and Schrickel 1946, p. 974). It should be added that stylistic characteristics must be above and beyond the inherent qualities of the materials used. The use of leather as a mask material, for example, involves constraints which cannot be considered stylistic.

The basic definition of style is extended into the field of ethnic art by Franz Boas: "[Style can be considered to be] highly specialized local forms, so distinct in appearance that each type may with certainty be assigned to the region from which it comes" (1955, p. 145). *Region* here assumes a meaning beyond simple territorial considerations to include ethnographic and cultural components. A traditional style, then, is an expression and an integral part of the culture that produced it. As Herskovits says, "Style may be thought of as something that gives cultural identity" (Redfield, Herskovits, and Ekholm 1959, p. 54).

As ethnic art styles have a necessary cultural component, it would be relatively easy to identify regional and/or traditional mask styles if Mexico presented us with clearly defined cultures and cultural regions. However, the situation is not that simple. To begin with, there are over seventy different linguistic groups within Mexico, and sometimes there are various tribal groupings within a single linguistic group. While these groups are distinct from one another and possess their own traditions, there has been a great deal of cultural interaction from before the Conquest to the present day. Ideas, motifs, symbols, and styles have spread without regard to their origins; their diffusion has not been uniform or consistent.

An excellent example of this cultural diffusion in relation to masks was given by Frances Toor in *Mexican Folkways* (vol. 5 [1929], pp. 115, 142, 143). In one of the first studies on Mexican masks, Toor identified three contemporary masks as depictions of Ehecatl, the Aztec god of the winds. However, not all of these masks originate with the Nahua (Aztec) Indians as one would expect. The first was made by the Nahuas in Copanatoyac, Guerrero; the second was made by the Yaqui Indians of Sonora in the northernmost part of Mexico, and the third by the Zapotec Indians of the Ixtlán region of Oaxaca in the southern part of the country. Since it can be assumed that the Spanish and the Catholic Church did not introduce this pagan god to these other ethnic groups, these masks stand as prima facie evidence of Pre-Conquest diffusion and its continuing influence in modern times.

The large number of Indian groups and their various Pre-Hispanic interactions constitute only one of the stumbling blocks in determining traditional mask styles, for there have also been over 450 years of contact with European cultural and religious influences. This contact has been far from uniform or consistent. Some groups, such as the Coras, Huichols, and Seris, had only minimal contact up until recent years, and their indigenous cultures have stayed more or less intact. Other groups which were less remote or whose territory contained valuable resources experienced a far more direct and pervasive influence from the Church and the Spanish. Some Indians, such as those in Jalisco, have become almost completely acculturated and have retained little of their native culture. Others, such as the Nahuas in remote mountainous regions of Guerrero, have retained much more of their own culture, but even in these groups the native traditions vary dramatically from one village to the next. With the destruction of the great centers of Indian culture, these traditions ceased to have a central, living core and degenerated into local traditions with little or no interconnection among different parts of the same region. Many of these traditions were also suppressed by the Church and, therefore, went underground, where parts were lost or distorted. The presence and the force of the Church varied considerably from village to village and from region to region, so that the amount of remaining Indian culture also varies widely, depending more on the village than on the area.

One good example of a confusing mixture of cultural influences is illustrated by the story of Santiago Martínez Delgado, a mask-maker from Chapa, Guerrero (Fig. 28). Recently, he was commissioned by a dealer in masks to make several Eagle Knight (Caballero Aguila) masks, which are based on the Aztec warriors' traditional masks. Even though Chapa is a Nahua village (i.e., Aztec), the Eagle Knight mask is no longer traditional there, although it is still used in other villages in Guerrero and Puebla. So, in order to find a model of this mask, he ended up traveling to the Museo Cuauhnahuac, the museum in Cuernavaca, which was showing a collection of some of my masks. This type of decay of local traditions makes it almost impossible to ascertain regional traditions; the borrowing, of course, further complicates the situation.

Another major difficulty in identifying characteristics of mask style is the rapid social change occurring throughout modern Mexico. In the past, the balance between the indigenous and European cultures remained fairly stable on the village level generation after generation. Even if this balance varied greatly from village to village, there was at least a large degree of continuity within any particular village. Since 1910, however, the government's policy of benign ne-

28. Mask-maker Santiago Martínez Delgado. Shown posing with some of his masks, used in the Fiesta of September 16. Photograph by Ruth Lechuga. *Chapa, Guerrero, 1976.*

glect of Indians has been abandoned; the Ministry of Public Education has opened schools in even the smallest villages, contributing to the substitution of Spanish for native languages and accelerating the demise of Indian cultures. Television or at least radio has penetrated many of the most remote villages, bringing both the Spanish language and modern value systems. The young, in their efforts to become modern, no longer respect or study the old values and ways. Consequently, the traditions of masks and the art of making them have disappeared from many areas and are rapidly fading from others.

Many times over the last years, I found outstanding masks in small villages, but when I tried to find out who made them and what dances they were used in, no one knew. "Sí, señor, an old man who used to live on the hill used to own the mask, but he is dead now. No, I don't know if it was made in this village," is all too typical a response. Since masks are one of the most widely distributed of all Mexican ethnic arts, it is often impossible to find out where a mask was made and by whom, making all but the most general stylistic analysis totally impossible.

Further complicating the task of identifying traditional styles is the fact that such styles are not static and unchanging: the traditions themselves change. Fig. 29 shows a collection of Tlaxcala Carnival masks. The oldest of these masks were made of leather in the nineteenth century. Later, wooden masks became popular; more recently, these masks have movable eyes that wink when a string is pulled. While the history of the Tlaxcala masks is fairly well documented, this is not the case with the majority of other masks. The large, unpainted helmet mask shown in Figs. 30 and 31 was supposedly used in processions sometime in the past, but for some unknown reason, such masks went out of vogue and were stored outside, with the rain and the elements washing away their water-based paint. Excluding copies, no contemporary masks are made in this fashion. Other types of masks that are no longer being made include the large Dwarf masks from La Parota, Guerrero (Fig. 188) and the fine Barbones masks from the region of Ostotitlán (Fig. 32). Such stylistic variations can be particularly frustrating just when one feels that one has pinned down a particular regional style. (On the other hand, it is the variety of Mexican masks that makes them so interesting!) Examples of this are the Caimán figures of the Balsas River and other rivers in the state of Guerrero. Typically, these Caimán figures have an open space in the center so that they can be worn about the waist (see Fig. 303c). Just recently, however, I discovered what appears to be an older Caimán sculpture that was meant to be carried under the arm and did not have the typical center opening. Possibly this type was the precursor of the step-in Caimáns in some villages, while other villages have continued to use the older style for their contemporary figures. It is also possible that the under-the-shoulder Caimán is a separate contemporary style from another village and no developmental relationship exists. Thus, without extensive research on a village-by-village basis, it is a highly questionable practice to estimate ages of masks on the basis of stylistic variations. There are only a few cases where suffi-

29. Carnival masks. The small state of Tlaxcala has an old tradition of mask-making, and a great deal of time and money is spent to maintain it. The Carnival dances of this area seem to be surreal and sophisticated, but in reality they represent a petition for rain and fertility. In this set of masks, those on the top row (*a, b, c*) are of leather and were made in the nineteenth century. Mask *b* has a beard of pita fiber. In the center row, *d* and *e* are fine old *santero* carved masks with glass eyes. The woman character (*d*) has the typical dimples and ears. Masks *f, g, h,* and *i* are contemporary glass-eyed masks carved by Carlos Reyes Acoltzi and his son of Tlatempan, Tlaxcala, two of the few remaining *santero* mask-makers. Masks *g, h,* and *i* have eyes that can be opened and shut by manipulating the strings seen hanging from the chins. Masks *d* and *f* property of Mexican Folk Arts, Chicago; mask *h* from the collection of Paul Skinner. *State of Tlaxcala; (b, i) 30 cm.; (others) 20–23 cm.; wood, paint, leather (a, b, c), pita fiber (b), glass eyes (d–i).* I.A.C.

Figs. 30–31. Helmet mask, Bat Dance. During the Bat Dance (December 23) all animals, but the bat in particular, pay homage to the Christ Child. Fig. 30 shows the human side of this unpainted helmet mask and represents a bearded deity, perhaps the Lord of the Animals. A squirrel perches on the head, and a bat, a butterfly, a lizard, and a coyote are superimposed on the face. (The Aztecs called the coyote Huehuecoyotl, the god of dance.) Fig. 31 shows a bat making up the entire face, with crude human eyes carved into the wings and three small bats along the lower edge of the mask. From the collection of Larry Walsh. *Totozintla, Guerrero (Nahua); 84 cm.; wood (zompantle), unpainted. (Fig. 30) I.A.C. (Fig. 31) V.A.D.*

32. Barbones (Bearded Ones) masks, Dance of the Marquez and others. These finely carved masks are, I believe, of the same period as the silver masks seen in Figs. 21 and 154 and the large La Parota wood masks in Fig. 188. Judging from similarities in design and workmanship, all these masks appear to have been produced by a large family or school of excellent artisans who probably worked on an apprentice system. It is not known how large an area this school of artisans covered, how many carvers there were, or how long a time was involved. Recurring characteristics are the blue eyes, high cheekbones, long upper lip, and intricately carved beards of many styles. Eye slits appear either above or below the eyes. Mask *e* property of the University of Arizona. *Area of Ostotitlán, Guerrero (Nahua); 22–49 cm.; wood (zompantle), paint. I.A.C.*

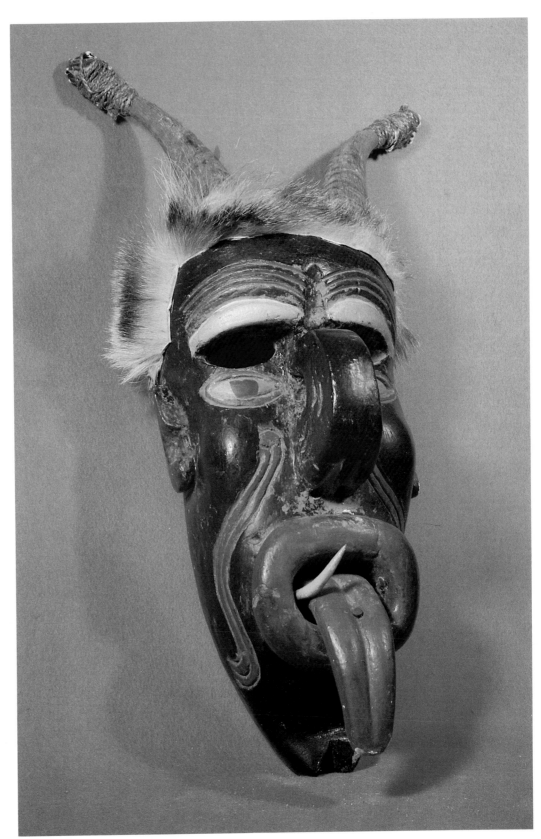

33. Carnival dancer. This masked Carnival dancer wears colorful plumes atop his Indian straw hat. His costly glass-eyed mask was carved by *santero* carver Carlos Reyes Acoltzi (see Fig. 147), who also did church carvings. Photograph by Ruth Lechuga. *Papalotla, Tlaxcala.* I.A.C.

34. Devil mask, Dance of the Tres Potencias (Three Powers). Unique to the town of Acapetlahuaya, Guerrero, are Devils with horn tips in a protective wrapping of paper and handmade string. This long face has a disproportionate mouth with a single tusk and the tongue extended to symbolize power and defiance. The cupped, handlelike nose has perforated nostrils that allow the dancer to breathe. The dancer's chin rests on a depression behind the upper lip. *Acapetlahuaya, Guerrero (Nahua);* 53.4 cm.; wood (zompantle), paint, animal fur. II.B.C.

36. Mask for Los Locos (Crazy Ones) Dance. A real artist recognized a fine opportunity here, as the natural formation of this piece of wood was used to fashion a striking mask without much carving. The wood was simply hollowed out to accommodate the dancer's face, and simple eyes and nose were added to complete the crude design. The mask is painted with modern enamel paints; the naïve, bold colors and the way they are used contribute to its effectiveness. Property of the University of Arizona. *Tlaniquitlapa, Guerrero (Nahua); 28 cm.; wood, paint.* I.B.C.

35. Character and dance unknown. This old mask by an amateur mask-maker is primitive and clumsy in execution, yet remains very forceful and effective. A double-headed snake passes through a mouth of crude teeth and ends with its red heads resting next to the white, projecting eyes. The protruding leather tongue signifies either power or defiance. This mask is of very heavy wood. Property of the University of Arizona. *Michoacán (Tarascan); 27 cm.; wood, paint, leather.* II.B.C.

cient documentation exists to permit one to make such estimates with any degree of accuracy.

The last major difficulty in identifying mask styles stems from the very popularity of masks in recent years and the fact that they have become a salable commodity. Many mask dealers are more interested in obtaining "merchandise" than in finding the ethnographic information that gives these masks meaning. Far too often one will find an obviously old and finely made mask with no information as to where it was made, what dances it was used in, who made it, etc. In other mask-making cultures, such as those of the Eskimo, the Northwest Coast Indians, and African tribes, this would not be as serious a problem as it is in Mexico, since those groups have distinctive traditional patterns and designs which allow for easier and more accurate identification, in many cases down to the particular village. Unfortunately, this type of identification is impossible with the vast majority of Mexican masks, and the lack of ethnographic data becomes a major tragedy.

Yet this is not the worst of the problem. A large number of masks are currently being produced for the tourist trade. In many cases, it is extremely difficult, except for the trained eye, to distinguish used masks from these well-made "aged" copies. Many fakes are made within the mask-making tradition, so that there are not always obvious stylistic or design characteristics that differentiate them from masks made and used by the people. Moreover, the craft of forging antiques has become an art in itself in Mexico. Acid is used to "age" the wood, and tool dents to simulate use, and sometimes artificial termite holes are added. There is no easy method of identification, for it takes years of experience to recognize the small details (wear characteristics, paints used in certain areas, etc.) that set old masks apart. Unfortunately, some large museums have been deceived and have included fakes within their collections. One of the major problems with these masks is the resulting confusion in the task of making a systematic study of authentic masks, their styles and usages.

All this does not mean that there are not regional differences in mask styles, for there obviously are. These will be discussed in Chapter 4. But the mixture of cultural traditions, the high degree of individuality, Mexico's rapid transition into a modern, industrial nation, the changes in mask styles, and the commercialization of masks make such a discussion general at best.

Despite the cultural complexity of Mexico today, there is, I believe, one informal structure that has a definite stylistic effect throughout the country as a whole: the existence of three distinct types of mask-makers. While I do not mean to suggest that this division is rigid or even explicitly acknowledged by the community, the mask-makers I have known fit into three different categories according to their backgrounds and mask-making styles: the *santero*, who makes both masks and church figures (see Figs. 29 and 33); the professional mask-maker, whose work tends more to reflect native traditions (see Figs. 1, 34, 110, 120, 121); and the amateur (see Figs. 35 and 36). These three types of mask-makers are discussed in Chapter 6.

2. Iconography

37. Devil masks, various dances. These six astonishing Devil masks by the highly gifted carver José Rodríguez were made between 1920 and 1950. Mask *a* is a simple human face with two gracefully poised dragons atop the head. Mask *b* is a darkly painted humanoid face with ferocious fangs and highly expressive serpents. Below the center of the chin is a coyotelike animal framed by variously posed lizards on projecting branches. Mask *c* may be a comic character, with its elongated eyes and four intertwined snakes all carved with great skill from a single piece of wood. The three lower masks show a Catholic influence in the devils mounted on top. Mask *d* is a pale human devil with animal ears and a European devil with feet poised flatly on the forehead. Mask *e* shows a dark human devil surmounted by a pink devil standing on yellow frogs with serpents curving down from its hands beside the face below. Both *d* and *e* show the strongly Asiatic features used by an earlier carver, whose work is shown in Fig. 38. Mask *f* has a strong facial expression and is crowned by a devil figure. All these masks show Rodríguez's careful conception of animal life and Indian symbolism. Masks *c* and *e* property of the University of Arizona. *(a, c) Calpisaco, Guerrero (Tlapanec or Popoloca); (b, f) Tecuitlapa, Guerrero (Tlapanec or Popoloca); (d, e) Acatepec, Guerrero (Tlapanec or Popoloca); 33–38 cm.; wood (palo amargo), paint (oil). (a–c)* II.A.C. *(d–f)* II.A.D.

THERE ARE A NUMBER of iconographic motifs that have captured the imagination of the Mexican people and are used as basic themes for mask design found throughout most of the country. While the method of rendering them varies drastically, the almost universal acceptance of these themes and motifs reveals much about the overall Mexican character.

Following is a brief discussion of a few of the more important and more widely used themes and motifs. A great many will be discussed in the chapters concerning regional styles and dances. Some of these, particularly those that seem to be Pre-Hispanic survivals, are dealt with in greater detail in Part III. The purpose of this discussion is to provide a general understanding of mask subjects, so that stylistic variations can be more clearly seen.

The Devil (El Diablo). There are two basic types of Devils: the traditional European Devils, as seen in the small devils atop the masks in Figs. 37d and 37e, and the wild, animalistic Devils, such as the one in Fig. 39. The animalistic Devils derive from pre-Hispanic "monster" or *nagual* masks. When the Spanish friars arrived in Mexico, they simply added horns to these pagan masks and renamed them Devils to assert the superiority of Christianity (see pp. 173–174).

Fig. 40 shows a set of Devil masks which combine European-style Devils with Indian animalistic spirits and Indian symbolism, as do the ones shown in Fig. 37. Fig. 41 shows a particularly grotesque Michoacán Devil. Other Devil masks are seen in Figs. 6, 14, 18, 34, 51, 61, 68, 70, 87, 106, 133, 179, 189, 193, 200, 201, 217, 218, 242, 250, 251, 269, 292, 306–308, and 312. Many animal masks are commonly called Devil masks today.

Except in the Pastorela Dance, the Devil figure is now viewed more as a prankster or clown than as a figure of evil. Often, a masked Devil will go around during a fiesta telling sexual jokes and grabbing women, saying, "The Devil made me do it!" Normally, this is regarded as great fun by all concerned.

Moors (Moros). In the Dance of the Moors and Christians and its many variants, the Moors, who are traditionally the villains, are represented as bearded men, whose portrayal ranges from extremely realistic to crude but recognizable. Moor masks may also be quite splendid, reflecting a love of pageantry, as is shown in the Sultan mask in Fig. 138*b*. The Morismo mask in Fig. 283 shows a freely conceived, happy rendition that is well executed. Fig. 280 shows a sad-faced Moor with a bloody, slashed face. Some distinctive variations of the Moor theme include the red-faced Moro Chino masks (Figs. 42, 284) and the highly stylized, unrealistic Moro Pasión masks (Figs. 43, 285), with their long, sometimes spiral noses, red faces with gold-painted projections, etc.

Animals. In many cases, animals play an important role in the remnants of indigenous religious practices and form important symbols in masks. As the various animal motifs are among the most widely used in modern masks (particularly in those regions where the indigenous culture has remained a dominant element in village life), this category is far too broad to be discussed here. It is dealt with at length in Chapter 9.

As mentioned above, many animal masks are commonly called Devil masks.

Viejos (Old Men). The Viejos are a common mask type in many areas, the Viejitos (Little Old Men) of Michoacán being the most famous. These masks are usually representations of old men and are worn by young men who imitate the mannerisms and movements of the Viejitos to the amusement of the onlookers. Typical Viejito masks from Michoacán can be seen in Fig. 311. Not all Viejito masks depict old men; in a few areas of Michoacán, these masks portray young men, and old age is implied only through the actions of the dancers. There are also very comic Viejo masks from Guerrero, reflecting the Indians' humorous (rather than depressing) view of old age. Another Viejo mask is shown in Fig. 211.

Malinche. Malinche was the Indian woman who served as Cortés's interpreter and who became his mistress. She is viewed as the betrayer of her country and as a woman whose uncontrollable sexual passion destroyed the Indian nations. However, when all is said and done, the Indians of Mexico have a certain amount of respect and admiration for Malinche because of the power she had with the Spaniards.

The Malinche mask is used throughout Mexico in the numerous variations of the Conquest Dance. Malinche is also found in a number of other dances, such as the Dance of the Negritos, where she represents the "wanton woman," the destroyer. She is normally depicted representationally with varying degrees of realism; however, animal and color symbols are often added to her face to reinforce her sexual aspect. Two very typical, red-faced Malinches are seen in Fig. 44; these masks have realistic, attractive features but with red paint, silver dimples, and *chintetes* (small lizards) added to signify lust. Malinche masks can vary greatly, as can be seen in Figs. 97, 215, 259, and 278.

Negritos (Little Negroes). The Negritos have wide distribution even beyond the popular Dance of the Negritos. In most cases, they function as clowns in much the same way as the Devils do. In fiestas, the Negritos tell sexual jokes,

38. Possible Devil mask. When this book was being prepared for publication, this mask and those seen in Figs. 1, 206, and 242 were found in Jaleaca, Guerrero, where they had been hidden or forgotten in old chests. I judge them to have been carved around 1850 or before, but no information is obtainable to date. Carved from a single piece of fine hardwood, all are extraordinarily preserved and show wear only around the holes where cords were attached to tie the mask to the wearer. Master carver José Rodríguez may well have been influenced by the work of this earlier carver, as we see here the same distinctly Asiatic features of high cheekbones and slanted eyes as on several Rodríguez masks in Figs. 17 and 37. Photograph by Ferruccio Asta. *Jaleaca, Guerrero (Nahua); wood, paint.* II.A.C.

39. Devil mask. The style of this Devil is unique to the village of Huitziltepec, Guerrero, which lies surrounded by fields, considerably inland from Zumpango del Río on the main road to Acapulco. The cockscomb was associated with the Devil in medieval European legend, but the overall character of this mask is definitely Indian, with its unrecognizable animal decorated with goatee, leather tongue, and animal teeth. A newer Huitziltepec Devil can be seen in Fig. 142 (third mask from left). *Huitziltepec, Guerrero (Nahua); 24 cm. (approx.); wood, paint, leather, animal teeth.* IV.B.D.

40. Devil masks, Chintetes (Lizards) Dance. Of heavy wood and many times repainted, these old masks combine Pre-Hispanic water symbols of snakes, frogs, and fish with the Christian Devil concept. The water symbols are superimposed on the faces of the upper masks, and they form the noses of all the masks. Mask *a* property of the University of Arizona. *Guerrero (Nahua); 21–25 cm.; wood, paint.* II.B.C.

41. Devil mask, dance unknown. A superb old Devil mask of unusually somber colors and well-carved facial features. The carving shows good definition and knowledge of form. The reverse side has a deeply cut-out under-jaw typical of Michoacán masks. The segmented, wormlike creatures that form the two sets of horns combine with the serpent in the mouth to give this Devil a particularly grotesque aspect. *Michoacán (Tarascan); height: 45 cm.; depth: 35 cm.; wood (zompantle), paint, leather.* II.B.C.

42. Moro Chino masks, Dance of the Moors and Christians. There are many styles of masks used in the Dance of the Moors and Christians, ranging from the realistic (as seen in Fig. 138) to the type of highly stylized interpretation seen here. Guerrero Moro Chino masks have the curly beards and the unexplained horizontal block forms across cheeks and brows seen here. The carving of these Moors is strong and sure, with the small beards thrusting forward to repeat the feeling of depth in the brow and cheek projections. The dancers look out through the mouth in these tall masks. Mask *a* property of the Smithsonian Institution; mask *b* property of the University of Arizona. *Quechultenango, Guerrero (Nahua); 38 cm. (approx.); wood, paint.* I.B.C.

43. "Pilato el Chico" Moro Pasión ("Little Pilate" Suffering Moor) mask, Dance of the Moors and Christians (variant). This very old mask was brought to me in 1971 from a *rancho* in the area of Coatepec Costales, where it is said to have been kept unused since the time of the great-grandfathers. The hard wood has an undercoat of Spanish whiting covered with many coats of thick paint, which is now cracked and chipped with age and heavy use. The long upturned nose is a typical characteristic of Moro Pasión masks, one which may be taken to the extreme, as can be seen in the Moro Pasión from Puebla (Fig. 285) with its elaborate, coiled nose. Moro Pasión masks are usually painted red, but in this older version, the mask-maker was content to color only the nose and add red dots to the flat cheeks. *Region of Coatepec Costales, Guerrero (Nahua); height: 25 cm., including beard; depth: 12.5 cm. (at nose); wood, paint.* I.B.C.

44. Malinche masks, Tenochtli Dance. Mask *b* is by far the older of these two, as can be seen by the very small eye openings. It is not known where this mask was made. The newer mask (*a*) is from Acatlán, Guerrero. Both are painted red to signify lust and wantonness, and they share the feature of superimposed *chintetes* (lizards) and silver or gold dimples. Mask *b* also has a bee on the nose, perhaps to signify "stings," i.e., Malinche's brutal actions against her own people. *Guerrero;(a) 16 cm., not including hair (b) 18 cm., not including hair; wood, paint, ixtle fiber.* II.A.C.

make ribald comments and gestures, and help maintain order in the crowd so that the other dancers can perform properly.

There are two possible sources for this mask theme. It may have originated in the importation of Negro slaves by the Spanish. Since the Dance of the Negritos is most popular in the coastal states where most of the slaves were settled, it is logical to assume that the dance springs from the presence of these slaves. However, the Negrito masks are spread far beyond the regions where the dance is practiced, and there is a second possible source. In the codices, the Aztec god Tezcatlipoca is usually depicted with a black face and fangs, as befits his role of god of the shadows and the night. Quetzalcoatl and Ehecatl also frequently have black faces and fangs in the codices. We can see in Fig. 45 a Negrito mask from Oaxaca with fangs at the sides of its mouth, which leads me to believe that Negrito masks developed from representations of Tezcatlipoca, Quetzalcoatl (see Fig. 46), and/or Ehecatl.

In the state of Mexico, the Negrito characters of the village of Capulhuac are used to keep animals out of the fields. They wear papier mâché helmet masks without tusks (Fig. 99).

Negrito masks are broadly representational in style but are often distorted to emphasize their comic aspects. They can also be quite individualistic; see Fig. 86.

45. Ehecatl/Negrito mask, Plume Dance. Plume Dance assembly showing a character wearing an Ehecatl/Negrito mask leading the dancers into place for the action to begin. *Teotitlán del Valle, Oaxaca, 1942.*

46. Quetzalcoatl with fangs, as seen in the Codex Vaticanus 3773, p. 34. From *Commentarios al Códice Borgia* (Seler 1963), vol. 1, Fig. 422.

Death (La Muerte). Death is another theme that has both European and Pre-Hispanic antecedents. The skull was a common motif in Mesoamerican art; in fact, some of the most striking Pre-Columbian masks represent skulls. The Spanish also brought the Death figure to Mexico in their allegorical morality plays, to instruct the illiterate Indians in Christianity. These plays are still performed throughout Mexico, the most notable being the Dance of the Tres Potencias (Three Powers). Whatever its origins, the Death figure is now in evidence in almost every facet of Mexican popular art.

Death is not a character that inspires fear and loathing; indeed, its function is quite similar to that of the Devil, although Death is not quite so comic and does not engage in the same level of buffoonery. The cavalier manner in which Mexicans view Death comes, perhaps, from the fact that up until recent years, life expectancy was short and death omnipresent; therefore Mexicans adopted a joking response to it as a way of distancing themselves from their fears.

Death masks are normally skull representations, painted white to simulate bone. In Fig. 47, we see a variety of Death masks, ranging from crude to sophisticated skull depictions, including two dualistic skull masks. Fig. 48 shows a beautiful Death carved by Filiberto López Ortiz, with a very effective stylistic exaggeration of the features, especially in the eyes and the red wool tassel decorations. Other Death masks are shown in Figs. 121, 309, and 310.

48. Death mask, Day of the Dead. This detail from Fig. 59 shows beautiful carving and painting, as well as the finely finished reverse side typical of masks by Filiberto López Ortiz. During the Day of the Dead (November 2) the wearer of this mask went from house to house begging for food or money. *Pinotepa Nacional, Oaxaca (Mixtec); 18 cm.; wood, paint, wool tassels.* I.B.C.

47. Death masks, various dances. The Mexican Indian's ingenuity with form and expression can be readily seen in this collection of Death masks, a motif with strong Pre-Columbian tradition that is still immensely popular in modern Mexico. At top left is a mask collected in Tixtla, Guerrero, in 1931. It is finely painted and has a high dome of leather. Dual Death masks as seen at the top and on the right are extremely rare. These come from the village of Atenxoxola (see also Fig. 207). The large mask at center, with the cloth hanging down from the chin area, is from Tlanipatlán and is deeply and knowingly carved. The most individual mask seen here is at lower right. It is worn with the dancer clasping the wooden peg seen protruding from below the chin. The mask comes from the village of Ocotepec. Masks at lower left and in center property of the University of Arizona. *Guerrero; 17–29 cm.; wood, paint, leather (top left), copper (lower left), cloth (center). (Dual masks)* I.B.D. *(Others)* I.B.C.

49. Our Lady of Guadalupe mask (*a*); Our Lord Christ Mask (*b*). These masks were kept in a glass case in the village church of Chiapa de Corzo, Chiapas, for many years, and it is not known how they were used—possibly for church processions. Reportedly, a visiting nun reprimanded the local priest about having masks in a church, and they were sold to a collector. The masks were reconditioned in 1972. The Virgin (*a*) is a serene mask with an unusually dark complexion for a *santero* mask of this figure. She has a head covering of blue with a pattern of gold stars. The pale Christ figure (*b*) has minutely carved beard and hair. The twisted *bejuco* (vine) crown of thorns is made of tiny wires. Both masks exhibit the style and rich materials used by the *santero* carver. Property of the University of Arizona. *Chiapa de Corzo, Chiapas (Chiapanec); (a) 19 cm. (b) 24.1 cm.; wood, lacquer, glass eyes, wire (b).* I.A.C.

Santiago Horse (St. James's Horse). A figure that has received national acceptance, reverence, and affection is the horse used in the Santiago Dance. The horse is usually a small wooden one carved in two separate halves. The head and front legs are fastened to the waist of the person playing the Santiago Caballero and the back section fastened behind the dancer so that the total effect is that of a mounted man. In some areas, only the front part of the horse is used (Fig. 197); a third type is a larger step-in structure. What makes this figure unique to me is the particularly strong veneration I saw given it in the village of Cuetzalan, Puebla, as noted on p. 152.

Christian Figures. Because the Church introduced a large number of morality and passion plays into Mexico as instructional devices and as a method of unifying Indian communities within the Christian tradition, a number of Mexican masks portray Christian figures, such as angels, Christ, and the Virgin. One should not assume that all of these masks are made by *santeros* in their realistic human style. Of course, in areas where the Church is strong, these masks are made by *santeros*, but in remote areas where the Church's influence is weak or intermittent, these figures have been integrated into indigenous traditions and often assume animal shapes. This is particularly true with groups like the Yaquis, the Mayos, and the Coras, whose animal renditions of the Jews and the Pharisees are particularly imaginative and totally nonrealistic (Figs. 71, 75–77).

Christian figures in the typical *santero* style can be seen in Fig. 155*a*, a fine old mask showing typical Christian fairness of skin, blue eyes, etc. Restrained, realistic Christians in the *santero* style are shown in Fig. 49; these should be compared to the highly idealized wax masks in Fig. 169, which are saccharine types with lush, wavy hair and delicate features.

Pre-Hispanic Survivals. Because of the over 450 years of Spanish and Christian influence on Mexico's indigenous peoples and because of scant documentation of native people's beliefs during most of this time period, it is extremely difficult to authenticate the survivals of Pre-Hispanic motifs, and still more difficult to ascertain whether these figures still retain a religious meaning. There are, however, a number of these motifs which I feel have survived as a part of Indian traditions. The majority of these are animal forms, such as the jaguar (*tigre*), since animals were less recognizable as pagan gods than anthropomorphic figures and were, therefore, not so readily suppressed by the Church. (Again, these animal forms and their meanings are explored in more detail in Part III). Other, nonanimal survivals that can still be recognized are the masks of Ehecatl, the Aztec god of the winds (Fig. 45), as noted by Alfonso Caso and Miguel Covarrubias; Xolotl, the Aztec god closely associated with duality and monsters (since his main guise was that of a dog, Xolotl is discussed in depth in Chapter 9; see Fig. 207); and the Tlaloc (rain god) figure with a twisted snake nose (Fig. 106). In all likelihood, some of the animal figures that are labeled Devils are also survivals of Pre-Conquest gods, but the lack of proper documentation precludes any such identification.

50. Rhythm-makers/masks, Owl Dance.
These unique hollow columns had a dual purpose in the Owl Dance. One of the carvings was placed on the ground in the center of the circle of dancers, and drumsticks were used to make noise in time with the dancing by scraping the concentric grooves on the wings of the owl. Only for a brief time was the heavy column lifted onto the head and shoulders of a dancer to be used as a mask. Column *a* is probably the older, and its composition is far more finely integrated, showing compact movement of the forms from bottom to top. The human face at the bottom is the actual mask, with eye slits on the eyelids. The pink horizontal elements atop the head suggest part of an insect form. The next connected element is a green grasshopper whose legs reach down and fold around the forehead of the human face. The grasshopper is a split image, a popular design element among the Northwest Coast carvings (Boas 1955, p. 223). Perched on top is the sturdy owl with its striated wings used to create the cadence for the dance. From the rear this carving is the same except that the owl is shown from the rear with its tail feathers fanning out. The human face at the rear has no eye slits, so the mask must be worn with the owl facing forward. Column *b* is a loosely organized design. Two human heads are placed one on top of the other with horizontal plates to separate them in a rather arbitrary fashion. A bloodsucking bat spirit supports the owl, which is tall but delicate in proportion to the carving. The entire column is supported by a round base that includes three flattened animal hooves. An oddity of this column is that it has eye slits on both the human faces, although the dancer could have been able to use only the lower slits while wearing the mask. Column *b* property of the Smithsonian Institution. *El Limón, Guerrero (Nahua); (a) 119 cm.; (b) 130 cm.; wood (zompantle), paint.* v.a.d.

3. Mask Design

51. Devil masks, Devil Dance. These highly individualistic Devils from Milpillas, Guerrero, with their flatly applied, brilliant colors, are not typical of Guerrero. Rather, they suggest the forms and colors of masks from Michoacán, which is not surprising, since Milpillas is near the border of that state. The placement of the colors is similar to that of the extraordinary lacquer mask from Michoacán seen in Fig. 268. *Milpillas, Guerrero; (a) 18.5 × 20.5 cm.; (b) 19 × 16 cm.; wood, paint.* II.B.C.

SINCE the overwhelming majority of contemporary Mexican masks are made of wood, the following discussion is predominantly concerned with wooden masks; there are simply too few masks made from other materials to permit a comprehensive survey of their design characteristics.

Size and Form. Masks vary in size from small figures measuring only a few inches to huge carvings of lightweight wood which tower several feet above the wearer. Fig. 52 shows tiny Tejorón masks, only 11.1 cm. high, which are worn with many scarves wrapped to hide the wearer's face (Fig. 53).

Medium-sized masks, those which are made to approximate the size of a normal face, are usually attached to the wearer's head with a cord made of leather, ixtle, straw, or cloth, which goes across the back and over the top of the head to hold the mask on. Holes are often bored or drilled at the sides and at the top of the center for this purpose. In a well-made mask, a good balance is achieved in the design so that the mask will stay in place. Some masks are simply tied across the face under the nose to the back of the wearer's head. Others may be kept in place by the user's hand, small masks being held in one hand, while masks too large to be comfortably attached are held in both hands.

The largest masks are often designed to fit over the head as helmets. Fig. 50a shows a huge helmet mask which measures 119 cm. (nearly four feet) in height. This towering creation, from El Limón, in the region of Ayutla, Guerrero, was used in the Owl Dance (Dance of the Tecolote). It was worn on the head for only a short time, then placed in the center of a circle of performers who danced around it. This mask also had another use: a stick was worked across the owl's corrugated wings to make noise during the dance.

In Zitlala and several neighboring villages in the state of Guerrero, we find large, heavy Tigre helmet masks made of leather (Figs. 55, 184). Old helmet masks from the area of Axoxuca, Guerrero, are also made of leather, but with wooden noses and horns (Fig. 22). Papier mâché is also used in making helmet masks, as demonstrated in Fig. 99.

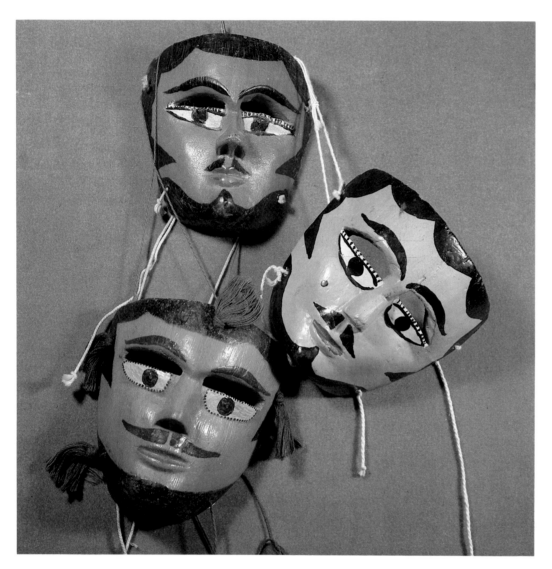

53. Tejorón mask, Dance of the Tejorones. This photograph was taken during Carnival in Huaspaltepec, Oaxaca, a Mixtecan village of the coastal area. The Tejorón wears a tall feather headdress and a tiny mask, with many scarves swathed about the face. Some of the scarves have been pushed below the chin so that he can smoke a cigarette. Photograph by Ruth Lechuga. *Huaspaltepec, Oaxaca; 12 cm.* I.A.C.

52. Tejorón masks, Dance of the Tejorones. These three precisely painted masks come from the Mixteca Baja area of Oaxaca. Their small size makes the dancers wearing them look extraordinarily tall. The dancers' heads are swathed in scarves to hide the edges of the mask (Fig. 53). *Tejorones* are members of dance societies that exist in a number of Mixteca Baja settlements. They perform at such events as childbirth or when damage is done by a snake, bull, jaguar, etc. Although these masks are of male characters, female masks of this type are also made; they are worn by male dancers dressed in the traditional woman's huipil and wrap-around skirt. Men wearing the male, moustached masks also dance at times in the woman's costume, thus emphasizing the transvestite implication. Top and bottom masks property of the University of Arizona. *San Cristóbal, Pinotepa Nacional, and Pinotepa de Don Luis, Oaxaca (Mixtec); 11.1 cm. (approx.); wood, paint, yarn (bottom mask).* I.A.C.

54. Mask for Deacoyante Dance. This small mask has sharper features than the Tejorones seen in Fig. 52, but the color and style are very similar. *Santa María Nutio, Oaxaca (Mixtec); 27 cm., including headdress; wood, paint, tissue paper.* I.A.C.

55. Tigre mask, Tigre Dance. This Tigre mask shows one of the many variations of this important animal in Mexican mask art. A very stout helmet, the mask actually served as armor during the early May fiesta when the dancers beat each other over the head with knotted rope. (See also p. 157.) Fig. 184 shows how masks like this are made. Customarily, they have deepset mirror eyes, which are long lost from this particular Tigre. Property of the University of Arizona. *Zitlala, Guerrero (Nahua); height: 26 cm.; depth: 23 cm.; leather, wild boar bristles, paint.* IV.B.C.

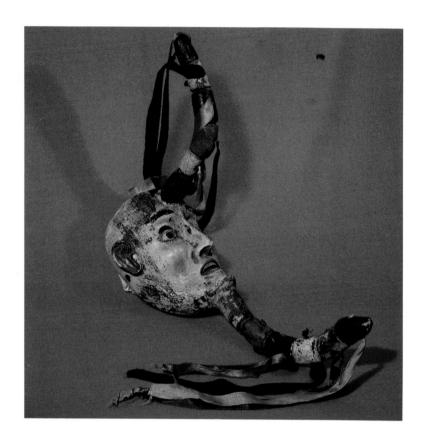 

56–57. Masks for Pastorela Dance. Each of these rare, very old masks has a projection from the forehead, the significance of which is unknown and which does not appear to be an animal form. Fig. 56 represents a female with light complexion and brown eyes. This mask also has a chin projection. Fig. 57 is also female, with fair complexion and blue eyes. The expression of this older mask is rather strained and fearful. From the forehead springs the unexplained projection bearing a ruddy, young female face. *Area of Axoxuca, Guerrero; (Fig. 56) 47 cm., including chin protrusion; (Fig. 57) height: 25 cm.; depth with protrusion: 36 cm.; wood (zompantle), paint, ribbons (Fig. 56). (Fig. 56)* I.A.C. *(Fig. 57)* I.A.D.

The creative designs of masks may include representations of one or more human faces. Single-faced masks are of course the most common, although double-and triple-faced masks are also found in contemporary Mexico.

A wooden mask usually covers the face well and is often carved so that there is an indentation on the reverse side to allow for the wearer's nose. The depth of the masks varies greatly. Often nostril openings are carved through the mask to give air. Even miniature Tigre masks intended not to be worn but to be sewn to costumes (Fig. 202), have the backs carved out. Many masks made to be worn show the mask-maker's concern for the wearer's comfort; the insides are well smoothed and even painted or covered with cloth. Fig. 59 shows the careful work of young Filiberto López Ortiz from Pinotepa Nacional, Oaxaca, whose masks were clearly designed with the wearer's comfort in mind. Some masks, however, are very rough on the inside and may have no indentation for the wearer's nose or holes for breathing.

Hair. The hair on wooden masks is often carved and then painted. It is not unusual for a good mask-maker to depict the hair as a sculptor would, either with scratched lines, curved or straight, on a two-dimensional surface or in

58. Double mask, Fish Dance or Caimán Dance. From what we know of Indian symbolism, it appears that the face at left is mirrored by his double on the right, with the Caimán, who is his real double, superimposed. *Ixcapuzalco, Guerrero (Nahua); wood, paint.* II.A.D.

59. Masks by Filiberto López Ortiz. These varied character masks from different dances were carved by a gifted young mask-maker, who was a barber by profession (see Fig. 151). His fame had begun to spread to Mexico City when he was killed in a land dispute, well before he reached his prime as an artist. Three Tigres (upper left, upper right, and center) showing great diversity of style are seen with a Negro mask (lower left) and two Carnival masks (top and lower right). At the bottom is an exceptionally well carved Death mask (shown in color in Fig. 48). All are carved with great feeling and flow of form in very hard guanacaste wood. Top mask property of the University of Arizona. *Pinotepa Nacional, Oaxaca (Mixtec); 17–25 cm. (approx.); wood (guanacaste), paint, wool tassels. (Top, bottom, lower left, and lower right)* I.B.C. *(Upper left, upper right, and center)* IV.A.C.

61. Devil mask, Dance of the Moors and Christians (variant). This mask was probably made in the 1920's, and time has given the surface a rich crackle texture. At one time horns may have been attached to the mask, as there are anchoring spots for them beneath the sheepskin on the forehead. The large hook nose and cheeks have parallel wrinkles brushed inside with red paint. The pupils cover the entire outer area of the unrealistic eyes. *Guerrero (Nahua); 29 cm.; wood (zompantle), paint, boar tusks, wool (sheepskin), horsehair.* I.B.C.

60. Hermit masks, Pastorela Dance. These semi-helmet masks are typical of those carved twenty to fifty years ago in the Cuetzala, Guerrero, area. They are heavy and squat in design, and the carving of beard and hair is relatively simple. Mask *a* property of Monte E. Hart, Cuernavaca, Morelos, Mexico. *Cuetzala, Guerrero (Nahua); (a) 41 cm.; (b) 44 cm.; wood, paint.* I.A.C.

63. Goat mask, Goat Dance. It is not known what type of hardwood was used to fashion this heavy old Goat mask. It has been re-painted a number of times. The striking design features horns that curve in a simple, sweeping arc and are squared off on the inner side. Eyeholes are placed high on the face. *Tlapehuala, Guerrero (Nahua); 24 cm.; wood, paint.* IV.A.C.

62. Parachico masks, Parachicos Dance. These fine old Spanish-style masks were worn with a wig of natural-colored ixtle fiber (Fig. 96) in a dance that began in Colonial times. It is said that a Guatemalan woman named Doña María de Angelo initiated the dance to help cure her sick son. Wearers of the large mask in the center and the one on the upper right were the lead characters in this dance, which was given during the last six days of January. The old Parachico masks (such as the one at upper left here) have eyes made by heating scrap glass and forming it to fit the eye sockets, with the pupils painted on the reverse side of the glass. Newer masks (such as the others here) have commercial glass eyes. Mask at upper left property of the University of Arizona; mask at lower left property of the Smithsonian Institution. *Chiapa de Corzo, Chiapas; 19–22 cm.; wood, lacquer, glass eyes, false eyelashes.* I.A.C.

65   **67**

64. Indian Soldier mask, Battle of the Fifth of May. This mask and the one in Fig. 91 were used in a dance depicting a battle between French and Indians that has been performed in Zacapoaxtla, Puebla, for many years. This fighting Indian has paint sparingly rubbed on cheeks and forehead. The mask has square-cut eyeholes, a bold round mouth, and horsehair crudely attached for eyebrows and beard. *Zacapoaxtla, Puebla (Nahua); 21 cm., not including beard; wood, paint, horsehair, leather.* I.B.C.

65. Character and dance unknown. Nothing is known about this esthetically pleasing, freely conceived mask. Its asymmetric design, the contrasting shapes of eyes and mouth, and the irregular jaw are a strong and primitive combination. Collections of the International Folk Art Foundation in the Museum of International Folk Art, Santa Fe, New Mexico. *State of Puebla; 23 cm.; wood, paint, animal hair.* I.B.C.

66

66. Azteca masks, Azteca Dance. These very fanciful masks are a surprise when compared to the many more realistic masks found in Mexico. The movement of the extremely disproportionate noses is reflected in the contours of the long tongues. Painted pink, the faces are adorned with bizarre facial features in reds and blacks. Mask *a* property of the University of Arizona. *Hidalgo; height: 24 cm.; length: 36 cm. (approx.); wood, paint, leather.* I.B.C.

67. Helmet mask, Bat Dance. This helmet mask shows a bat superimposed on a bearded human face so that the wings of the bat are transformed into the moustaches of the face below. A small underground rodent, called a *tuza*, becomes the figure's phallic nose. The dancer looks out through holes on either side of the *tuza*'s head. The reverse side of the helmet (not pictured) is a male visage, perhaps a Lord of the Animals figure. Property of the University of Arizona. *Tixtla, Guerrero (Nahua); 47 cm.; wood, paint.* II.B.C.

beautifully formed raised masses which flow very effectively in the desired direction (figs. 32, 60). Other masks have flat painted areas to designate the hair or use supplementary materials such as wool, ixtle, animal hair, commercial hair, etc. (See Chapter 7 for further information about the materials used in masks.)

Eyes. There must be a way for the wearer to see through the mask except in those rare cases in which the mask is held over the head or in front of the face. In the majority of wooden masks, the eyes are carved and painted; the wearer looks out through a slit above or below the eye. Parachico masks from Chiapas exhibit half-moons carved above or below the eyes (Figs. 62, 96) and the Tlacololero masks of Guerrero have a circle cut in each cheek (Figs. 143, 216). Sometimes there are no eye openings, and the wearer looks through the mouth, as in the old Devil masks from Guerrero (Fig. 106) and some Tigre masks from Jalisco, Guerrero, and other states (Figs. 81, 82, 176, 202, 264).

A smaller, though nonetheless considerable, number of masks have the entire eye carved out in a circular, square, or almond shape. An interesting example of carved-out eyes is Fig. 64, an Indian Soldier mask. A very expressive mask (Fig. 65) has square cut-out eyes in contrast to the triangular cut-out mouth.

In many Mexican masks the eye openings seem extremely inadequate. One would think the dancers could not see at all. When one considers that drunkenness is part of the ritual aspect of the ceremony, it is not hard to picture the general blindness (see p. 157). Many very fine old masks have exceedingly narrow eye openings (Fig. 44*b*).

Noses. The nose is probably the most important element on the carved wooden mask for imparting information concerning the identity of the mask. Sometimes, because of the lack of a large enough piece of wood, the mask-maker must put the nose on as a separate piece. One does, however, find masks with the nose carved from the same large piece of wood as the rest of the mask (Fig. 267). For symbolic reasons, the nose may be carved in the shape of a small animal or human figure. Particularly among the Bat masks, a large bat is often combined with the human face, a part of the bat body forming the human's nose (see Figs. 226, 227). Conventional noses are found in masks in which symbolism does not play a part. The nose can also be an erotic feature (see. p. 216). Long noses have been phallic symbols in Japanese, Balinese, and Javanese masks since the earliest times.

Mouth, Teeth, Tongue. Wooden masks display endless types of mouths, often revealing extraordinary imagination on the part of the carver (Figs. 64, 212). Teeth, when indicated, may be individually carved of the one piece of wood of which the mask itself is made, or may be of other materials, such as animal teeth, animal claws, corn kernels, or even real human teeth. Each of the extraordinary rain-petitioning masks by José Rodríguez was made from a single piece of wood (Fig. 17). Tongues are sometimes carved of the same piece of wood or may be added as a separate piece. (For additional details, see the section on supplementary materials in Chapter 7.)

68. Devil masks. These masks exhibit some of the finest carving and conception in Nahua masks. Each has a human face (now termed a Devil) with animals superimposed on the planes or as part of the features. Masks *a*, *e*, *f*, *j*, and *k* depict various forms of lizards; *f* is one of the finest combinations of facial and animal features to be seen. Mask *d* has an enormous tarantula or spider, while the face on *g* is almost completely hidden by a frog. Mask *i* has deer antlers over the nose and a wonderful facial expression. Devil *l*, like *g*, is almost completely hidden, this time by a large turtle body. These masks come from the remote Nahua settlements of Copanatoyac, Hueycantenango, Huitzapula, and Colotlipa in the state of Guerrero. Masks *a–e*, *h*, *k*, and *l* property of the University of Arizona; mask *j* property of the Smithsonian Institution. *Guerrero (Nahua); 26–40 cm.; wood, paint.* II.A.C.

77. Chapakobam (Pharisee) mask. This fine, very old Mayo Easter Week Pharisee mask was obtained in a shop in New Mexico, where its identity was not known. The fur of the helmet is scraped away over the face and ears. Note the perforated eyes. Today there would be far less care lavished on the detail in the well-painted eyebrows, colored paper trim, etc. *Area of Navajoa, Sonora (Mayo).* I.B.C.

small wooden face mask in the form of a man or a goat. Horse or goat hair is inserted to represent the beard and eyebrows. Yaqui masks generally have horsehair as a fringe, whereas Mayo masks generally have finer goat hair. The upper hair of Yaqui masks is clipped at eye level (Fig. 74); Mayo masks leave the hair long and flowing (Fig. 72). The masks are normally painted black, although white, brown, and other colors are sometimes used. They are further embellished with geometric and representational designs that have their origin in face painting; almost invariably these designs include a cross in the middle of the forehead and some type of geometric border. These designs can be either inscribed or painted. Typical Mayo Pascola masks can be seen in Figs. 72 and 73; Fig. 74 shows two Yaqui Pascola masks. See also Figs. 123 and 140.

The second type of mask is the Chapayeka/Chapakobam (Pharisee) mask, as it is called in Sonora, or the Jew mask, as it is called in Sinaloa. These masks are used in the dramatization of the Passion Play and represent both evil characters who persecute Christ and clowns. There are two general styles of these masks: wooden masks depicting humans or European devils, and fantastic fur hide masks. The one common element of both types is that the entire head is covered, even where the mask itself is only a face mask. The "human" masks are vaguely realistic, with the face either unpainted or painted white. Often cheeks, eyebrows, and moustaches are painted onto these masks. The second type of Pharisee mask is a helmet mask made from goat hide depicting a creature that seems to be a cross between an animal and a human being (Figs. 71, 75–77). The hide is shaved, and the upper face and eyes are painted in. The nose consists of an unshaved strip of fur, a flap of leather, or in some cases a carved wooden nose. Occasionally, cow horns are added to make the mask appear more like a devil. Ears, when they occur, are made from leather and are usually painted. Some of these masks are outstanding in design and style.

The Huichols of Nayarit and Jalisco. Traditionally, the Huichols make only one mask, that of Tate Nakawé (Grandmother Growth), which is used in the "First Fruits" ceremony. When I first visited the Huichols in 1937, the Tate Nakawé mask was unpainted, as is shown in Fig. 78. Recently, however, the Huichols have been making these masks to sell to tourists and have started to paint them, using their traditional face painting patterns similar to those shown in Fig. 108.

The Coras of Nayarit. In contrast to the drab masks of the neighboring Huichols, the masks of the Coras are brilliantly colored and highly imaginative. The Cora masks, which are used during Holy Week celebrations, depict fantastic animals. In Fig. 172, we see a mask that appears to be a cross between a deer and a caimán. These masks are made of cardboard covered with tissue paper and occasionally use fiber or animal hair as a supplementary material. One common characteristic of these masks is that they are painted with bright colors, often in broad stripes that have no relationship to a realistic portrayal. The masks are large face masks that normally extend beyond the face on both sides.

Guerrero. Guerrero is predominantly populated by Nahua Indians, although small groups of Tlapanecs, Cuicatecs, Mazahuas, and Popolocas also live within the state. Most of the Guerrero masks are produced by the Nahuas. In my opinion, the Guerrero masks surpass those of any other state in Mexico in terms of the number of masks produced, the survival of Pre-Hispanic influences, and the high quality of the work. The very number and variety of these masks, however, prevent any detailed analysis of their stylistic characteristics except on the most superficial level.

A good example of the wide diversity in Guerrero masks can be seen by comparing a number of the Tigre masks produced by this region. In Fig. 79, we see one of the famous Tigre masks from Olinalá, Guerrero. The Tigre masks from this town, which is also famous for its lacquer ware, have a distinctive style and are finely finished and carefully lacquered (Fig. 79). Other characteristics are the ridges which border the mouth, the painted leather ears, the use of boar bristles for whiskers, the red leather tongue, the glass eyes, and the piglike conception of the Tigre (real jaguars [*tigres*] not having been seen there for many years). In Fig. 80, on the other hand, we see a very old wooden Tigre mask from Tianguizolco, Guerrero. In many ways, this mask looks far more catlike than the preceding one. Fig. 81 shows a third Tigre mask, from Hueycantenango,

78. "First Fruits" Fiesta. A masked dancer and some participants at the Huichol "First Fruits" Fiesta. *La Mesa, Nayarit, 1937.* I.B.C.

80. Tigre mask, Tigre Dance. The Tigre mask has taken on innumerable forms, as it comes from the imagination of a skilled carver, who may never have seen a real jaguar. Here we see a benign pussycat, which is hardly fearsome, with its small nose and ears and naïve whiskers. This heavy mask is very old and has been newly repainted. *Tianguizolco, Guerrero (Nahua); 30 cm.; wood, paint.* IV.B.C.

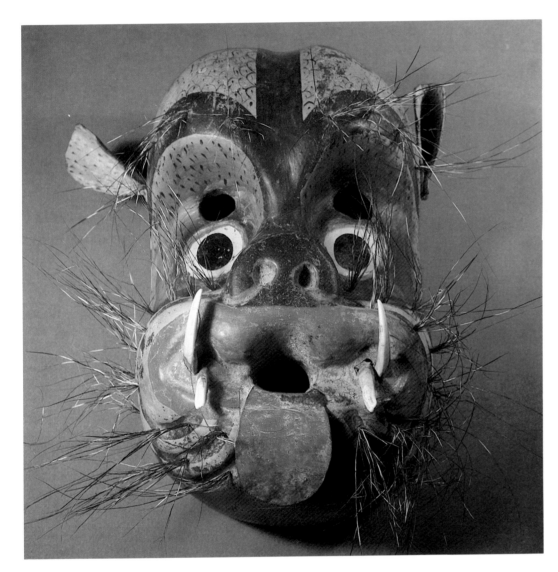

79. Tigre Mask. The famous Tigres of Olinalá, Guerrero, can always be recognized by their distinctive style, of which this is a typical example. The fine folk artists of Olinalá produce these painted masks, many of them lacquered, for use in a number of villages in the area. There are several Olinalá Tigre designs, all with piglike countenances. Property of the Smithsonian Institution. *Olinalá, Guerrero (Nahua); 32 cm.; wood, paint, boar tusks, wild boar bristle, leather.* IV.B.C.

81. Tigre mask. The cleft on the forehead is a typical feature of Olmec sculpture. *Hueycantenango, Guerrero (Nahua).* IV.A.C.

82. Tigre masks. These exotic and original hardwood Tigres come from a remote interior Nahua village. Both masks were worn high on the head so that the dancer could see out through the mouth. Mask *a* property of the Smithsonian Institution. *Quechultenango, Guerrero (Nahua); (a) 44 cm.; (b) 42 cm.; wood, paint.* IV.A.C.

83. Armadillo mask, Rabbit Dance. This sympathetic Armadillo mask has eyeholes on either side of the rabbitlike ears. The feet are shown as rather large, as the armadillo is known for its extraordinary digging ability. This type of mask was one of several styles used for the Rabbit Dance in Northwestern Guerrero (see also Fig. 84). *San Miguel Totolopan, Guerrero (Nahua); 32 cm.; wood, paint.* IV.B.C.

84. Armadillo mask, Rabbit Dance. This highly decorative Armadillo shows a strong sense of style developed by the artist. The shell of the animal has wide center bands with striking black triangles (compare Fig. 85), while the outer bands are decorated with grey dots. The head is neatly tucked in, and the tail is insignificantly small. The close association of the rabbit and the armadillo described elsewhere is a Pre-Conquest survival with fertility symbolism. *Ixcapaneca, Guerrero (Nahua); height: 30 cm.; depth: 16 cm.; wood, paint.* IV.B.C.

Guerrero. This mask is finely modeled, with the mouth ridges used to give it a ferocious aspect. The eyes, however, are completely different from those of the two masks discussed above, and they give this mask a somewhat oriental look. Note, too, the different way the nose is rendered. A fourth and radically different conception of the Tigre can be seen in the masks from Quechultenango, Guerrero (Fig. 82).

From this example, I think it is apparent that styles vary more from village to village and from one mask to another in Guerrero than in the other regions we have examined thus far. This divergence precludes minute stylistic comparisons and couches the entire discussion in far more general terms.

In comparing the masks of Guerrero to those of other states, one can say that the subjects of these masks far more often involve animal motifs, although one occasionally finds animal masks of high quality in Puebla, Oaxaca, and Michoacán as well. Guerrero also produces masks incorporating more different types of animals or animal parts in the same mask design than other states. Many of these masks are made by masters of the art who excel in making smooth transitions from one animal to another to form the overall design. One such master was José Rodríguez, the great itinerant mask-maker who moved from one *cuadrilla* to the next in the most inaccessible, remote mountain area to the south of Tlapa, Guerrero. His work can be seen in Figs. 15, 17, 18, 37, 150, 219, 222, 248, and 313. In masks like those made by Rodríguez, the various animals are used as symbols, and the entire mask becomes a symbolic statement. This type of sophisticated use of animal symbols is normally found only in Guerrero. As mentioned previously, many of these animal masks are commonly called Devil masks.

In addition to the unique use of animals, there are also a number of mask types found only in Guerrero. One of these is the Armadillo mask formerly found in El Limón, Guerrero. There are three basic forms of this mask: the helmet mask covered with real armadillo hide (Figs. 236–237), the frontal mask with pieces of armadillo hide applied (Fig. 233; see also Fig. 195); and the carved Armadillo with a hole cut in the middle of the sculpture so that it can be worn about the hips (Figs. 234, 235). There are also other types of Armadillo masks found in the general area of Teloloápan. These are smaller wooden face masks depicting the entire animal, used in the Rabbit Dance. The interpretation of the armadillo varies from village to village (Figs. 83, 84).

Other mask designs found in certain areas of Guerrero are the Moro Chino and Moro Pasión masks from the Dance of the Moors and Christians (see Figs. 42, 43, 284, 285).

Another type of mask found principally in Guerrero is that used in the Caimán Dance; it is decorated with pochote spines (Figs. 199, 247). As with the Armadillo theme, there are also representations of the Caimán (Crocodile) with an open space in the center so that it can be worn about the waist (Figs. 243, 303*c*). For years, I thought that the Caimán pochote mask and costume (Fig. 187) were unique to Guerrero, until I chanced upon a newspaper article that showed

85. Pitfall and armadillo, as seen in the Manuscrito Troano, Plate IX. After Thomas 1882, p. 98, Fig. 15. The striking black triangles across the center area of the armadillo show an Indian design sense that continues today, as shown in the modern Armadillo mask in Fig. 84.

a similar but different Caimán costume and mask from the Huastec area of the state of Veracruz. This surprised me very much until I found out that this mask and costume were made in a very small Nahuatl-speaking village called Tempoal, indicating that this motif had once been part of the general Nahua culture.

Michoacán. The state of Michoacán, which is predominantly populated by Tarascan Indians, is the second most important mask-producing state in Mexico. These masks can be categorized into two major style groupings: (1) the highly finished and somewhat restrained human representational masks (typified by the Viejitos, the Negritos, and the Christian religious masks), and (2) the wild, animalistic Devil masks.

The Viejitos (Little Old Men) are the best-known of all the Michoacán masks, especially since the Viejitos Dance has become one of the major tourist attractions of the state. These masks, while representational, are generally stylized caricatures. As can be seen in Fig. 311, they usually have large eyes and a wide, toothy grin. They are often painted white when they are carved in wood. Old clay Viejito masks from Quiroga, Michoacán, on the other hand, are often painted in darker flesh tones. Often, white "hair" is attached to the wooden masks to further reinforce the characters' age. The face itself is distorted to bolster the comic effect.

The Negrito masks are highly finished and well modeled and are generally more realistic than the Viejito masks. Although the noses and the mouths are finely and realistically fashioned, the eyes are out of proportion, and in many cases the irises are painted a bright blue. The lips are sometimes painted red, and the faces are lacquered black. The overall effect is quite individualistic. Fig. 86 shows two Negritos from Cherán, Michoacán, photographed in 1935.

The Christian masks of Michoacán are now quite rare, as the artisans seem to have stopped making them in the 1920's. The ones that are still in existence are highly realistic and seem to have been made by *santeros*. These masks exhibit a high degree of craft and ability that is characteristic of this region's mask-makers.

In comparison to the tight, restrained style of the masks discussed above, the Tarascans of Michoacán show great imagination in making Devil masks (Fig. 87; see also Figs. 41, 218, 306, 307, 312). While these masks have animal motifs, as do the Guerrero animal Devils, they often may be distinguished by their multiple, forward-projecting serpents and two or three sets of horns. In addition, a large number of these Michoacán Devils have mouths that appear to be opened in the midst of a scream; large, sharp fangs; and protruding tongues. Most often, they are lacquered. In many masks, a more traditional European Devil is incorporated into the design.

Oaxaca. In terms of quantity, Oaxaca is perhaps the third most important mask-making state in Mexico. In all likelihood, this is a direct result of the large number of Indian groups that still maintain their native languages and customs. This complicates the job of assessing mask styles and trends. In the areas discussed up to this point, we have been analyzing the masks of a single or

86. Negrito masks, Dance of the Negritos. Dancers with finely carved masks, costly headdresses, and lavish ribbon adornments. *Cherán, Michoacán, 1935 (Tarascan).* I.A.C.

87. Devil masks. Here we see some of the infinite forms the Devil takes in the rich imagination of the Michoacán carver. This group is essentially anthropomorphic with zoomorphic features, with the exception of masks *c* and *g*, which are clearly animal, and *b*, which is entirely human. Starting at the top and moving from left to right we see: (*a*) a Devil with real horns; (*b*) a lacquer mask from Uruapan used for the Hortelaños Dance; (*c*) a Pig Devil from San Francisco, Michoacán; (*d*) an old lacquer Devil from Uruapan; (*e*) an old Tarascan Devil of complex form; (*f*) a hardwood mask with unusual detachable horns; (*g*) an old Devil from Zacapu, Michoacán. Mask *c* property of Mexican Folk Arts (Chicago); masks *d, e, f* property of the University of Arizona. *Michoacán (Tarascan); 21–37 cm.; wood, paint, lacquer, animal horns, leather. (a, d, e, f)* II.B.C. *(b)* I.A.C. *(c)* IV.A.D. *(g)* IV.A.C.

88. Negro-Mestizo mask, Day of the Dead Dance. This mask, from a Negro village near the coast and the Guerrero border, is strongly reminiscent of the simplicity found in some African sculpture. The corn kernel teeth, round eyes, deer antlers, and horsehair are distinctive features that give the mask force, despite its flimsy base material. *Estancia Grande, Oaxaca; 29.2 cm.; corrugated cardboard, paint, deer antlers, horsehair, corn kernels.* II.B.C.

89. Dance and character unknown. The power of this mask lies in its crude execution, with few sculpted features and the application of iguana skin and iguana spines to represent teeth along the protruding upper lip. Eyes and see-out holes are one here, so that the mask comes to life when the dancer's eyes are visible. *San Dionisio del Mar, Oaxaca (Huave); 24 cm.; wood, iguana skin, iguana spines.* I.B.C.

predominant Indian group, such as the Tarascans of Michoacán or the Nahuas of Guerrero. The state of Oaxaca, however, has three major linguistic groups (the Mixtecs, Triques, and Zapotecs) and a large number of smaller ones, including the Amuzgos, Chatinos, Chontales, Huaves, Chochos, Chinantecs, Mixes, Tlapanecs, and even a branch of the Zoques. Over the years, the motifs and designs of these groups have diffused throughout the entire area to the point where it is often impossible to identify distinct styles for different groups, with the single exception of the Huaves, who live in a remote coastal area.

Masks from Oaxaca tend to be cruder than those of Guerrero and Michoacán. There does not seem to be as much overall emphasis on the mask as a developed art form as in the other areas. Oaxaca masks tend to be less realistic and less finely crafted in terms of modeling, surface finish, and painting. A good example is the Negro-Mestizo (Day of the Dead) mask from Estancia Grande (Fig. 88), made from folded pieces of cardboard with eye and mouth holes crudely cut out. The painting appears to have been done by the individual mask user, rather than by a professional mask-maker. Other typical Oaxaca masks are found in Figs. 89 and 178.

Oaxaca masks tend to reflect native humor and life. One example of this can be seen in Fig. 267, a comic mask from Cuilapan with a long, phallic nose that serves as a musical instrument: a *raspador*, or noisemaker. The sound is produced by scraping a stick across the ridges. Both the mask itself and its "music" are considered great fun by the spectators.

Like most regions, Oaxaca has had a number of *santeros* who have produced highly realistic masks and whose style is distinctive. See, for example, the fine mask from Juxtlahuaca shown in Fig. 146 and the exceptional work of Filiberto López Ortiz of Pinotepa Nacional, shown in Figs. 48 and 59.

The only Oaxaca Indians who have retained a unique style are the Huaves. They tend to use animal materials and motifs in their masks; the three most important are the turtle, the snake, and the armadillo. Characteristically, a turtle shell may be used to produce a work of art as in Fig. 174*b*. This use of animal materials extends even to human masks, in which armadillo skin may represent the beard and hair. Another characteristic Huave mask is the rump Serpent mask from San Mateo del Mar (Fig. 90), carved to resemble the head of a snake and worn on the dancer's buttocks.* Rump masks are found in only a few areas

90. Serpent rump mask. This Huave Indian rump mask with snake-head design is tied behind the dancer. The only other modern rump mask I have seen is the Pig rump mask from Ocozocoautla, Chiapas, shown in Fig. 94. Property of the University of Arizona. *San Mateo del Mar, Oaxaca (Huave).* IV.A.C.

---

* In the English language newspaper *The News* (June 18, 1978, Vistas section), Cayuqui Estage tells about the festivities for Corpus Christi in San Mateo del Mar in 1963 and 1964. During the late afternoon of that holiday, the Dance of the Serpent's Head took place. In this dance a rump Serpent's Head mask was worn by one of the two chief dancers, the Serpent, who wielded a large wooden sword. The second dancer, the Archer, sallied forth from the ranks, menacing the Serpent with the point of his arrow and striking the Serpent's wooden head with his whip. During the ensuing chase, the Archer beheaded the Serpent in symbolic manner, removing the Serpent's hat and placing it upon the point of his arrow. With cheers from the watching Indians, he then returned the hat to the Serpent, striking the wooden rump mask three times as he circled him. Thus renewed life was bestowed, magic had been performed, and the long-needed rains would come. The rump Serpent mask shown in Fig. 90 may not have been used in the Huave Corpus dance but is entirely typical.

of Mexico and are part of a "Pacific Basin" complex described by Michael Kan in *Early Chinese Art and the Pacific Basin* (Fraser, ed., 1968, pp. 109–111).

Puebla. As the Indians of Puebla are predominantly Nahuas like those of Guerrero, one would expect them to produce high-quality masks that are realistic and have a sophisticated use of animal symbolism. To a degree, this expectation is correct, as can be seen in Fig. 244, showing a fine, rather naturalistic Dog with *caimán* ears. These old Puebla masks are carved almost paper thin in a fine-grained hardwood.

In Fig. 161*a* we see an Apache mask that was used in the Carnival celebration in Huejotzingo. The underlying leather face of this mask is the same as that of the Serrano masks which are used for other characters in the same Carnival celebration. Differentiation between these masks is achieved through the use of supplementary materials and the painted skin tones. The Serranos have light-colored facial hair with long eyebrows, moustaches, and goatees. The Apache masks have dark-painted skin tones with gold interlocking circle patterns similar to face painting and usually a brass ring through the nose.

Another distinctive style of mask still in use in Puebla today is the Santiago mask of Cuetzalan, which has a characteristic large, sharply pointed nose and is painted a bright red. These Santiago masks show none of the high skill of the older Puebla masks. They have limited delineation of facial characteristics, except for the noses, and are commonly decorated with ribbons during the Santiago Dance. Other distinctive, unique Puebla masks can be found in Figs. 64, 65, 91, 92, 270, and 291.

Tlaxcala. Tlaxcala is famed for its Carnival masks; it is also one of the few states where a history of the development and usage of masks exists. Most informants believe that leather Carnival masks, such as the ones shown in Fig. 29*a*, *b*, and *c*, were in use around 1800. These were quite realistic and were made by pounding leather over a stone or wooden mold, as are the Huejotzingo, Puebla, Carnival masks of today. A slit was made from mouth to chin and sewn together with a thong to help form the face. When beards were used, they were made of pita fiber. According to the same informants, these masks were not satisfactory. After being used for five or six hours, they became sticky, hot, and bad-smelling, so the dancers were very happy to switch to wooden ones.

The early wooden masks were carved in a naïve manner, with painted eyes. It was not until they began to be made by the more experienced and sophisticated *santeros* that the masks acquired a very finished look, with a fine professional paint job and glass eyes with eyelashes, which is now considered to be the Tlaxcala style. The fine, old man and woman masks in Fig. 29 (*d* and *e*) date perhaps from the beginning of the twentieth century.

The latest innovation in these masks (Fig. 29*g*, *h*, and *i*) is movable eyes with false eyelashes; the cord by which the eyes are manipulated can be seen hanging below the chin. A spring keeps the eye open, and the cord is used to shut it, so that it appears to wink at the viewer. These masks for the most part represent city people and are notable for the prevalence of gold teeth. They are

92. Masks possibly for Day of the Dead Dance and Procession (November 2). These two disproportionate masks have no mouths, possibly because the dead do not speak. An extraordinary departure from the anthropomorphic can be seen in the noses: one, a coiled and painted snake, and the other, a 40.6-cm. tree branch, whose slight bend gives life to an otherwise lifeless mask. *Possibly area of Cuetzalan, Puebla; (a) 23 cm.; (b) 28 cm.; wood, paint. (a)* II.B.C. *(b)* III.B.C.

91. General mask, Battle of the Fifth of May. The carvings of this long-faced General, probably a Frenchman, is bold and primitive, and very little paint remains on the mask. There are still several wooden teeth in the mouth. For another mask from the same dance, see Fig. 64. Property of the University of Arizona. *Zacapoaxtla, Puebla (Nahua); 26 cm.; wood, paint, horsehair, leather.* I.B.C.

94

93

95

93. Carnival dancers. These dancers wear fine attire and carry umbrellas, in a dance which has ancient rain-petitioning significance. Their beautiful masks, with glass eyes, are of the type seen in the studio in Tlatempan in Fig. 147. Photograph by Ruth Lechuga. *Amaxac de Guerrero, Tlaxcala, 1977.* I.A.C.

94. Pig rump mask. This rump mask was worn by the character Maoma (Mohammed), but is also called Goliath. Its wearers also wore Parachico face masks. This rump mask is rather artless and heavy but has been lovingly embellished with a great variety of materials, including curved glass eyes and straw eyelashes. The mask is inscribed inside "1970 recuerdo [remembrance of] José Domingo H." Property of the University of Arizona. *Ocozocoautla, Chiapas (Zoque); 29 cm.; wood, paint, leather, mirror, wire, paper flowers, ribbons, straw, glass.* IV.B.C.

95. Cow mask. This very expressive mask was worn in a dance for the Fiesta of San Sebastián. The Cow appears in this fiesta together with traditional Parachico dancers (see Fig. 96), who have similar hair headdresses made of ixtle fiber. Property of the University of Arizona. *Suchiapa, Chiapas.* IV.A.C.

96. Parachico dancer. He carries a tin rattle and wears an ixtle fiber wig. See Fig. 62 for other Parachico masks. *Chiapa de Corzo, Chiapas, 1941.* I.A.C.

97. Malinche mask, "Malintsi Este Dance" (Lenten dance). Malinche is usually depicted with far more derision than we see in this forty-year-old Zoque mask. The serious yet plastic face has been carefully smoked to a flat black, with only faint patches of the red undercoat showing through. This mask was collected in 1970 by Dr. Tom Lee. The Indians, particularly the Zoques, hung masks in the smoke of their kitchens so that they would acquire a sooty black color. *Rayon Mescalapa, Chiapas (Zoque); 18 cm.; wood, paint (undercoat only), soot.* I.A.C.

painted with oil paint and/or enamel. Fig. 147 shows mask-maker Carlos Reyes Acoltzi and his two sons. Reyes and one other master carver (who now lives and works in the city of Puebla) are the only remaining makers of these fine, expensive wooden masks, which are still used in Tlaxcala today.

In addition to these extremely realistic masks, the dancers normally wear frockcoats, black trousers, dress shirts, and white gloves, and carry umbrellas (Fig. 93). This surprisingly sophisticated costume seems wildly out of place in the small provincial towns of Tlaxcala where the dance is performed, and one feels that one has just walked into a Fellini movie. Fifteen years ago, men also took the parts of the women, wearing dresses, hats, and kerchiefs over their faces instead of masks. While this dance appears very modern and sophisticated, there is probably a shamanistic undercurrent to it. The umbrellas carried in the fiesta that is conducted in the midst of the dry season may be a plea for rain. This interpretation is further reinforced at the end of the dance, when dancers wearing plumed hats (Fig. 33) carry pairs of whips made of ixtle, which they place on the ground in an arrangement that suggests serpents. As is pointed out in Chapter 9, serpents are symbolic of rain and water, and whips are often used as a substitute for them.

Chiapas. In identifying traditional styles, Chiapas presents the same type of difficulty as Oaxaca, in that there are a great number of different Indian groups in the state and that generational and village differences are often greater than tribal ones. It can be said that Chiapas masks are somewhat better crafted than those of Oaxaca, although they do not generally have the fine modeling of facial detail found in other states. A good example of this is the Cow mask used in the Fiesta of San Sebastián in Suchiapa, Chiapas (Fig. 95).

Chiapas does have highly original masks that stand out as being unmistakably from this state. These are the famous Parachico masks from Chiapa de Corzo (Fig. 62), which are extremely realistic and well finished, and have glass eyes. Even beard detail is carved into the masks. Also note the use of false eyelashes to create more realism. One of these masks is shown in use in Fig. 96. The Sak-Hol mask is also unique to Chiapas. It is a half-mask that seems to be derived from Indian traditions rather than from European origins (Fig. 134). Another unique mask from this state is the Tzotzil leather Carnival mask from Huistán shown in Fig. 161i. Generally, these Carnival masks do not show any facial details except for the sharp nose, the almond eyes, and the small round mouth. Facial painting patterns and a false moustache and goatee are sometimes added to make the mask more colorful. Another distinctive Chiapas mask is the reserved, restrained Zoque Malinche mask shown in Fig. 97, finely carved and carefully smoked over a cooking fire to an inky black. Cardboard Zoque masks can be seen in Fig. 274.

State of Mexico and Federal District. Excluding those from Mexico City (whose population is drawn from all the states of the country), the masks of the state of Mexico and the Federal District tend to represent human subjects rather than animals, as in Guerrero, or Devils, as in Michoacán. Mask styles vary sub-

98. Centurion helmet masks. These rare masks are from the eighteenth or nineteenth century, with richly carved headdresses painted in the "Estofado" manner with polychrome colors and gold leaf. The disproportionate fangs and nonhuman ears suggest evil. The Centurions played the brutal guards of Christ during Holy Week ceremonies. Over the painted eyes of the mask on the left is curved glass that was melted tó shape by the mask-maker, a feature found in other masks of this age. Both masks have movable jaws tied with thongs through holes in the side of the head. *Area of Toluca, state of Mexico; 58 cm. (approx.); wood, paint, glass, gold leaf.* II.A.C.

99. Negrito (Negro Sordo) mask, Dance of the Negritos. This mask, made by Adelaido Alvaro, is being held by Santos Tesillo, ex-mayordomo of the Dance of the Negritos in Capulhuac, Mexico. Dancers wearing black papier mâché helmet masks like this one guard the fields against animals. Probably they also fulfill the role of the black-faced clowns who are commonly used to clear the areas where the dancers perform in many parts of Mexico (see Fig. 45). Information and photograph courtesy of Eduardo Dagach. *Capulhuac, state of Mexico.* I.B.C.

stantially. Some masks, like the fine, old Centurions (Fig. 98), were painted in the churchlike "Estofado" manner. Today, masks from this area are made far more roughly. The Negrito masks by Adelaido Alvaro of Capulhuac, Mexico (Fig. 99) are papier mâché helmet masks in which only the nose is articulated, with slits for eyes and mouth. Considering the plasticity of papier mâché and what other groups (like the Coras) do with this medium, the starkness of these

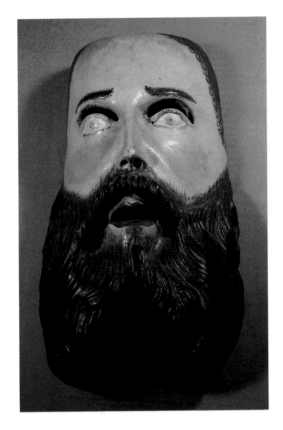

100. Probably Emperor Maximilian mask.
Masks from Morelos are rare. The village of Axochiapan particularly had a masked dance tradition. Today a few dances are still performed, but the masks are now usually of cloth, paper, or other cheap material. In 1974 I saw a dance of Las Moras (Female Moors), but no masks were used except by the King of the Moors and the King of the Christians. This mask is said to have been collected in 1925 by a Mexican resident of Cuernavaca. It probably represents the Emperor Maximilian. Apparently Maximilian left behind in this area of Morelos some blue-eyed followers from his forces, known as "Zuaves." Another, very similar mask from this period has been found, having like coloring but a slightly different beard. Both masks are in superb condition but were made for use, as they have crescent-shaped eye slits above the eyes. These masks have been given to the museum in Cuernavaca. Property of Museo de Cuauhnahuac en el Palacio de Cortés, Instituto Nacional de Antropología e Historia, Centro Regional Morelos-Guerrero. *Tepalcingo or Axochiapan, Morelos (Nahua); 34 cm.; wood, paint.* I.A.C.

masks suggests that they are not designed to resemble actual Negroes so much as one of the ancient black gods—Tezcatlipoca, Quetzalcoatl, or Ehecatl (see Chapter 2).

More realistic and more commercial are the wax masks from Santa María Astahuacán, Federal District, and from Chimalhuacán, State of Mexico. Figs. 166–168 show the process of making these masks, which are formed over a plaster mold.

Other Mask-making Areas. There are yet other areas of Mexico that produce masks, although none as important as those described above. The state of Morelos is one of these areas. Logically, one would suppose that, since its population is predominantly Nahua and it is bordered by Guerrero on one side and by Puebla on the other, Morelos should produce a large number of masks; unfortunately, this is not the case, probably because Morelos is so close to the capital and is criss-crossed with roads, and is therefore highly acculturated. However, a few excellent masks have been found in this state during the last fifteen years (see Figs. 100, 212). Morelos is most famous for the Chinelo* masks of the Tepoztlán area (Fig. 101). These Carnival masks are made from window screening stretched over a wooden mold and trimmed with black, red, or white beards and eyebrows. The major decorative accomplishment of the Chinelos is to be found in their rich velvet costumes and beaded hats. Recently, these hats began to feature small inset lights that can be turned off and on by the dancer.

Jalisco is another state in which masks have almost ceased to be produced, and only a small number of the old ones still exist. Perhaps the most characteristic of the masks of Jalisco are the long-nosed leather Devil masks shown in Fig. 70. Another type of Jalisco mask is the crude human-faced mask with lizards carved in its cheeks (Fig. 102). In style, this mask is more reminiscent of Guerrero than of neighboring Michoacán.

The masks from Veracruz are crudely representational of human faces and are not generally finely finished or painted. In the masks of Noalinco, Veracruz (Fig. 103), there is a tendency to exaggerate the eyebrows, and the painted striped patterns of the moustaches and eyebrows suggest a possible African influence. As Veracruz had one of the largest concentrations of African slaves of the Mexican states, these stripes may well be a survival of African face-painting designs. Veracruz masks sometimes also incorporate animal figures, although without the complexity or precision of the Guerrero and Puebla animal masks. Quite often, there are snake motifs, although these snakes probably do not function as water or rain symbols as do snakes in masks from drier areas. The symbolism here probably relates to the abundance of poisonous snakes in the area, with the snakes on the masks serving as talismans.

---

* The meaning of "Chinelo" is obscure. One informant stated that the name derived from the clogs, called *chinelas*, which were originally worn by the dancers. These clogs were supposedly purchased in Puebla, and since Puebla is famed for its *china poblana* (Pueblan Chinese) costume, the clogs and thereby the dancers took on the "Chinese" appellation. There has been no verification of this story, however.

101. Chinelo Carnival dancer. These dancers wear masks of window screening shaped over a mold for their pre-Lenten festivities. Great care and expense are lavished on their beaded hats and velvet costumes. Photograph by Toni Beatty. *Tepoztlán, Morelos, February 1977.* I.A.C.

102. Character and dance unknown. It becomes very difficult to determine the age of a mask that has been under protection in a collection. When this one was brought to our door in 1969 it looked familiar. After purchase, I found it pictured in *Mexican Folkways*, vol. 5, no. 3 (1929), p. 116. At that time it was owned by a Sr. Jubilo. Nothing more is known about it except that in the 1929 photograph the missing teeth and worn nose were exactly as they are here. The earless mask has a lizard and a frog carved onto the cheeks. *Jalisco; 28 cm.; wood, paint.* II.B.C.

103. Wooden mask. The colors used in this distinctive mask are largely red and white. Courtesy of the Instituto de Antropología, Universidad Veracruzana, Jalapa, Veracruz. *Noalinco, Veracruz (20 km. north of Jalapa).*

104. Carnival masks, Macho Cabrillo (Goat) Dance. These small goatman masks have both a cheerful and a sinister aspect. The faces are carved with twisted noses, a feature also seen in the masks of other cultures, such as the Seneca, the Northwest Coast Indians, African tribes, and the Eskimo. The significance of this nose in these Hidalgo masks is unknown, but facial expressions are generally exaggerated for Carnival festivities. Mask *a* property of the University of Arizona; mask *b* property of the Smithsonian Institution. *El Nante, Hidalgo (Otomí); 16 cm. (mask only); wood, paint, goat horns, wire, ribbon, bells, horsehair.* II.B.C.

Otomí masks from El Nante, Hidalgo, are small goatlike human masks of hardwood, with little articulation of facial features except for the nose, which is often twisted, as in Fig. 104.

The last mask-making state to be mentioned here is Guanajuato, which produces millions of papier mâché masks that are sold throughout Mexico. Generally, these are brightly painted Devils and Death masks. Both types are extremely popular with Mexicans, but tourists generally avoid the Death masks and buy only the Devils, a reflection of different cultural attitudes toward death. Two fine wooden masks from León, Guanajuato, may be seen in Fig. 155.

The Mayans of the Yucatán Peninsula, whose ancestors produced some of the finest of all the Pre-Conquest masks, do not make any masks now, as far as I can determine. This is surprising, given the fact that their indigenous traditions are still strong.

PART II: THE MAKING OF MASKS

105. Character and dance unknown. Mask *b* is from the late nineteenth century and is very finely crafted, with cloth beneath the paint and touches of gold leaf. It was purchased in Atzacualoya, Guerrero, from an elderly Indian, who had no information about it, although he had had it for a long time. Masks *a* and *c* are later copies of this style and much cruder in execution. In the Codex Borgia we see the face of the Earth God Tlaltecuhtli looking out from the open jaw of a *cipactli* (Fig. 249 of this volume)—a convention similar to that used here and in the Frog Devil Masks in Fig. 248. All of these may have a similar meaning surviving from Pre-Hispanic times. Mask *a* from Collections of the International Folk Art Foundation in the Museum of International Folk Art, Santa Fe, New Mexico; mask *c* property of the University of Arizona. *Guerrero; (a) 80 cm.; (b) 101 cm.; (c)75 cm.; wood, paint, cloth (b), gold leaf (b).* II.A.C.

106. Devil mask and costume. This open-mouthed, bovine Devil mask retains the Pre-Conquest conception of Tlaloc, the rain god, as a twisted snake (closely associated with water) forms the nose. The staff and the costume are basically European in nature, except perhaps for the pair of open-mouthed serpents attached on either side of the staff. See Fig. 107 for a Pre-Hispanic clay vessel representing Tlaloc with his twisted snake nose. Property of the University of Arizona. *Chilacachapa, Guerrero; height of mask, including horns: 39 cm.; depth from nose to back: 29 cm.* IV.B.D.

THE OBJECTIVE of Part II is the documentation of the art of mask-making. Since mask-making is a traditional art form in Mexico, with hundreds of years of history, it is impossible to understand contemporary masks completely without understanding their historical context. Consequently, Part II is divided into three chapters: Chapter 5, "Links to the Past," a brief synopsis of relevant Pre-Conquest and Colonial mask-making traditions; Chapter 6, "Mask-makers," a discussion of modern artisans; and Chapter 7, "Mask Materials," a description of the materials, tools, and techniques that are in use today.

5. Links to the Past

MEXICO is and has always been a mask culture, and its tradition of mask-making stretches back for thousands of years. Many "modern" mask types, mask symbols, and mask-making techniques derive from this Pre-Hispanic heritage. Contemporary masks must be viewed as part of this tradition if they are to be fully understood.

The objective of this section is to provide a brief discussion of Pre-Conquest and Early Colonial masks that have influenced contemporary masks. This discussion is a limited one, in part because of the scarcity of historical records, which makes definitive correlations almost impossible. Only a few of the Pre-Conquest masks have survived; these are generally made from clay or stone and do not represent the full spectrum of mask types. The early Spanish chroniclers tended to pay scant attention to masks in their descriptions of the gods and rites, and most of the Indian pictorial codices were burned. Over 450 years of cultural interaction with the Spanish, the Catholic Church, and African slaves further complicate any historical analysis; a detailed discussion of these influences is far beyond the scope of this book. I have included here only those materials which I feel are relevant to modern Mexican masks.

ANCIENT MASKS

Face Painting. The inclusion of face painting as a mask type may seem odd, but the function of a mask is to disguise and transform its wearer. Face painting in its ritualistic and ceremonial aspects has the same goal and so should be classified as a type of mask. In all likelihood, the first mask was the painted face, as natural dyes (such as ash, vegetable juices, and colored clays) were readily available, and people did not require great technological skill to utilize them. The face has comparatively flat surfaces on which to paint, and it is generally considered the center of an individual's personality or soul. The face is the feature that must be changed if that personality is to be replaced and transformed.

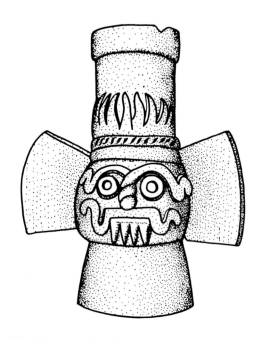

107. Clay vessel with the face of Tlaloc, god of rain. In Museum für Völkerkunde, Berlin. The drawing is ⅛ natural size. After *Comentarios al Códice Borgia* (Seler 1963), vol. 1, Fig. 301.

108. Huichol face painting. A Huichol Indian with his face painted for the peyote ceremony. The face paint is made from a yellow root said to be obtained in the state of Zacatecas during the peyote-gathering pilgrimage. *1937.*

109. Seri face painting. An old blind woman shows Seri face painting of simple everyday variety. *Punta Chueca, Sonora, 1963.*

Although far more sophisticated masks were available at the time of the Conquest, face painting was also used. In the Florentine Codex (Sahagún 1951, p. 120), we read: "And when they [the captives] were being cast into the fire, there then went dancing [one arrayed as a] squirrel. He was bedecked with a small feather crest; he had a crest. The painting on his face was in two colors. He wore a small box upon his back as he went, in which was a small dried rabbit."

Face painting is still practiced in Mexico today among the Indian groups that have had minimal outside contact, such as the Huichols (Fig. 108) and the Seris (Fig. 109). The Mayos and the Yaquis also use face-painting motifs on their Pascola masks (Figs. 72, 74). In addition to face painting, another custom similar to that mentioned above in the Florentine Codex may have also survived, as it is still common to find clowns (Huiquixtles) carrying dried, stuffed squirrels and other animals as they clear the field for other dancers.

In ancient Mexico, the body was often painted as well as the face, as is noted in the *Historia de las Indias*: ". . . three days before the fiesta the priests were painted, some white, some black, others green, others blue, others red . . . In short, they were very strange, because in addition to the many colors, 1,000 figures were made on the body, of devils, serpents, tigers, lizards and similar things. They danced all the day before stopping" (Gómara 1966, 2:426).

Although a few Mexican Indian groups (such as the Coras and the Tarahumaras) continue to paint their bodies for fiestas, the preceding passage is of interest mainly because of the mention of the creatures which were painted on the bodies. These creatures remain important symbols in contemporary masks and are discussed in greater detail in Chapter 9.

Fig. 110 shows a carved wooden Maromero (Tight-Rope Dancer) from Igualapa, Guerrero, whose costume chiefly consists of body painting, complete with the representation of an ancient green jade necklace.

Bone Masks. Bone was, of course, readily available to the ancients and could be easily worked with simple tools. Further, bone had intrinsic, magical properties within the shamanistic religious framework of Indian Mexico; it embodied the soul, the spirit of the animal. Since shamanism was largely concerned with controlling natural forces (such as the abundance of animals) in order to ensure survival, it is logical that bone was an important mask material.

One of the earliest artifacts that can be tentatively identified as a mask was fashioned from the fossilized vertebra of a llama to resemble the head of a coyote (Fig. 111). Found in Tequixquiac, state of Mexico, it is thirteen centimeters in height and dates from around 12,000 to 10,000 B.C. Whether this vertebra is or is not a mask is open to debate, but I feel that it probably is. Its small size is not significant, since masks of this size and smaller are still used in Mexico today. It is also not significant that there do not seem to be any holes on the outer edges of this mask for fastening it over the face, since bone masks used today are secured in a different manner (Fig. 112). Whether one can see out through this mask can only be determined by wearing it; in Pre-Conquest times, there were a large number of small masks without any eye openings at all. These were hung

110. Maromero (Tightrope Dancer) masks and Maromero somersault figure, Lenten Fiesta and Fair. During the Lenten Fiesta in Igualapa, Guerrero, two dancers, wearing the old masks seen here, manipulated the somersault "dancer" by the pole that pierces its body. The loosely jointed doll swings with great movement and added fun and excitement to this famous fiesta. These three pieces are probably fifty years old. Collections of the International Folk Art Foundation in the Museum of International Folk Art, Santa Fe, New Mexico. *Igualapa, Guerrero (Nahua); (a) 25 cm.; (b) 65 cm.; (c) 29 cm.; wood, paint.* I.A.C.

about the neck or waist and called amulets. More recently, small masks have been sewn onto costumes to serve as protection against evil spirits, as can be seen in Fig. 202.

A modern bone mask is shown in Fig. 112. It is from Mochitlán, Guerrero, and is made from the pelvis bone of a cow or other large mammal. Another pelvic bone mask is one made by the Northwest Coast Indians (Fig. 113), which demonstrates the diffusion of shamanism in the Americas. (See Chapter 8.)

Crowns. One element of shamanism that has had wide distribution throughout American Indian cultures is the use of crowns. While no Pre-Conquest crowns have yet been found, possibly because they were made of perishable materials, there are many indications of their existence. Fig. 114 shows contemporary crowns made by the Seris of Nayarit and the Nahuas of Guerrero. Similar crowns are to be found among the Buryat and the Altai of Siberia (Fig. 115). Andreas Lommel (1967, pp. 108–109) tells us that after a Buryat shaman undergoes a special ritual initiation, he receives an iron hat shaped like a crown and made of a hoop with two cross hoops attached to it. Among the Altai people, these crowns were sometimes worn instead of masks.

Leather and Skin Masks. The evidence that Pre-Hispanic Indians used masks made from leather is given by Francisco López de Gómara: "All garb themselves in their finest array; some stain themselves with soot, others cover

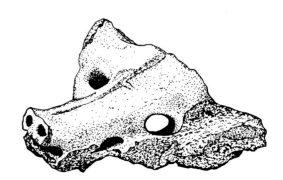

111. Fossil vertebra of a llama fashioned to resemble the head of a coyote. In the National Museum of Anthropology, Mexico City. After a photograph by Irmgard Groth, Bernal 1968, p. 32. *Tequixquiac, state of Mexico; 13 cm.; bone. 12,000–10,000 B.C.*

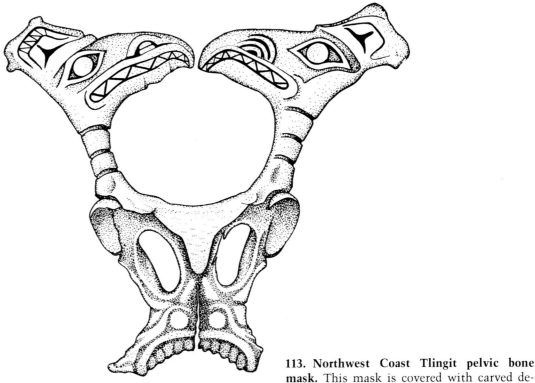

113. Northwest Coast Tlingit pelvic bone mask. This mask is covered with carved designs. After Covarrubias 1954, facing p. 40.

112. Mojiganga Procession mask. This masked musician plays a drum and participates in the Mojiganga Procession. Both men and women take part in this procession, which announces the fiesta and the dances that follow. The mask is made from the pelvis of a cow or other large mammal. (See also Figs. 113, 156.) Photograph by Marcos Ortiz. *Mochitlán, Guerrero, 1974; pelvis bone.* IV.B.C.

themselves with leaves and others don leather masks" (1965, 1:69). Because of the perishability of leather, none of these masks have survived, nor were they described in sufficient detail to make possible any comparisons to modern leather masks. Leather masks were probably more widely used than those fashioned from gold and other precious materials, though the latter are most noted in the commentaries.

In Pre-Columbian times, masks were also made from the human skin of sacrificial victims. In the *History of the Indians of New Spain*, Fray Toribio de Motolinía wrote, "They beheaded two female slaves at the top of the steps before the altar and the idols. There they flayed their bodies and faces and cut off their thigh bones. In the morning the leading Indians put on the skins, even the skin of the face like a mask" (1950, p. 66). This practice is also confirmed by other sources.* The sacrificial victims represented the gods themselves; thus these skin masks, which were the faces of the gods, constituted the ultimate religious transformation for their wearers.

---

* In the *Florentine Codex*, for instance, we read "Here [this one] was waiting. He had his mask made of the skin of the thigh [of her who had been the likeness of Toci]; and he put on his peaked cap, which was curved back and ser- rated. . . . Now he departed, in order to bear his mask, made of the skin flayed from the leg [of the woman who had represented Toci], off to the enemy's land" (Sahagún 1951, pp. 112, 114).

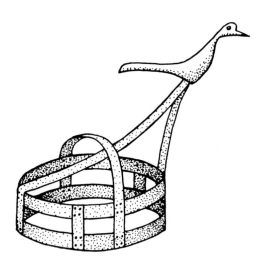

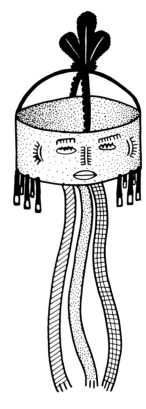

114. Seri crown (*left*); Nahua crown (*right*).

115. Altai crown. After Lommel 1967, p. 109.

Wooden Masks. As wood is the most popular material used in masks to-day, it is logical to assume that it was also a common mask material in ancient Mexico. In illustrations in the codices we see towering masks and headdresses, undoubtedly made from lightweight wood and probably decorated with huge superstructures of bark paper. Because of climatic conditions, none of these wooden masks have survived, and it is impossible to establish any direct correlation to modern masks.

Helmet Masks. When I first saw carved wooden helmet masks from several small villages in the state of Guerrero, I was confused and surprised, never having previously heard of or seen them in any dance during my years in Mexico. Immediately I thought of the large European Carnival masks of France and Italy and guessed that the idea might have been brought to Mexico. However, the appearances of these masks made this seem unlikely, for, though no one in the village remembered when or how they had been used, the masks depicted animals and, most particularly, the Lord of the Animals, a central Indian motif (Figs. 116–117).

I then found that these masks do have Pre-Hispanic antecedents. The first mention of the use of helmet masks is found in Gómara: "Many come with feather helmets or masks, made in the form of the heads of eagle, tiger, alligator and wild animals" (1966, 2:139). More direct evidence of their use is found in the small archaeological figures which were discovered in several different localities. Figs. 118–119 show a clay sculpture of a dancer from the late Classic period (A.D. 600–900) from southern Veracruz. Like other sculptures from the same period, it represents a figure over whose head fits a removable clay helmet mask.

116–117. Helmet mask, Bat Dance. Here are two views of a fine old helmet mask that shows great ability in composition and execution. In Fig. 116 we see the inevitable male face, whom we believe to be the Lord of the Animals, who accompanies the animals in so many Mexican masks. Atop the head is a baby bat, which faces backward, as can be seen in Fig. 117. Fig. 117 shows a large bat with wings spread. The genital area of the bat becomes the mouth of the human face, with teeth (a vagina with teeth?). The human countenance behind the bat body has eyes with slits for the dancer to see through. Property of the University of Arizona. *San Francisco, Guerrero (Nahua); height: 49 cm.; circumference: 104 cm.; wood, paint. (Fig. 116)* II.A.C. *(Fig. 117)* V.B.D.

The removable masks on these figures often represent skulls. Some contemporary Mexican wooden helmet masks also have a skull on one side, with another figure, very often a bat, on the reverse side (Figs. 120–121). The Pre-Columbian removable helmets, on the other hand, portray only one face each, not two. The actual use of these small clay figures is not known, but it can be assumed from their elaborate costumes and headdresses that they had ceremonial significance.

Contemporary helmet masks may be made of wood, leather, or papier mâché. We know of a wooden Tigre mask with a leather back added to make it into a helmet mask. The heavy leather helmet mask shown in Fig. 55 is so thick and stiff that it must be soaked in water before it can be worn. The old so-called Vaquero leather helmets (Fig. 22) have wooden noses and horns. A papier mâché helmet mask is seen in Fig. 99.

Wax Masks. Wax is a fragile material that in my opinion was used in Pre-Hispanic times, both alone and as a base for mosaic on wooden masks. Professor Jorge Angulo, former director of the Cuahnahuac Museum of Cuernavaca, informs me that in the excavation of a tomb in Zaachila, Oaxaca, stone mosaics were found scattered on the floor of the tomb with vestiges of the wax mask in which they were embedded still remaining. The wood had long since disintegrated. Wax was abundant in ancient Mexico. At the time of the Conquest, Motolinía commented: "There is a great deal of wax and honey in these mountains, especially in Campeche. They say that there is as much honey and wax there, and just as good, as in Safi, Africa" (1950, p. 220). One can assume that this bounty was used by Pre-Conquest Indians.

118–119. Pre-Conquest clay figure with mask. The removable mask is shown in place (Fig. 119) and removed (Fig. 118). From the collection of Dr. Kurt Stavenhagen, Mexico City; photograph by Wiltraud Zehnder.

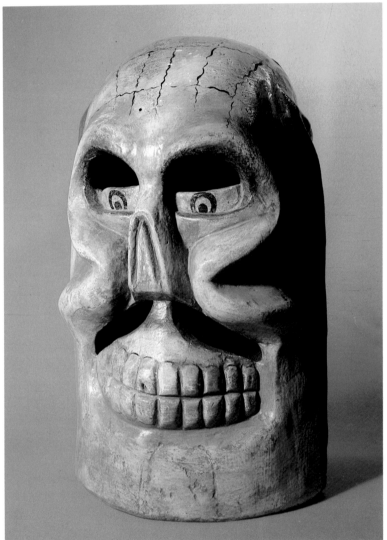

120–121. Helmet mask, Bat Dance (December 23) and Devil Dance (La Navidad, September 8). The bat and the human face are always an interesting combination in Mexican masks, as can be seen in Fig. 120, showing one view of a splendid helmet mask. The ribcage of the bat here bridges the human nose, while the bat legs are transformed into moustaches. Fig. 121 shows the reverse side, a strong Death mask in the tradition of a Pre-Hispanic motif that pervades many genres of folk art in modern Mexico. The only bat characteristic seen here is incorporated into the nose of the skull. *Tlacozotitlán, Guerrero (Nahua); 54 cm.; wood, paint.* II.B.C.

Wax is commonly used as a mask-making material today, as in the masks from Santa María Astahuacán, Federal District, which are formed over a plaster mold in a process described in Chapter 6 and shown in Figs. 166–168.

Stone and Clay Masks. Because of the durability of clay, we have direct and unequivocal evidence of mask use in Mexico by the Pre-Formative people who inhabited the area of Tlatilco about 1500 B.C. These people left behind small clay figures of shamans holding masks in their hands: these masks were probably used in magical ceremonies. Other figures include masked dancers with decorations wrapped about their legs (Fig. 122), reminding one of the butterfly cocoons used by the Mayo Indian dancers of Sonora today (Fig. 123). It is not known what material was used in making the Tlatilco masks—possibly clay, since this is a clay region, although it might just as well have been wood.

In contrast to the masks described above, the surviving clay and stone masks are commonly classified as mortuary masks, as they were usually discovered in tombs. As shown in Fig. 124, some of these masks have no eyeholes and were probably specifically made for the dead. Others, such as the Guerrero and Chontal masks and the beautiful Olmec mask shown in Figs. 124–126, do have eyeholes, whose presence suggests other possible uses. One might well think that such masks were worn by the living, as they have eyes cut to see through, a place for the nose, and even nostril holes drilled so that the wearer could breathe. The sides of such masks may also be perforated so that they could be tied over the face. There are three possible explanations for this type of construction. The first possibility is that these masks were made for, and worn by, the living and were simply buried with their owners. Second, they may have been used on wooden idols within the tombs, idols that have long since disintegrated.* Finally, all this splendid work may have been done so that the wearer could wake up comfortably after death in another world.

Stone masks have been made of jade, diorite, porphyry, granite, quartz, and alabaster. Many mortuary masks, however, were made of clay (Cordry 1973, p. 2). One interesting Pre-Hispanic use of masks is found in the clay funeral offerings that depict a dog wearing the mask of the deceased (Fig. 127). These offerings, which are particularly prevalent in Colima, illustrate the belief that the Aztec god Xolotl in his guise as a dog leads the deceased in the journey to the underworld. Miguel Covarrubias writes, "The clay dogs, made obviously as a funerary offering, are modeled with extraordinary realism; they are shown standing, seated on their hind legs, curled asleep, rolling on their backs, with bones in their mouths, barking, and so forth" (1957, p. 93). Other animals were also portrayed wearing masks (Fig. 128), possibly as part of a shamanistic ritual with the human face disguising the animal nature behind it, or with the shaman taking the characteristic of the animal whose power he utilized.

122. Pre-Classic clay figurine with leg decorations. From the collection of Miguel Covarrubias. After Covarrubias 1957, facing p. 14. *Tlatilco, Valley of Mexico, Middle Zacatenco Period.*

---

*The use of masks on idols was probably a common practice, as noted by Fray Juan de Torquemada: "They arrayed this Idol in vestments of the God Quetzalcohuatl.... and they dressed it with great ceremony, and covered its ugly face, with an uglier and more horrible mask" (1969, 2: 290).

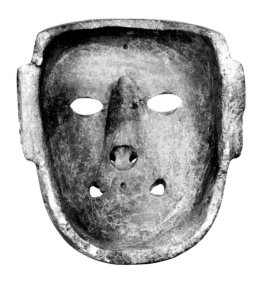

124. Olmec stone mask. Courtesy of the Instituto de Antropología, Universidad Veracruzana, Jalapa, Veracruz. *Las Choapas, Veracruz.* I.A.C.

123. Pascola dancer. This dancer wears a small mask (see also Figs. 72 and 73) and a belt with bells. In his hand is a special Mayo rattle. The cocoon leggings are possibly a survival of Pre-Cortesian leg ornaments seen on early figures from Tlatilco (see Fig. 122). The Mayo cocoon leg rattles, or *teneboim*, are from a "giant silk moth (whose silk is not utilized), Rothschildia Jorulla. The moth attaches cocoons to shrubs where Mayos and Yaquis gather them in the spring" (Fontana, Faubert, and Burn 1977, p. 48). Pebbles and sand are put into the cocoons. *Pueblo Viejo, Sonora, 1938 (Mayo).* I.B.C.

125–126. Exterior and interior of Olmec stone mask. Dated approximately A.D. 600–800. Courtesy of the Instituto de Antropología, Universidad Veracruzana, Jalapa, Veracruz. *Las Choapas, Veracruz.* I.A.C.

While very few stone masks are made today, clay was commonly employed as a mask material in the state of Michoacán up until very recent times. Fig. 160 shows a typical example of one of these clay masks; notice the delicacy of execution. Some of the famous Michoacán Viejito masks were also made of clay. But today, clay is most commonly used as a mold for making papier mâché and leather masks. The common papier mâché Carnival masks, sold in almost any market in Mexico, are made over these clay molds in Toluca and Guanajuato. Some of these molds, as well as the masks, are works of excellent craftsmanship.

Masks of Precious Materials.   The most important of the Pre-Conquest masks, at least in the eyes of the conquistadores, were those fashioned from gold, turquoise, mother-of-pearl, emeralds, etc. The early Spanish accounts abound with references to these masks and the materials that they were made from. One typical account is as follows:

127. Pre-Columbian clay funerary offering. Miguel Covarrubias describes this sculpture as a "dog wearing a human mask, with holes in the ears for earrings. Other animals shown in collections of Colima effigy-vessels are storks, parrots, a turtle with a dog's head, snakes, fish, sharks, a crab, a tarantula, shells, and snails— the representative fauna of the country" (Covarrubias 1957, pl. 93). Courtesy of the Museo Nacional de Antropología, I.N.A.H., S.E.P. *State of Colima.* v.a.c.

> *". . . they had and worshiped 2,000 gods, of which the principal ones were Vicilopuchtli and Tezcatlipucatl . . . They were of stone, well pro-portioned, although with ugly and frightening faces, as large as fully-grown giants; they were covered with mother-of-pearl, many pearls and pieces of gold were inserted through the outer layer, mounted and glued with a paste they call* tzacotli. *Birds, serpents, animals, fishes, flowers, roses made in mosaic style with turquoise, emeralds,* chalaydony, *ame-thysts and other fine stones, were beautifully executed, and the mother-of-pearl was revealed which shone greatly. Each of these idols had a thick chain of gold girded around its body, in the manner of a snake, and at the neck a thick necklace of gold down to the shoulders, from which hung ten human hearts, also of gold, with mirror eyes, that by night and by day shone greatly and in the darkness caused great terror; at the back of the head it had a face of a dead person; very dead, but none the less frighten-ing.*
> *(Cervantos de Salazar 1936, 2 : 45).**

Another sixteenth-century chronicler, an eyewitness to the Conquest, tells of Cortés climbing the steps of the Great Temple in Tenochtitlán, where, with an iron bar, he attacked the stone statues of the gods, especially that of Huitzil-opochtli, the Aztec tutelary god, which he hit between the eyes: ". . . and this way he removed the gold masks with the bar . . ." (Tapia 1971, p. 585).

A surviving mosaic mask made of precious materials is shown in the Oc-tober 1968 *National Geographic*, where it is described as follows: "Mosaic mask

---

* Some other accounts of masks made from precious materials, are as follows. Torque-mada comments upon the masks given as gifts to Juan de Grijalva by a cacique: ". . . three or four masks, parts covered with turquoise stones . . . set in the manner of mosaic work . . . and parts covered with leaves of gold . . ." (1969, 1: 354). In the *Historia General de las Indias*, masks made of precious materials are included in a listing of the ransom that Grijalva obtained. It reads:

> . . . *Two gilded masks.*
> *A mosaic mask with gold.*
> *Four masks made of gilded wood, of which one had two straight rods of tur-quoise mosaic, and the other had ears of the same, only with more gold . . .*
> *(Gómara 1966, 2: 17).*

128. Archaeological figure of a turtle. This little three-legged animal had a shaman's horn on its brow and wears a human face mask. (See discussions of horned masks on pp. 173–174.) One can see very clearly where the horn was, and one can only regret that this member was broken at some remote time. *West Coast; 12.5 cm.; clay.* V.B.D.

129. Mosaic mask in the Pre-Columbian tradition. This mask, made in recent times, follows the ancient mosaic tradition of Mexico. The wood base has turquoise inlaid around the eyes and on the upper cheeks, but plastic is used for the rest of the mosaic with such ingenuity that the mask remains both beautiful and effectively strong. It is not known whether this mask was ever used for a dance or whether it was made purely for sale. *Ixcateopán, Guerrero (Nahua); 21 cm.; wood, paint, turquoise, plastic.* I.B.C.

may have fitted a wooden figure used in religious ceremonies. Chips of turquoise and red shell encrust a serpentine base; obsidian pupils peer from mother-of-pearl eyes. The life-size mask came from the Pacific Coast State of Guerrero, a hundred miles from Teotihuacán but once under its sway." *

The making of such masks required not only great wealth but also a high degree of craftsmanship and religious motivation on the part of the Indians. After the Conquest, as their wealth and religious motivation disappeared, so did the high level of craftsmanship. Masks made of precious materials are no longer a major part of the mask-making tradition, though a few have been made in modern times. See, for example, the silver masks in Figs. 21 and 154, made between 1890 and 1910. It is surprising that these masks, which weigh up to 1.7 kilos each, have survived, rather than being cut into pieces to be sold.

---

* Bart McDowell, with photographs by B. Anthony Stewart, "Mexico's Window on the Past," *National Geographic*, October 1968, p. 501 "

In recent years in Ixcateopán, Guerrero, beautifully executed copies of turquoise mosaic masks have been made, in which white or black plastic is used together with real turquoise to simulate the ancient masks; these are sold to tourists (Fig. 129).

PRE-CONQUEST USES OF MASKS

The existence of masks made from gold, jade, turquoise, and other precious materials indicates that the Indians of ancient Mexico must have placed tremendous importance on masks. Fig. 130, from the Codex Tro-Cortesianus, shows a Mayan artisan who appears to be working on a mask, suggesting that mask-making was a large industry that involved many highly skilled craftsmen. Yet, while it is obvious that masks played a major role in the religion, there is very

130. Mayan craftsman at work. After the Codex Tro-Cortesianus, p. 65. Alfred M. Tozzer states that figures such as that being worked on here are "braseros" (1907, pp. 108, 109). Eric Thompson has suggested that they are wooden idols (1970, p. 191). I suggest that they are probably masks.

131. Eagle Knight mask, Azteca Dance. This old, well-worn mask was used in the Toto-zintla-Tixtla-Huitziltepec area of Guerrero. The carving is finely conceived and executed with unusual sweeping feathers at the rear of the mask and large red and green ear ornaments. The mask represents a warrior of the ancient Chichimecs who fights against the Christians. *Guerrero (Nahua); 42 cm. (approx.); wood (zompantle), paint.* II.A.C.

132. Xolotl as the double of Tezcatlipoca. Shown by the deformed foot sign at bottom right. As seen in the Codex Borbonicus. After *Comentarios al Códice Borgia* (Seler 1963), vol. 2, Fig. 213.

little information extant about the circumstances in which they were used. Most of the ceremonies in which masks were employed were quickly suppressed by the Catholic Church because of their "idol-worshiping" nature. Consequently, only a few of these old usages can be shown to have had any direct influence on contemporary uses. In keeping with the intent of this chapter, only those Pre-Conquest uses of masks that seem to have influenced modern usage will be presented in the text. I have, however, included a brief discussion of some of the "nonrelevant" uses in the notes for the interested reader.

Warfare. In Pre-Hispanic Mexico, warfare was almost continuous. Most of these wars were not territorial conflicts, but wars whose main purpose was to capture sacrificial victims; they are commonly called "flower wars." Warriors normally wore terrifying masks depicting jaguars, eagles, and other beasts to inspire fear in the enemy, as the wearer was thought to assume the qualities of the animal/god represented in the mask (Cordry 1973, p. 2).

The use of Eagle and Jaguar masks is found today in the Azteca and Tenochtli dances, garbled versions of the fall of Tenochtitlán in which the struggle between the Aztecs and Cortes's army is recreated (Fig. 131). Irene and Arturo Warman suggest in *Lo efímero y eterno del arte popular de México* (1971, 2:743) that Conquest dances are probably variants of the Dance of the Moors and Christians, introduced in Mexico during the early sixteenth century, but both the eagle and the jaguar were animal symbols most closely equated with war and power in the Aztec mind, and the use of these masks suggests a survival of this concept.

Representations of the Gods. In religious rites in ancient Mexico, masks were worn not merely to represent a particular god but to transform the wearer into that god. This is not actually a specific use of masks but the primary function of all masks. The numerous gods in the Pre-Hispanic pantheon were differentiated from one another by the assignment of distinct characteristics to each. The Aztec god Xolotl, for example, was associated with the dog; Tezcatlipoca, with burning or mirror eyes and the jaguar; and Quetzalcoatl with the plumed serpent. Also, the gods were identified by specific vestments and objects held in their hands (Caso 1958, p. 21), in much the same way as the Catholic Church used to identify its saints. The coloring of these symbols was also important; many gods were associated with identical objects, but of different colors.

Modern masks frequently incorporate many of these identifying symbols. Because of the long time span and the lack of documentation, it is impossible to state whether these symbols are direct survivals or simply represent traditional motifs that have been passed down from generation to generation but have lost their original meanings. The similarity of some masks to older prototypes and their use in some of the contemporary dances strongly suggest that there are many such "survivals" in modern masks. Part III deals with this issue in greater depth.

One example, however, of a possible direct survival (as opposed to a symbolic one) is the Sak-Hol (White Head) mask used in the Fiesta of San Sebastián in the Tzotzil village of Zinacantán, Chiapas (Fig. 134). This is a simple leather mask, covered with tinfoil; it covers only the upper half of the face. Although half-masks are extremely uncommon in Mexico today, there are many Pre-Columbian archaeological figures with masks covering just the upper or lower half of the face. It could be argued that the Sak-Hol mask may be a variant of the half-masks used in Pre-Hispanic Mexico (Fig. 135a). The remoteness of Zinacantán leads me to believe that this could be an indigenous survival.

Protection. In Pre-Hispanic Mexico, masks were often worn for protection against evil spirits, against illness,* and in funeral rites.† Of these three uses of masks, the only one that seems to have a possible connection to modern use is that of protection against evil spirits. According to Sahagún (1953, pp. 27–28), during the Aztec New Fire ceremony (which was performed every fifty-two years to rekindle the sun), pregnant women and children wore masks of maguey leaves, to protect them from changing into wild beasts and mice, respectively. The connection of this practice to modern masks comes not in the ritual itself but in the use of maguey as a mask material.

While I have not encountered any masks specifically of maguey leaves, there is one mask from San Juan de las Colchas, Michoacán, made from the heart (*quiote*) of the maguey (Fig. 173). The maguey plant has always been considered a magical plant with special properties; thus its use as a protective agent is readily understandable. Some of the names of the over two hundred species of maguey are very revealing of this aspect of the plant: *maguey manso* (tame maguey), *maguey bravo* (savage maguey), *maguey bruto* (beastly maguey), and *maguey curandero* (healer maguey). Since most makers of wooden masks believe that masks embody the magical properties of the material they are made from, it is logical to assume that this modern mask is also thought to incorporate some of the characteristics of the maguey itself.

Entertainment. In Pre-Conquest Mexico, as today, there were some dances which must be classified as entertainment, although they may also have

---

* As noted in *Datos para la historia de la farmacia pre-cortesiana*, "For as long as the illness of some individual lasted, his face was covered with masks of Huizilopochtli or of Tezcatlipoca" (Rea 1953, pp. 10–11). In the *Historia General de las Indias* Gómara comments upon how masks were utilized as a precaution against illness: "When the King of Mexico is sick, masks are put on Tezcatlipoca or Vitcilopuchtli or on another idol, and they are left there until he recuperates or dies" (Gómara 1966, 2: 394). These two statements are quite different. In the first, the mask of the god is put on the individual. In the second, a mask was put on one of the idols mentioned, but this statement does not tell us what mask was thus used. One wonders if it could have been a stylized mask of the king. When the king died, Gómara continues, a mask "painted with devils" [pagan gods] was placed over his face.

† When mortuary bundles were the custom, a mask of stone, wood, or possibly copper was tied to the top of the bundle. "Of the ceremonies with which they buried the lords, and those who were not, in this New Spain . . . All assembled together, they put the dead body in order, wrapping him up in fifteen or twenty exquisite capes woven with a design . . . , and when he was shrouded and his face covered, they placed a painted mask on top" (Mendieta 1945, 1: 178).

134. Sak-Hol (White Head) mask. Used by the Tzotzil Indians of Zinacantán, Chiapas, for the Fiesta of San Sebastián. Mask and information courtesy of Walter "Chip" Morris.

133. Devil masks. These masks are now termed Devil masks because of the Spanish influence but may at one time have represented something else. Each figure holds in its mouth a snake that becomes its nose. A hint as to their possible Pre-Hispanic meaning is given in the Florentine Codex:

"And [an image of] Tlaloc was set in place. Before him was [a vessel of] water. It was full of serpents and frogs. And they who were called *Maçateca* swallowed the serpents [while still] full alive. Each one severally held them only in their mouths, not with their hands. They took them only in their teeth, when they seized them in the water, there before [the image of] Tlaloc. And the Maçateca went eating the serpents with which they went dancing.

"And he who first finished with a serpent—who swallowed it—then raised a shout and a cry; he circled the temple. And they offered gifts to those who swallowed serpents." (Sahagún 1951, pp. 163–164)

"And thus they swallowed frogs, likewise alive. When this was similarly done, these very same macateca performed [the swallowing]." (Ibid., p. 188)

This ritual is similar to a dance for rain done by the Hopi of New Mexico.

Mask *a* property of the University of Arizona. *(a) Apaxtla, Guerrero; (b) Cuetzala, Guerrero; (c) Copalillo, state of Mexico; (d) Michoacán; (a) 44 cm., including horns; (b) 31 cm.; (c) 44 cm.; (d) 35 cm.; wood, paint (a, b, d), animal teeth (b, d).* II.B.C.

135. Some Pre-Conquest styles of masks. (*a*) A small mask worn over the upper part of the face. The man looks through the mouth, but it is not entirely clear from the drawing whether the chin is carved or whether it belongs to the wearer of the mask. For a modern mask with similar characteristics but with a carved chin, see Fig. 226. (*b*) A mask of Tlaloc from the same codex of a more openwork character. We don't know whether the nose is carved or belongs to the wearer. (*c*) An animal mask of which we have almost exact counterparts today. It is probably a wolf or coyote. (*d*) A very cleverly devised skull. It probably is not all carved but rather is a mouth mask (see below). (*e*) A figure of a double-faced torchbearer. We cannot tell whether there is a large helmet mask hiding the head of the wearer or whether one face is that of the wearer, with a mask on the back of her head. This figure shows the idea of duality. (*f*) Probably a mouth mask in the shape of a bird. It would have been held in place by a leather strap or a piece of wood held in the wearer's teeth. Such masks exist today in Indonesia and Africa, though they are no longer used in Mexico. (It is possible that the whole face and mouth ornament here is a single mask, but it appears more likely that a mouth mask is involved.) (*g*) A Mayan with a mask. This representation may depict a long, narrow mask of a type no longer in use in modern Mexico; or it may simply be a depiction of the wearer's face and the mask at the same time through an artistic convention similar to our use of dotted lines to indicate interior surfaces. Masks *a*–*f* after the Codex Nuttall (Nuttall, ed. 1974); mask *g* from Stela 11, Yaxchilan (after Kubler 1962, plate 76).

Anne C. Paul writes of similar cut-away masks on a Maya vase: "The most intriguing and unusual items of dress which these figures wear are the human-image face masks; these masks partially reflect the profiles of the men who wear them. Apparently made of wood, they are attached to the headdresses and exhibit slight variations in construction. The example on Person 3 is moveable; it is hinged at the mouth and is activated by means of a cord which is attached to the chin and held in the wearer's left hand. The other masks also appear to be hinged although no pulling-cords are indicated. The masks on Persons 6, 8 and 11 have goatees. Those on Persons 6 and 11 have traces of a moustache, and those on Persons 9 and 11 have teeth set into both the upper and lower jaws" (Paul 1976, p. 121).

had subsidiary functions.* One such dance that existed in ancient times and whose variants are still practiced today was described by Fray Diego de Durán: "Another dance is performed; that of the old Humpbacks who wore masks representing old men. It was extremely gay, merry, and funny in the native fashion" (1971, p. 297). Because of Durán's use of the word *corcovados*, which can mean either "humpback" or "bent over," it is not known whether he was describing the Humpbacks Dance, which is still performed in Oaxaca, or the Viejitos Dance, in which the "old men" are bent over. It is possible that these two dances are variants of the dance that Durán observed.

Another modern dance with Pre-Hispanic origins is the Stilt Dance. Although there are no descriptions of how this dance was performed before the Conquest, there are a number of depictions in various codices of dancers performing on high stilts, such as the woman from the Codex Tro-Cortesianus pictured in Fig. 136. In Fig. 137, we can see a modern performance from the Indian State Fair of Oaxaca in 1941.

COLONIAL INFLUENCES

It is difficult (if not totally impossible) to identify accurately all the cultural influences on the Indians and their folk art that were introduced during the Colonial Period. It is even more difficult to gauge how these influences affected the various Indian groups and their mask-makers, as many of these groups lived in remote, inaccessible places and spoke only their own languages. We can, however, identify three major cultural influences—the Spaniards, the Catholic Church, and the African slaves—although these influences were not distributed equally throughout Mexico.

The Spaniards had a strong secular folk-art tradition, particularly in regard to masks. In the New World, this tradition was manifested in the form of *mascaradas*, which are described as follows by Irving A. Leonard:

> The commonest public spectacle was the máscara or mascarada. It was, essentially, a parade of persons dressed in varied costumes and wearing peculiar masks, who promenaded about the streets by day or night, on foot, or mounted on horses or other animals; if after dark, they carried

---

* An ancient entertainment dance with such a subsidiary purpose is reported in the *Book of the Gods and Rites and the Ancient Calendar*: ". . . another man appeared, representing a person with a cold, coughing constantly, feigning a chill, making wild and funny gestures. Then the actors were a large fly and a beetle; they came out imitating these creatures in lifelike fashion. One of them buzzed like a fly when it comes near meat, while the other watched him and said a thousand funny sayings. Then this other, disguised as a beetle, poked about the rubbish. All these native farces were highly amusing and pleasant, but were not acted out without pagan meaning, for they stemmed from the fact that the god Quetzalcoatl was held to be the advocate for tumors, eye disease, colds, and coughing. Thus, in these same farces they included words of pleading directed to this deity. They begged for help, and so it was that all those suffering from these ills and diseases came with their offerings and prayers to this idol and his temple" (Durán 1971, p. 135).

*lighted torches, giving the city an unaccustomed illumination. They rep-
resented historical, mythological, and Biblical personages, gods of primitive religions, astrological planets, allegorical figures of Virtues, Vices,
and other abstractions, and almost any bizarre creature, real or imaginary, was a welcome novelty. Impersonations reflected themes which
varied from the sublime to the ridiculous, from the refined to the grotesque, and from the exalted to the most satirized. To an illiterate public
the* mascarada *was like an animated magazine bringing before their avid
eyes a semblance of things real and imagined; it instructed, it diverted, it
entertained, and it often expressed their moods, their reverence, and their
resentment.*

Those mascaradas *featured the garbs of many nations, and a partial-
ity for that of the Turks, still threatening in Europe, was second only to
the costumes of Indian tribes nearer home. The impersonation of familiar
and exotic types did not, however, exhaust possibilities, for the participants frequently marched in the simulated forms of birds, animals, and
imaginary creatures.*

(I. Leonard 1959, pp. 118–120)

The second major influence was the Catholic Church. The missionary zeal
of the Church produced the most direct contact with the native populations, as
it tried to suppress Indian religions and replace them with Christianity. There
was no Indian group that did not have at least some contact with the Church,
which had a rich, complex iconography complete with religious celebrations
and processions. "The Church . . . did not fail to recognize this general passion
for pageantry which it shrewdly utilized to its own advantage by sponsoring
processions displaying the richly clothed images and ornate symbols of the
Faith with all the pomp, splendor and wealth at its command" (I. Leonard 1959,
p. 118).

The last major influence was that of the African slaves. Although slavery
never reached the proportions in Mexico that it did in the United States, large
numbers of Africans were brought to Mexico to work the sugar cane. The
Blacks, with their strong African mask-making tradition, were quickly integrated into the Indian communities, and even today there are a number of Indian
groups that must be classified as negroid (see Cordry and Cordry 1968, p. 299).
Since the effect the two groups had on each other was not documented by the
Spaniards or the Church, it is difficult to say how much or how little African
traditions influenced Indian mask-making.

In the Early Colonial Period, the processions and the masks were probably a
mixture of Indian and European traditions, but as the Colonial Period wore on,
masks acquired more of a Spanish character. We are told by Manuel Romero de
Terreros y Vinent (1923, pp. 23–24) that in a fiesta for the glorification of San
Isidro el Labrador on January 24, 1621, an elaborate procession paraded through
the streets of Mexico City. On one of the floats, the allegorical figure of Fame

136. Woman walking on stilts. She is wearing an animal headdress for a ceremonial rite. After the Codex Tro-Cortesianus, Folder 36, top. "The special evils that happened during the Muluc years were a scarcity of water and an abundance of sprouts in the corn. The old women had to perform a special dance on high stilts and to offer dogs made of pottery with food placed on their backs" (Morley 1956, p. 215).

137. Masked stilt dancers. These dancers are from Santa María Roala (near Zaachila), Oaxaca, photographed at the Indian State Fair of Oaxaca, 1941. Stilt dancers still perform in this village for the Day of San Pedro, June 29.

138. Pilate mask and Sultan mask, Dance of the Moors and Christians. These Moor masks are semi–helmet masks in that the rear is carved to fit partially over the dancer's head and he looks out through ample curved openings above the eyes. These masks have not been used for more than twenty years and have been well cared for. The fine carvers from the village of San Martín Pachivia, Guerrero, produced masks for many other settlements, such as Ahuacatitlán, where these two masks were collected. The dark-faced Pilate (*a*) is truly splendid, with his intricate crown and wavy hair, while the Sultan (*b*) can be recognized by his turban, decorated with half-moons and stars. *Ahuacatitlán or San Martín Pachivia, Guerrero; (a) 74 cm.; (b) 63 cm; wood, paint.* I.A.C.

wore a silver mask made by the silversmith Juan Rodríguez Abril, a clear example of the carry-over of the Indian tradition.

Many of the Colonial masks also began to be covered with gold leaf. The masks in Fig. 98 are probably from the late eighteenth or early nineteenth century and are said to represent the centurions who guarded Christ. Later masks that reflect the Colonial style are to be seen in Figs. 138 and 286 (Moors from the Dance of the Moors and the Christians). Very few real Colonial masks exist today.

However, the Spanish influence did not totally overwhelm and replace the Indian. While the Indians readily accepted the pageantry, glamour, and beliefs of the Church, many retained parts of their own religious systems below the surface. The fact that early Christian missionaries tended to merge pagan festivals and usages into the Christian calendar and hagiography allowed a great number of Pre-Conquest beliefs to survive, in many cases producing a strange coexistence of Christian and Indian beliefs, in which individuals may participate and believe in elements of both systems without seeing any conflict. In most cases, however, the Indian beliefs are fragmentary, since they depend solely upon oral tradition.

In a very few, isolated cases, native religious practices have survived almost intact; one striking example of this is the Judea fiesta celebrated by the Cora Indians of Nayarit. Originally, the Judea was a re-enactment of the Passion Play taught to the Coras by Jesuit missionaries. When the Jesuits were expelled from Mexico in the early nineteenth century, this Easter Play quickly reverted to something far closer to the Indians' real beliefs. Today, the Judea consists of two opposing armies, the Pharisees and the Romans, in mock combat. These "soldiers" are painted from head to toe in striking designs, wear brilliantly colored papier mâché animal masks (Fig. 172), and engage in ritual drunkenness and simulated public masturbation. Observers not aware of the "Christian" theme of this event would probably think that they were witnessing a strictly pagan fertility ritual. In this case, Pre-Hispanic traditions and beliefs have never been completely integrated with Christian beliefs.

139. Hermit mask, Pastorela Dance. Carved with sincerity rather than sophistication, this semi–helmet mask has a primitive charm reminiscent of some Byzantine icons. The paint is applied thinly and without undercoat, probably for financial reasons. *Region of Acapetlahuaya, Guerrero; 35 cm.; wood, paint.* I.A.C.

6. Mask-Makers

MASK-MAKING is a disappearing art whose traditions are rapidly being lost as a result of the social changes occurring in Mexico today. Remote villages which required a two- or three-day horseback ride to visit in the 1930's and 1940's now have roads and some type of regular bus service; their traditions are no longer protected by isolation. Even the land of the Huichol Indians, which was safeguarded by the rugged mountains of the Sierra Madre Occidental, has recently been penetrated by roads and planes and is being opened to modern influences.

The increase in population due to better medical care and the shift from subsistence agriculture to modern farming techniques have caused a major flight of people from the countryside to the cities. Today, it is rare to encounter a village which does not have at least a few members living in an urban area. As many of these members are viewed as "progressive" by the other village members, their visits to relatives and friends not only serve as direct sources of cultural diffusion but also reinforce the prejudice that too often exists about the Indian way of life in today's Mexico.

Changes in the educational system have also hastened the cultural integration of indigenous groups into the mainstream of Mexican culture. In the past, most of these villages had either limited educational programs or none because of the lack of funds and teachers. In recent years, the government has launched a major effort to teach Spanish and provide a basic education for these groups. In many cases, this has resulted in the functional loss of Indian languages by the young and in the corresponding loss of the culture's traditions.

One of the most profound agents for change has been the wide acceptance and use of radio and television. After a village receives electricity, the first modern appliance to be purchased is often a television or a radio. Not only do television and radio place further emphasis on the use of Spanish as the primary language; they also speed the substitution of modern values for traditional ones and accelerate the flight from the villages to the cities.

140. Mask-maker Don Placido. The mask-maker is shown blocking out a Pascola mask. A finished, painted model is seen in the foreground. *Antanguisa, Sonora, 1938 (Mayo).*

141. Mask-maker Fidel de la Fuente. This mask-maker makes Devil masks with many horns and small devils emerging from the face. In this town on September 16 there is a contest of Devils, and the young men help each other to finish the masks until the evening before the festival, each adding details of beard, hair, and metallic paint according to his taste. Because of this competition, new masks are made each year. Later they are sold or kept by the participants as mementos. Photograph by Ruth Lechuga. *Teloloápan, Guerrero, 1976.*

142. Boy with several masks. Here we see the son of mask-maker Eliseo García in front of his father's house with a group of masks. The first and third masks here are of the types seen in Figs. 193b and 39, respectively, although the spirit helper is missing from the Vulture mask. *Huitziltepec, Guerrero, 1970.*

143. Mask-maker Cruz Teodora. A fine Guerrero mask-maker, said to have been about forty-five to fifty years of age in 1931, when this picture was taken. On the right is a Tlacololero mask, which in Guerrero is the only type of mask to almost always have large round eyeholes on the cheeks. The mask alone on the lower step is an interpretation of Christ and is now the property of the Heye Foundation's Museum of the American Indian in New York.

140

142

141

143

As the erosion of the languages and traditional values of indigenous villages increases, the function and the importance of masks within those communities are also eroded. Fewer and fewer young people see any necessity or value in becoming mask-makers. Thus, in many villages the craft of mask-making is restricted to old men and is disappearing.

In an effort to document the craft of making masks while it was still possible, I initiated a partial survey of existing mask-makers with the assistance of María Teresa Pomar and her helpers, in order to augment the field observations that I have made over the last forty years. This survey, which was in the form of a questionnaire, concentrated on the materials, paints, glues, and tools used by individual mask-makers, as well as when and in which dances their masks were used, and whether they were sold to other towns for use in their fiestas. Questionnaires were completed by forty-two modern Mexican mask-makers from eight states, as follows: thirteen from Michoacán, ten from Oaxaca, ten from Guerrero, three from Zacatecas, two each from Hidalgo and Querétaro, one each from Puebla and Chiapas. This distribution more or less reflects the distribution of mask-making in Mexico today, with the addition of Veracruz and some mask-making groups, such as the Huichols, the Coras, the Yaquis, and the Mayos, which were outside the survey area. The individual responses of the forty-two mask-makers are included in the Appendix.

Many years of study could be devoted to gathering data on the work of the scores of fine mask-makers who worked from ten to fifty years ago and more. Except in rare instances,* one cannot find even their names, although at times it is possible to identify the work of a sculptor by the style of carving. It is interesting to discover that one man's good work spread to nearby villages and often covered a wide radius. Of the forty-two mask-makers surveyed, sixteen sold their masks to markets other than local, which indicates the inherent difficulty in tracking down any particular craftsman. Masks are one of the most widely circulated of all folk arts.

In my years of investigating masks, I have been fortunate enough to become familiar with the work of numerous mask-makers, many of whom have since died. A good number of the craftsmen who made the masks shown in this book died from ten to forty years ago, and their successors know little of the old traditions. Fig. 144 shows Nalberto Abrahán, one of the ablest Indian wood carvers I have seen in Mexico. This photograph was taken in Tixtla, Guerrero, in 1945, and I never have forgotten Abrahán or his magnificent carved wooden masks and dolls. When I was able to return to Tixtla in 1972, it had changed from a small

---

* One instance where the names of past mask-makers were recorded was in Acapetlahuaya, Guerrero, where they were written into the municipal record. According to Arturo Reyes, one of my informants, these were as follows:

"1. Pablo San Pedro. 1755. He was also known as Pablo Santero, because he sculpted many saints. It is said that all he needed to do was to see a person once and he could sculpt them in wood.

"2. Sebastián Neri. 1860. He was a mask-maker.

"3. Guillermo Pico. 1887. Mask-maker for dances.

"4. Florentino Casino. 1925. Mask-maker for dances."

145

144. Mask-maker Nalberto Abrahán. Abrahán not only made excellent masks but also carved extraordinary wooden dolls, photographs of which are to be published at a later date. He died in 1966 at the age of eighty-eight. In 1972 we returned to Tixtla and found his son, who was also a mask-maker (see Fig. 145). *Tixtla, Guerrero, 1945 (Nahua).*

145. Mask-maker Ruperto Abrahán. Ruperto Abrahán was the son of the very fine mask-maker Nalberto Abrahán (Fig. 144). Ruperto died in 1974 at the age of seventy-four, but a third-generation son, also named Ruperto, is said to be working as a mask-maker in Tixtla. *Tixtla, Guerrero, 1972 (Nahua).*

Indian village to a sizable town. I tried to find Abrahán or his descendants and finally located his seventy-two-year-old son Ruperto, who said that his father had died in 1966 at the age of eighty-eight. Ruperto was also a mask-maker but had very little inherited talent. He did, however, make good Tlacololero masks, such as the two he is shown with in Fig. 145. Ruperto died in 1974, and one of his sons is now carrying on the tradition. It remains to identify and record the few remaining good old mask-makers in Mexico; when they are all gone, the links with past customs will also disappear.

TYPES OF MASK-MAKERS

As mentioned briefly in Chapter 1, the mask-makers I have known throughout Mexico fit into three categories according to their background and their mask-making style. First is the *santero*, who makes masks and church figures. He usually has the approval and assistance of the local priest and therefore has access to good paint, glass eyes, commercial hair, and even gold paint or tinsel paper. Above all, he may have a few good tools, since he carves large church figures. This mask-maker produces fine, well-finished masks which are used by the people of his village and are in demand by those villages near and far where his fame has traveled. These sophisticated masks may have movable eyes, eyelashes, and gold teeth. People pay as much as one hundred pesos per mask to have these repainted each year and also pay high prices for costumes of a suitable quality, appropriate for use with the masks. The *santero* has good paint and

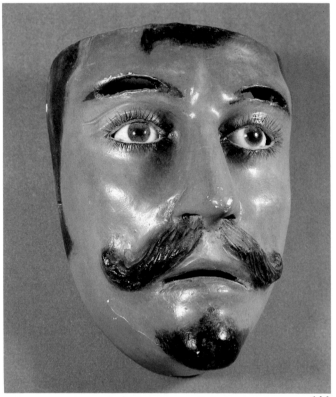

146

147

148

146. Character and dance unknown. Obviously the product of a *santero*, this realistic face is well carved and painted. The brown eyes and dark complexion are unusual for a *santero* mask, as the ideal for these carvers is usually a European/Spanish fair complexion with blue eyes. *Juxtlahuaca, Oaxaca (Mixtec); 20 cm.; wood, paint, glass eyes.* I.A.C.

147. Church sculptor and mask-maker Carlos Reyes Acoltzi and his sons. Shown in their workshop, "El Arte." In 1975 we heard that there was only one son working with his father. (See Fig. 29 for other Acoltzi masks; see also Figs. 33, 93.) *Tlatempan, Tlaxcala, 1971.* I.A.C.

148. Character and dance unknown. This beautifully mended lacquer mask was seen in the house of a mayordomo, where an old woman "apparently owned it privately and held it in great veneration. After taking the mask from the chest where her clothes were kept, and laying aside the many wrappings of cloth and paper, she said: 'It is like a saint.' Then she kissed the mask and talked to it softly in Zoque. This mask belonged to her great-great-grandmother, and it had the fine patina and appearance of the wooden santos of the 18th century. In Copainalá the same masks are used in various dances and are often rented for a peso each" (Cordry and Cordry 1941, p. 60). *Copainalá, Chiapas (Zoque); 19 cm.; wood, lacquer.* I.A.C.

149. José Rodríguez. An old photograph of the extraordinary mask-maker José Rodríguez and his young family taken in a Chilapa, Guerrero, studio (date and photographer unknown). Rodríguez lived and worked in the *cuadrilla* of Santa Anita and other *ranchos* and villages of Guerrero, and he died many years ago. This picture belonged to an aged cousin of Rodríguez and was brought to us in Cuernavaca. The dates of his life have not been determined. One bench he carved was dated 1919, but no other dates have been found. It is to be hoped that more information will eventually be uncovered.

knows how to use it. Generally, the standard of the *santero* is one of realism (see Figs. 49, 270, 291).

Santeros producing masks as of 1978 are to be found in Juxtlahuaca, Oaxaca; the city of Guanajuato; and Chiapa de Corzo, Chiapas. There are also Carlos Reyes Acoltzi and his son, who are currently working in Tlatempan, Tlaxcala. Their very highly finished masks are widely respected and are used during Carnival in various towns in the state. They are used on Carnival Tuesday in San Bernardino Contla; on the first Sunday of Lent in San Francisco Tepeyanco; and on Carnival Sunday in San Juan Totolac. Fig. 29 shows the two general mask types, with and without beard, with stationary glass eyes and eyes that blink when a string hanging below the chin is pulled. Reyes has very professional carving tools from Mexico City, although he probably uses a machete to form the original block. He also has a special room attached to his house that he uses as a workshop (Fig. 147).

Second is the professional mask-maker who has neither the *santero*'s training nor his standard of realism. Rather, he came to be a mask-maker by virtue of having considerable aptitude for the craft as well as varying degrees of artistic, creative talent. He may or may not have inherited the profession from his father and/or grandfather. His masks may have a wonderful naïve quality which makes one think of Byzantine or early Christian art (Fig. 139), or they may be very skillfully and imaginatively executed, realistic portrayals (Fig. 148).

This mask-maker is likely to know the symbolism of each mask and how to use the symbols, incorporating them into the design. By making many masks over the years, he may have developed a readily recognizable style. Moreover, he may sell his masks to other villages, where they may be used for characters other than those for which they were originally intended. One typical example of this is the animal masks made for an Animal Dance with definite Pre-Hispanic origins (Fig. 222). These masks often turn up elsewhere as Devils for a Devil Dance.

In this category, one of the most extraordinary mask-makers during the last centuries in Mexico was José Rodríguez (Fig. 149), who lived and worked as a goatherder in small, remote *cuadrillas* (settlements) in the eastern, Tlapa side of the state of Guerrero thirty to fifty years ago. His masks were so respected that in villages where he worked, whole sets of masks have been kept in chests in the church or on the municipal building walls for all these years. He was said to have lived first in a community called Cuadrilla Santa Anita. This small community and the others where he worked, which do not appear on most maps of Guerrero, have kept their traditions intact to an extraordinary degree.

Rodríguez created the twenty-five masks used in the Diablo Macho Dance, which was performed in Santa Anita on June 5 as a prayer for rain. Each mask is unique and has many symbolic water creatures and a semihuman face, as can be seen in Fig. 17. These probably originally represented gods rather than devils, as has been mentioned. Rodríguez's knowledge of animals, snakes, lizards, frogs, and bats was great as was his knowledge of the supernatural.

151. Filiberto López Ortiz and his wife. This very gifted mask-maker was most unfortunately killed in a land dispute a few years later. (See Figs. 48 and 59 for examples of his work.) *Pinotepa Nacional, Oaxaca, 1965.*

150. Owl masks, Tecolotillo (Little Owl) Dance (August 14). José Rodríguez must have spent an unusual amount of time creating this set of Owls, with their particularly careful painting and beautiful color schemes. The owl was associated with death in rural Mexico, and these have a particularly frightening aspect that brings to mind the proverb, "When the owl screeches, the Indian dies." Santamaría (1959, p. 1018) writes of a custom called *poner el tecolote* ("to place the owl") in which a crucifix was placed at the head of a dead person, while a candle was placed at the feet. The combination of the lizard with the owl seen here is one of those mysterious animal relationships whose meaning is no longer known. Mask *c* property of the University of Arizona. *Parotillas, Guerrero; (a) 36 cm.; (b) 44 cm.; (c) 34 cm.; wood, paint (earth colors).* IV.B.D.

153

152. Possibly Carnival mask. Although it is the work of a nonprofessional carver, this mask has a naïve charm in its distinctive use of color and simple carving. The numeral 4 repeated on the face appears to be merely a random decoration. The mask was probably used in Carnival, although the former owner said it was used during Holy Week ceremonies. *Tancanhuitz, San Luis Potosí (Huastec); 30 cm.; wood, paint.* I.A.C.

153. Matachines Dance mask. This unpretentious mask was made by a nonprofessional, yet is very expressive in its simple carving and in the use of plain, available natural materials. Collections of the International Folk Art Foundation in the Museum of International Folk Art, Santa Fe, New Mexico. *Villa García, Zacatecas; 26 cm.; wood, paint, animal fur, cotton yarn.* I.A.C.

José Rodríguez also made masks for a settlement called Parotillas for the Tecolotillo (Little Owl) Dance, performed on August 14. The three Owls in Fig. 150 are very original in design, and the handling of the paint shows great talent. Commercial paint is primarily used on these masks, but some of the Rodríguez masks are painted with earth pigments.

These first two groups of mask-makers can be classified as professionals, even though those in the second group do not have the official sanction and support that the *santeros* have. These two groups represent the mask-makers involved in our survey. It is interesting to note that twelve of the mask-makers who completed the questionnaires had fathers who were also mask-makers and seven had grandfathers who had been mask-makers.

The third type of mask-maker is the amateur, a poor man who can't afford to purchase or rent a mask but has made a vow to the patron saint of his village to dance on the Día del Patrón. His mask may be an artful, naïve creation (Fig. 299), or it may be entirely without esthetic merit. Very likely, it will be crudely carved and unpainted, except for a bit of shiny oil paint borrowed from a neighbor (Fig. 175).

7. Mask Materials

CONTEMPORARY MASKS are most commonly made of wood; however, a wide variety of other materials are used as well. Most of these basic materials are traditional and have been in use since before the Conquest. Of course, some changes have occurred, as a few new materials have been adopted and the use of some Pre-Hispanic materials (human skin, precious stones, etc.) has been discontinued. (See Chapter 5 for a more complete discussion of Pre-Conquest masks and materials.)

The following is more than just documentation of modern mask materials, for each material imposes inherent limitations upon the artist. Further, special qualities are often thought to reside in certain materials, and mask-makers have devised special ways of handling these materials to preserve these qualities. Therefore, to understand the masks of Mexico, it is mandatory to know and understand the materials used in their production.

WOOD

Most of the reasons for the popularity of wood in mask manufacture are obvious: availability, relative plasticity, the ease with which supplemental materials can be attached, comparative durability, and the fact that a finished mask can be produced with a minimum of tools and, in some cases, with a minimum of training. Many Indian groups also attribute spiritual qualities and forces to particular trees, a belief which is probably a holdover from Pre-Hispanic times,[*] and masks made from the wood of these trees acquire their attributes and powers. Many masks have to be cut from a specific wood in order to be deemed effective. It is not surprising that the groups holding these beliefs have also developed special rituals for harvesting the wood.

154. Silver mask for rain-petitioning dance. This intricately worked, bearded mask, one of a set of rare silver masks (see Fig. 21), has squash blossom earrings, a popular design motif adopted from Mexico by the Indians of the Southwestern United States. The squash blossom motif was originally Moorish and was brought first to Spain and then to Mexico. The richly decorated brow, teeth, and beard show exceptional workmanship and attention to detail. *La Parota, Guerrero (Nahua); 43 cm.; silver, cloth (lining).* I.A.C.

---

[*]Certain woods in Pre-Conquest times were thought to have a life or spirit of their own. Masks may have been carved at times on the live trees so as to absorb some of this living power, a practice used by the Iroquois and some African tribes.

Rituals of Wood Harvesting. In some regions of Mexico, the cutting of trees to be used in making masks is undertaken only at specific times. In some parts of Guerrero, for example, trees have traditionally been cut during the *luna menguante* (waning of the moon), preferably at sunrise during the month of January. The Totonacs in Veracruz believe that "any wood will last longer if the tree is felled in November, when the moon is in conjunction" (Kelly and Palerm 1952, p. 72). Elsewhere, it is believed that wood must be cut during the full moon. A fine old Bat mask from Xotoltitlán, Guerrero, which I acquired is made from zompantle (colorín) wood, which is usually very light; but this mask is very heavy, which is said to have resulted from cutting the wood during the full moon.

Some rituals have a much more mundane cause, however. In Michoacán, according to a friend who lived there for many years long ago, legend had it that the woodcutters sought wood for masks only in the rainy season. The reason, though, was more practical than symbolic. The cutting was restricted by the government, but during the rainy season the inspectors remained in their warm houses and could not hear the blows of the axe over the roar of the thunder. Restrictions on the felling of trees still carry severe penalties, and one Guerrero mask-maker told me he was trying to get an exemption from such worrisome regulations.

The tree used in the Dance of the Voladores is also cut under special circumstances. The woodcutters give the tree a drink of tepache and ask its pardon for the cutting (Durán 1971, p. 163). Furthermore, additional ceremonies must be carried out before the tree is used in the dance. The possible consequence of omitting such ceremonies was reported in the Mexican newspaper *Excelsior* on August 14, 1966. The article tells of an accident which took place while a dance was being performed in Saltillo, Coahuila. Two of the dancers were killed and two were injured when they fell from the pole, which they had climbed during the dance. According to the leader of the group, the accident was due to the omission of the religious ritual honoring the pole. The base of the tree should have been sprinkled with the blood of a hen and a litre of mescal. Since a hen could not be found and only the mescal was used, the tree was offended.

Also, woodcutters and mask-makers sometimes prepare themselves according to traditional rituals and practices. One woodcutter who believed that trees must be cut during the full moon remarked that, while cutting, "Our ancestors took herbs [probably hallucinogenic] but now we drink mescal."

Eighty-two-year-old Maximiliano Calderón, from the village of Ixcapaneca, Guerrero, said that in former years, when the people made masks, they would fast. They were also drugged with mushrooms taken either from trees or from the ground on June 24, the day of San Juan Bautista. A liquid was then extracted from the mushrooms and combined with other ingredients. A carver would drink the mixture before undertaking the making of a large number of wooden masks. Likewise, another Indian, now too old to carve, said that in his youth mushrooms were taken while fasting before beginning a mask. Unfortunately, it

Table 1. Woods Used in Mask-making

Chiapas	poplar
Guerrero	zompantle, *siringuanillo*, *clabellino*, plum, *parota* (conacaste), avocado, *camaroncillo*, *zopilote*, *sabino*, *palo hediondo*, copal
Hidalgo	pine
Michoacán	*cirimo*, copal, zompantle, *jaboncillo*, poplar, *tepamo*, avocado, pine
Oaxaca	copal, pochote, *sompan*, *huamúchil* (*guamúchil*), zompantle, pine, willow, *palo mulato*, *parota*, *tutucunyi* (white wood), ash, *huaje*, *sapote*, *cremilín*
Querétaro	ash
Zacatecas	willow

is difficult to get information concerning current practices involving the taking of hallucinogens because those who may know are afraid to talk, fearing interference by the authorities.

Types of woods used. Table 1, based on our survey of living and working mask-makers, gives the woods that are currently being used in the various states of Mexico.

One of the most widely used woods is zompantle (*Erythina americana*, Mill.), commonly known as colorín. It is a very light, soft wood with a heart that is spongy like cork. There are eleven varieties in Mexico, widely distributed. The zompantle tree has two qualities which made it very important to the mask-maker. One is that it is practically indestructible. Branches planted in the ground, even long after they are cut, will sprout into small trees. Thus, the tree is believed to have an immortal quality. The other important characteristic is that it produces a small red hallucinogenic bean. This bean probably is one of the hallucinogens used in the past to produce the desired visions while making a mask. It was used for similar purposes in Pre-Hispanic times.* Unfortunately, some areas have suffered from a scarcity of zompantle wood. I know of one in-

---

*At the time of the Conquest of Mexico, a wooden rack was placed in front of the main temples. Skulls of sacrificial victims were put on this, and it was called a *zompantle*. I always wondered why the skull rack was called zompantle and why that wood was used. It does not seem possible that this soft wood was used for such a purpose, i.e., to perforate skulls, until one realizes that the mystic ideas that held things together and united them are the important ones at work here—specifically, the idea of the everlasting quality of the tree.

Wood was a sacred, powerful, living thing partly because of the belief in the mystic union of all things and partly because of the numerous sacred ceremonial objects that were made of wood. Zompantle, in particular, was sacred because of its hallucinogenic property and its apparent immortality.

The small hallucinogenic red beans from the zompantle tree were called *tzite* by the Mayans (Recinos 1950, p. 87–89) and were said to have been used to create the first man. The Mayans also used *tzite* for divination.

155. Pastorela Dance masks. These two sharply contrasting masks were probably used in the same dance. The finely carved mask at left (*a*) shows the *santero* features of realistic style, fine materials, and fair complexion with blue eyes. The tin crown is adorned with a cast-off bicycle light. The Hermit mask on the right (*b*) is crudely carved and adorned with simple fiber and leather. It shows hard wear, unlike the *santero* mask, which has been very well preserved. The Hermit mask is accompanied by a large wooden rosary of beads and cross strung on a twine of twisted fibers. Both masks property of the University of Arizona. *León, Guanajuato; (a) 48 cm., including crown; (b) 27 cm., not including beard; (a) wood, paint, galvanized tin, plastic, mirrors; (b) wood (zompantle), paint, ixtle fiber, leather.* I.A.C.

156. Mojiganga Procession masks. The larger of these two mammal pelvis bone masks was worn during the Mojiganga Procession, where noisemakers were used to set the mood and summon the people to the fiesta (Fig. 112). The smaller mask is a child's mask for the same occasion. (Fig. 113 depicts a similar bone mask of the Northwest Coast Tlingit Indians.) Property of the Smithsonian Institution. *Mochitlán, Guerrero (Nahua); (a) (top) 18 cm.; (b) 48 cm.; (a) small animal pelvis; (b) cow pelvis.* IV.B.C.

158

157. Tigre mask, Tigre Dance. This copper Tigre was probably made before 1910, during the same period that brought forth other copper and silver masks in Guerrero. A few of these rare masks of several sizes came onto the market in 1975 and 1976; then the type disappeared entirely again. Recently, a friend stopped by Chiepetepec, where this one was made, to ask about copper Tigres and found no one who knew of them. This mask is hammered out of a single piece of copper, with coiled wire ears and earrings added. Chiepetepec seems to have produced the only Tigres with two sets of ears, as seen here. The coiled wire ears are reminiscent of the monkeys and bells produced in Xochipala (Fig. 158). *Chiepetepec, Guerrero (Nahua); 25 cm.; copper, paint.* IV.B.C.

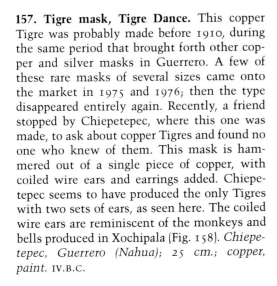

158. Copper and silver ornaments and bells. These small ornaments, whose age is not known, were found in Xochipala, Guerrero, and were circulated by several vendors during the years 1976–1977. In the foreground are silver monkey ornaments of several sizes. (Two similar monkeys of the larger size can be seen as earrings on the La Parota silver mask in Fig. 21*d*.) In the background are copper bells, long green with age, in the forms of monkeys, frogs, coyotes, and *caimanes*. *Xochipala, Guerrero; 1–4 cm. (approx.); silver, copper.*

stance in which mask-makers from the famed mask center of Olinalá, Guerrero, had to travel to Apango, Guerrero, to carve their masks because there was not enough zompantle for their work in Olinalá.

A wood that was formerly employed for masks in Acapetlahuaya, Guerrero, was from the tree called *palo hediondo* (*Cassia emarginata*, L.). The name derives from the fact that the leaves, when crushed, are foul-smelling. To work it, the wood was cut when the moon was waning, preferably in the month of January at sunrise. After cutting, the wood was soaked in water containing one or more herbs to prevent splitting when the masks were carved. One herb thus used was called *jarilla negra* (*Dodonaea viscosa*, Jacq.), according to Maximino Martínez (1959, p. 105).

OTHER MATERIALS

Bone. The earliest masks were probably made of bone. This material was readily available, and furthermore had great symbolic significance due to man's close relationship with animals. (See Chapter 5.) Some bone masks still exist today. In Fig. 156, we see such a mask from the state of Guerrero fashioned from the pelvis of a large animal, probably a cow or ox. A similar mask, although more elaborated with carved designs, was made by the Tlingit Indians of Alaska (Fig. 113).

Copper and Silver. Masks are seldom fashioned from metal today. A rare, indeed unique, set of twelve silver masks (ten male and two female) was made in La Parota, near Campo Morado, Guerrero. One mask, which depicts an old woman (Fig. 21*c*), has the date 1902 hammered on the reverse side of the chin; the others probably date from 1890 to 1910. As shown in Figs. 21 and 154, these masks were made with the repoussé technique from a very heavy gauge of sheet silver; they weigh up to 1.7 kilos each. The ears were soldered on, as were the silver earrings, in the form of monkey heads and flowers, which are 3.5 cm. in length. The backs of these masks are lined with cloth for greater comfort.

Copper masks are more plentiful than silver ones. The copper masks shown in Fig. 20 were made during the same period and in the same manner as the silver masks from La Parota: repoussé technique with a heavy-gauge metal and cloth linings. These were probably once blessed or offered to the gods, as is suggested by the faint smell of copal incense lingering in some of the cloth linings. These copper masks differ from the silver ones in that the faces are painted and they do not have earrings. The copper Tigre mask from Chiepetepec, Guerrero (Fig. 157), however, has two sets of ears, the lower pair being fashioned from coiled copper wire and having earrings. Most copper masks found now come from the Campo Morado, Malinaltepec, Chiepetepec, and Pascala del Oro areas of Guerrero. Judging from their condition, the bulk of these masks were probably made in the early part of this century.

The metalworking techniques used in these masks were also used to make silver and copper bells that are similar to the earrings mentioned above.* These bells are from the Xochipala area of Guerrero (Fig. 158). The most common designs are frogs, butterflies, crocodile heads, monkey heads, and coyote heads. Most Indian informants state that these bells were originally made for necklaces. However, when I first witnessed a performance of the Dance of the Moors and Christians in Carácuaro, near Pátzcuaro, Michoacán, in 1935, the dancers used small silver bells in the shape of fish as decorations on their costumes. This leads me to believe that many of these copper and silver bells were originally used on dance costumes. The date of the Xochipala bells is not known, but great quantities have been found in recent years in large jars in the foundations of a very old church being torn down. It is interesting to note that the silver mask shown in Fig. 21*d* has earrings identical to the monkey bells mentioned above.

Stone. In Pre-Hispanic times, stone was often employed for masks, as is noted in Chapter 5. It is seldom used today, but one modern stone mask has been collected from Texcaltitlán, near Toluca in the state of Mexico. This mask, shown in Fig. 159, is made from a light porous stone called *tezontle,* which was used for building facades in Colonial times. Other types of stone are used for mask molds, as seen in Fig. 162.

Clay. Clay was also utilized in Pre-Hispanic times for making masks and other figures. However, due to the weight and the impracticality of this material, it is not commonly used today. In some areas of Mexico, one still can find contemporary clay masks. I have seen an Ehecatl mask of black clay with white tusks, made in the early 1940's, in San Bartolo Coyotepec, Oaxaca. It is said to have been made for the traditional Valley of Oaxaca Clown character who ap-

---

* The technique of metal wire coiling (copper, silver, and even gold) was used in various lo- cations throughout ancient Meso-America.

159. Doctor mask, Doctor Dance. From the Toluca area, this is the only modern stone mask I have seen. The Doctor Dance has five characters: the Doctor, the Male Nurse, the Wife of the Male Nurse, Don Cleto (who owns the dog that chases the Tigre), and the Tigre. The dark red, porous *tezontle* stone used here is the same as that seen on many Colonial building facades in Mexico City. Today masks for this dance are said to be of commercial rubber. This stone mask is lined with animal fur and leather to protect the dancer's face. The character has forms on either cheek that may be either sideburns or some animal representation. Property of the University of Arizona. *Texcaltitlán, state of Mexico; height: 32 cm.; width: 23 cm.; stone (tezontle), paint, fur, leather.* I.B.C.

160. Mask for Tastoanes Dance. This very heavy, old clay mask is lined with cloth to protect the dancer's face. The face is strongly modeled and very expressive. *Michoacán (Tarascan); height: 17 cm.; thickness: 1.5 cm.; clay, paint, cloth.* I.A.C.

pears in the Plume Dance and other locally performed dances. (Fig. 45 shows a similar mask made of wood and worn in the Plume Dance in Teotitlán del Valle, Oaxaca, in 1942.) Fig. 160 shows a clay mask for the Tastoanes Dance from Michoacán. It is carefully lined with cloth and has withstood years of wear and tear. The face of this mask is definitely that of an old man; however, a clay mask used for the same dance in Juancito, Michoacán, depicts the face of a young man. In the latter case, the wearer shows through magnificent pantomime the process of becoming an old man.

Molds made of clay have traditionally been used in mask manufacture and are still common today (Fig. 171). There are excellent, very old clay molds from Toluca, state of Mexico, used in making inexpensive papier mâché masks sold at Carnival time in many areas of Mexico, most particularly and in greatest quantities in Celaya, Guanajuato.

Leather. Leather, another material used since Pre-Hispanic times, is utilized today by mask-makers in several areas of Mexico. Examples are a fine Apache mask (Fig. 161d) from Tixtla, Guerrero, which was collected in 1945, and two excellent old Devil masks from the Guadalajara area (Fig. 70).

There are many variations of simple, rather flat, fur-trimmed leather masks from the Tecuani (Wild Beast) Dance that is enacted in the area of El Potrerillo, as well as many other parts of Guerrero. (Wooden masks are also used.) One character in this dance is the Rastrero, or Tracker, who hunts the Tigre (Fig. 2). He wears a mask with yellow- or white-painted eyeglasses, reminiscent of some Eskimo masks which have eyes outlined with dark lines of fur. It is believed that the glasses give him magic vision. Another important character in the Tecuani Dance is the Dog, Maravilla, who sometimes has a leather mask, although more often a wooden one. In Figs. 238–239, we see an ingeniously made leather Maravilla mask. The talented leather craftsman has determined an extraordinary pattern for a realistic head with large ears—all fashioned from a single piece of leather and so designed that it will stay on without benefit of cords.

A famous, very heavy leather mask used as armor is the Zitlala, Guerrero, Tigre helmet mask shown in Fig. 55. It is painted yellow or green and probably once represented the green or the ripe corn. It has deep-set mirror eyes and whiskers of boar bristles. Another heavy leather mask is the small, very old mask with gesso surface and colored paint from Santa Cruz de las Huertas, Jalisco (Fig. 163). This mask, which is used in the Tastoanes Dance, has a very long, phallic nose made of plaster and leather and an enormous wig. Its use of gesso over the leather is unusual.

In Venustiano Carranza, Chiapas (previously called San Bartolomé de los Llanos), deerskin masks are worn in the Carnival (Fig. 161k). Another leather Carnival mask, from the Tzotzil village of Huistán, Chiapas, is shown in Fig. 161i; it is neatly made and brightly trimmed with bells and *papelillo* beads. Still another Chiapas leather mask is called Sak-Hol (White Head) and is used for the fiesta of San Sebastián in Zinacantán. It is a simple, flat leather mask with silver paper or tinfoil glued to the front surface (Fig. 134).

161. Various characters and dances. This collection of twelve leather masks shows the variety of forms this material can be fashioned into by skilled Mexican artisans. Mask *a*, at the upper left, is an Apache Carnival mask collected in Huejotzingo, Puebla, in 1945. In this town the Carnival festivities depict the Cinco de Mayo (Fifth of May) battle in which the Mexicans defeated the French. Today only small holes remain on the mask to show that it once had moustaches and eyebrows, and the gilded nose ring is also gone. Several overlapping gold painted circles are still visible on the cheeks. Mask *d* is another Apache mask, collected in Tixtla, Guerrero, in 1945. It is fashioned from two pieces of heavy leather joined down the center of the face and skillfully sculpted into the facial features. The bearded mask at the lower left (*i*) is a very well made example of a Tzotzil leather Carnival mask from Huistán, Chiapas. The face is made of one piece of heavy leather with cut-out eyes and mouth and a triangular nose, which has been cut out and sewn on. Isinglass (mica) has been carefully attached from the inside to fill the eye sockets. Decoration is added in the form of small black painted *papelillo* beads made of paper, bells, and a horsehair beard. Mask *j* represents a Rastrero from the area of El Potrerillo, Guerrero. Bits of red leather, white seeds or beads for teeth, and shredded leather hair and beard are attached to the flat leather face. Mask *k* is a Tzotzil Carnival mask from Venustiano Carranza (formerly San Bartolomé de los Llanos), Chiapas. This is the only deerskin mask we have ever seen. The final mask (*l*) is from Ayutla, Guerrero, and was used in the Viejitos Dance. It was made over a mold and is the only mask in this group which is carefully lined with cloth. Noteworthy are the expert painting and the expressive eyes. The beard is of ixtle fiber. All other masks pictured here are Carnival masks from various parts of Guerrero. Masks *b, c, e, f, g, h, l* property of the University of Arizona; mask *j* property of the Smithsonian Institution. *Various regions; 16–29 cm. (approx.); leather with various supplemental materials.* (*d, e, i, j*) I.B.C. (Others) I.A.C.

162. Stone mold and leather Carnival masks. This stone mold and the leather masks made from its form come from a small town near Atlixco in Puebla. Clay, plaster, and wood are also used for mask molds. Property of the University of Arizona. *Huiluco, Puebla (Nahua); 20 cm. (approx.). (a, c)* I.A.C.

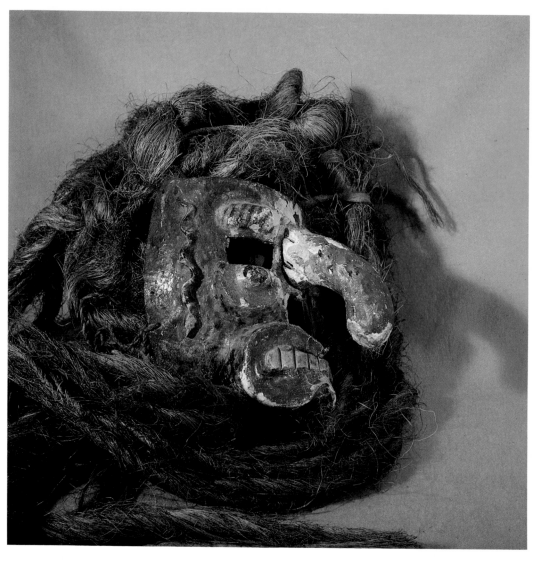

163. Mask for Tastoanes Dance. Heavy leather is here coated with clay and ponderous broken color to achieve a monstrous human face with disproportionate features and a mop of wild ixtle hair. Such boldly erotic features are not common in Mexico, but the *chintete* (lizard) and small snake seen on the cheeks do often appear also on Malinche masks. This mask is very old. *Santa Cruz de las Huertas, Jalisco (Tarascan); height: 19 cm.; depth at nose: 19 cm.; leather, clay, paint, ixtle fiber, gesso.* II.B.C.

164. Gourd mask. Ex-Cordry collection, ex-Raúl Kamfer collection. Photograph by Carmelo Guadagno. Courtesy of Museum of the American Indian, Heye Foundation, N.Y. *Michoacán (Tarascan); height: 13.3 cm.; width: 19 cm.; gourd, paint.* I.B.C.

165. Hortelaño (Field Worker) masks, Hortelaños Dance. Children are participants in many Mexican fiestas, and these small, highly individualistic masks are used by them for the Hortelaños Dance in the Barrio of Magdalena in the city of Uruapan, Michoacán. Large noses made of small gourds are wired on, while the disproportionate features are enhanced by eyebrows, moustaches, and beards of horsehair and sheepskin. It is interesting to note that, for this agricultural dance, the masks are made from an agricultural product, the gourd. This choice may have had something to do with sympathetic magic in former times. Masks *b* and *d* property of the University of Arizona. *Uruapan, Michoacán (Tarascan); 18 cm. each (approx.); gourds, sheepskin, horsehair, glue.* I.B.C.

Gourds. In some areas of Mexico, gourds are utilized for making masks. One such gourd mask was made in Olinalá, Guerrero, for the little-known Turtle Dance. Another gourd mask, collected in Michoacán in 1935, is pictured in Fig. 164. Now in the Museum of the American Indian in New York, this small mask is fashioned of a section from a fairly round gourd with an applied wooden nose and touches of paint. A children's Hortelaños (Field Workers) Dance in one *barrio* in Uruapan, Michoacán, features amusing gourd masks (Fig. 165).

Wax. Wax is another material employed in both Pre-Conquest and contemporary masks (see Chapter 5). The following is a report by Ruth Lechuga concerning the manufacture and usage of wax masks in Santa María Astahuacán, Federal District, and in Chimalhuacán, state of Mexico. The masks referred to can be seen in Figs. 166–168.

The wax masks from Santa María Astahuacán, D. F., used during Carnival date back several generations and are representative of an ancient tradition. They are presently used with a charro costume. Mr. Candido Castillo Cerillo learned the trade from his father and was the mask provider for all neighboring towns. He died recently, but his widow, Angela Torres de Castillo, their son Delfino Castillo, and their niece María del Refugio García de Medina now manufacture the masks, assuring the tradition's survival. They maintain they are the only ones who know how to make them, and people from all the towns within postal zone 13, such as Tláhuac, Tlaltenango, Santa Cruz, and others, order their masks through them. The masks used in each place are slightly different. In Santa María Astahuacán, for example, they prefer broad beards, decorated with curls. In some towns they might order them very white; in others, such as Santa Cruz, very red.

The Castillo family uses plaster casts which they make. A piece of manta cloth is placed over the mold, followed by the color. This seems to be a secret. While they described their work in great detail, they would not specify which substances were used, and mentioned only a powder and a solvent. Various layers of wax are applied, until the desired thickness is achieved. The cloth is encased in the mask. This part of the work must be done at midday; otherwise the wax is too hard when it is cold. The wax used must be top-grade beeswax. To buy it one asks for cera en marqueta *(a cake of crude wax).*

The eyes, mouth, and nose are painted at the end. This first process, called hacer las pelonas, *is to make the unadorned masks. The eyebrows, beard, and moustache are then made in a process known as* encarñar, *"to make curls." The bristles from cows' tails are used for the hair, and these bristles are wrapped around them, and the needles are pulled out. The resulting curls form the base of the beard, which is sewn to the mask, and the other decorations are sewn on top. A ribbon is sewn to the top edge of the mask and is tied around the dancer's head. A large charro hat hides the ribbon when the mask is used. The hat's strap is tied below the chin, securing the mask close to the face. The mask is heated slightly, either on the stove or in the sun and when soft is molded directly to the dancer's face.**

Wax masks, more crudely made than those from Santa María Astahuacán, are used for the Jardineros (Gardeners) Dance of the famed black pottery village of San Bartolo Coyotepec in the Valley of Oaxaca. This dance is one of the many variations of the Dance of the Moors and Christians, which was introduced by the Spanish friars and has survived for centuries in Mexico. There are three principal characters in the wax-masked version of the Jardineros of San Bartolo

---

* Ruth Lechuga, personal communication; translated by Marta Turok.

166–168. Artisan Angela Torres Vda. de Castillo making a wax mask. Fig. 166 shows three stages of the wax mask process and the plaster mold (*left*). In Fig. 167 the artisan is seen removing the wax mask impression from the plaster mold. Fig. 168 shows two finished wax masks. Photographs by Ruth Lechuga. Fig. 168, mask *a*, property of the University of Arizona. *Santa María Astahuacán, Federal District, 1974.*

169. Christian King mask (*a*) and Christian Dama del Caballero (Cavalier's Lady) mask (*b*), Jardineros (Gardeners) Dance. From the famous black pottery area of Oaxaca come these carefully made wax masks. Both these Christians have the traditional fair skin, blue eyes, and light hair. The eyes are covered with isinglass (mica) for brilliance, and the beaten tin crowns are gilded and inlaid with pieces of mirror and colored glass. In Fig. 170 we see the Jardineros dancers from the same village performing in 1941 with less elaborate masks and costumes. The more elaborate masks and costumes of today are due to the betterment of this village's economic situation. Property of the University of Arizona. *San Bartolo Coyotepec, Oaxaca (Zapotec); 25.5 cm. (approx.), including crown; wax, paint, cloth (lining), tin, mirror, dyed pita fiber, glass, feathers (b), isinglass.* I.A.C.

170. Jardineros Dance. The first Indian State Fair of Oaxaca brought a number of Oaxaca's diverse Indian groups into direct contact for the first time. This group, from San Bartolo Coyotepec, are wearing simple wax masks and homemade costumes, which today have been replaced with more lavish ones (see Fig. 169). *Indian State Fair of Oaxaca, 1941.*

171. Cloth masks, dance unknown. These rather comic masks are made by gluing cloth in layers over a clay mold, such as the mold for a Pig mask from the same village seen in the foreground. Mask *a* is a round-eyed, boldly painted Parrot, while mask *b* is a human character with animal ears. The ixtle fiber hair is well mounted, and white cloth closes off the sides and bottoms of the masks. Cloth masks are very rare. From the collection of Ruth Lechuga. *El Doctor, Querétaro; 20 cm. (approx.), not including hair and white cloth; cloth (glued layer technique), paint, ixtle fiber. (a)* IV.A.C. *(b)* II.A.C.

Coyotepec, two of which are seen in Fig 169. The Christian King wears a painted tin crown with six points and stars, a brown wig of curled pita fiber, and reddish brown painted-on hair, moustache, and goatee. The Dama del Caballero wears a diadem with glyphs on the front and a reddish brown wig. According to our friend Anita Jones, who sent us the masks, these dancers hire themselves out to other villages from time to time. Fig 170 shows the Jardineros Dance as it was performed in 1941 in the same Oaxaca village.

When we first saw the Stilt Dance in Zaachila, Oaxaca, in 1941, the dancers used wax masks, as shown in Fig. 137. According to Anita Jones, the Stilt Dance is now performed in Zaachila on June 24 and 29. On the latter date, which is the Day of San Pedro, the dance takes place in the *barrio* of San Pedro with the music of a small drum and a flute. No wax masks or any other masks are used today in this dance. As mentioned earlier, the Stilt Dance is one of the few modern dances that can be traced back to Pre-Conquest times (Fig. 136).

Cloth. I am acquainted with two heavy cloth Tigre masks from Hueycantenango, Guerrero, and one Zoque Tigre mask from the village of San Fernando, Chiapas, constructed over a frame of vine and bamboo strips. The Hueycantenango Tigres are made of many layers of cloth glued together, resulting in a thickness of more than one-half inch; they are painted yellow with spots of black. No flexibility may be found at any point; rather, these masks are like heavy armor. They have wild boar tusks, leather ears, and mirror eyes; the wearer looks out through the mouth. Fig. 171 shows two rather comic heavy cloth masks from El Doctor, Guerrero, made in clay molds.

Window Screening (Tela de Alambre). One unusual material used in creating masks is window-screening or *tela de alambre*. The masks of the rich, velvet-costumed Chinelo dancers of Tepoztlán, Morelos, are made of this material. Window-screening is worked over a wooden mold and trimmed with a black, red, or white beard and eyebrows (Fig. 101).

Papier Mâché. Very interesting papier mâché masks are made in Jesús María, a Cora village in the heart of the mountains in Nayarit. These masks form a part of the mixture of Pre-Hispanic and Christian rites enacted during the Easter ceremonies. The Judases wear large masks, such as the Imaginary Beast mask in Fig. 172, each one the creation of the man or boy who wears it. At the end of the ceremonies, these masks are ritually destroyed by casting them into the river, where they disintegrate. In 1936, when I was in Jesús María, there was no mention of such masks. It has been suggested that, at some time since then, a teacher in the schools there may have taught papier mâché technique which took the form of mask-making. This is probably what happened, as the Coras previously used face painting and we have no record of their using masks until fairly recently.

The following account of how these papier mâché masks (which are called *hasha* in Cora) are made was recorded by Marina Auguiano and Guido Münch in Jesús María, Nayarit, during Holy Week in 1972:

1. One makes a clay mold two weeks in advance. Normally, each person

makes his own mask, unless he is without talent.

2. When dry, one glues pieces of cardboard to the mold with a flour and water paste. The mask is then left to dry.

3. The mold is destroyed, leaving the mask.

4. To simulate the hair, the "hair" that is found inside the organ cactus is used, as it looks authentic.

5. Deer antlers or imitations of them are covered with tissue paper and placed on the mask.

6. The mask is then covered entirely with tissue paper.

7. The teeth may be metal or, in the case of this fantastic animal (Fig. 172), wood covered with silver cigarette paper.

8. At dawn on Holy Thursday, the "Borrados" (the Judases) go toward the river Jesús María and paint their bodies, masks, machetes, and the turtle shells which they carry in their belts in black and white patterns. The white they obtain from earth lime, and the black from burned, ground corn.

9. On Good Friday, they decorate the masks, machetes, and turtle shells with colors: both ochre earth color and aniline dyes. They dissolve the aniline in water and spit it onto the masks.

10. On Saturday about twelve noon, the Judases take off their body paints in the river and then throw their masks and machetes in the river.

11. When the things are destroyed, the only items saved are the deer antlers (if authentic) and the turtle shells.

In some areas, papier mâché masks have supplanted wooden masks for practical reasons. In Acatlán, near Chilapa, Guerrero, I recently encountered one mask-maker who had always carved wooden masks in the past, but, due to difficulties in obtaining wood and to the time involved in carving a wooden mask, had decided to make all his masks of papier mâché. He used a convex face made from wood, with almost no facial features, as a mold; on this, he worked with paper and a paste of flour and water. He said he could make ten papier mâché masks in the time it would take to make one wooden one. Also, since papier mâché masks are less expensive and wear out quickly, they can be sold readily and more often than masks made of more durable materials,—perhaps another example of modern preplanned obsolescence.

The situation is the same for a sixty-eight-year-old mask-maker from Tlaniquitlapa, Guerrero, who had traditionally carved wooden masks. A few years ago, he decided to make masks of papier mâché and rent them for thirty pesos per three-day fiesta. He said that he would not do any more business with wood, as wooden masks do not wear out and replacements are rarely needed.

Maguey and Fiber. Maguey (*Agave americana*) is a material, like wood, that is thought to possess spiritual forces or qualities. As previously mentioned, in Pre-Conquest times, masks made from maguey leaves were used for protection of pregnant women and children in the Aztec New Fire Ceremony. A modern use of maguey can be seen in Fig. 173.

173. Hermit mask, Pastorela Dance. According-ing to informant Leonardo Valdez, this un-painted mask is carved from a very unusual white material called *quiote* (heart) *de maguey*. Property of the University of Arizona. *San Juan de las Colchas (near Uruapan), Michoacán (Tarascan).* I.A.C.

172. Imaginary Beast mask. An Easter fiesta mask of papier mâché, called *hasha* by the Cora Indians. (See the text for a description of the way such masks are made.) The material seen beneath the horns and hair comes from the inside of an organ cactus. *Jesús María, Nayarit (Cora), 1972.* IV.A.D.

In recent years, a large number of woven fiber masks have appeared in Mexico. These masks seem to be made solely for the tourist trade, as I have never seen or read about their use in any authentic dance.

Tin. Tin masks have always been rather a mystery, but there are some beautiful ones. We have been informed that there is a fine old tin mask in the Museum of Popular Art in Pátzcuaro, Michoacán. Recently a tin mask from the state of San Luis Potosí has been brought to my attention by María Teresa Pomar. Whether the tin masks were used in dances has always been doubtful.

SUPPLEMENTARY MATERIALS

Mask-makers often use supplementary materials in forming various parts of masks, especially wooden masks. This is often done when appendages are too large to be carved from a single piece of wood. Materials may also be added to achieve realism or to create an elaborate design. For example, Fig. 174a shows a mask made from a turtle shell, to which a carved wooden nose and mouth have been added. Or supplementary materials may be used to add symbolic significance to the mask. Tassels of handspun dark red wool are seen on the Tejorón and Negrito Carnival masks made in Pinotepa Nacional, Oaxaca. Their symbolic significance derives from the handwoven women's belts from which they are fashioned. For generations, the belts have afforded symbolic protection to pregnant women during eclipses (Cordry and Cordry 1968, p. 43).

The variety of materials which are added to masks is practically limitless. Bells and ribbons may be attached to the mask, as in Fig. 104. In addition, glass, leather, plant fiber, and even tinfoil taken from cigarette packs may be used. Spines from the pochote or ceiba tree (*Ceiba pentandra*, L.) formerly served as decorative features in trimming wooden masks, most commonly Caimán and Xolotl masks (see Figs. 199 and 247). These cone-shaped spines, from one-half inch to three inches long, grow on the branches and trunk of the tree (see Fig. 246). As discussed in Chapter 9, the pochote tree was commonly regarded as the Tree of Life throughout Pre-Hispanic Mexico and has great symbolic significance.

Supplementary materials may be attached at the top of the mask for hair. Animal materials such as sheep's wool, wild boar bristles, or horse tails are often used on masks as head hair, eyebrows, and beards. Hair may also be represented by maguey or ixtle fiber (Figs. 44, 96) or the finer, twisted pita, either in its natural color or dyed in various hues. Other plant fibers are similarly used in other areas of Mexico (Fig. 172). In Fig. 278, a copper mask representing Malinche displays thick locks of human hair. The horns in this mask are antlers from a deer.

Beards are made of plant fiber, animal skin, or even human hair. The same material used for hair is frequently used in making the beard. The longstanding practice of using animal hide for beards is illustrated in Fig. 175, which shows a comic mask from Tanlajas, San Luis Potosí.

Eyes are sometimes made from pieces of old glass bottles, which are heated and curved. Such eyes, with hand-painted iris and pupil on the under surface, have traditionally been set into the Parachico masks of Chiapa de Corzo, Chiapas (Fig. 62a). More recently, these masks have commercial glass eyes brought from Mexico City, where they are manufactured for large dolls and store-window mannequins. Some Tlaxcala masks have glass eyes with lids which the wearer opens and closes with the aid of a string; the actual apertures for seeing are half-moons located directly under the painted eyebrows. Commercial glass eyes are most commonly used by *santeros*, who have access to commercial products (Fig. 29, second and third rows). On some Tigre masks from Guerrero, the round eyes are covered with flat or curved glass (Fig. 176). Other Guerrero Tigre masks have mirrors over the eyes, requiring the wearer to look out through the mouth (Fig. 264). Masks with mirror eyes were also made in Pre-Hispanic times, as noted in Chapter 9. Eyes are sometimes accented with eyebrows of human hair. Moro Chino masks have rectangular wooden blocks, often painted gold or yellow, over their eyebrows and across their cheeks (Figs. 42, 284).

Fig. 233 shows masks from the area of Ayutla, Guerrero, that have cheeks, foreheads, and chins covered with armadillo hide. The skin of a deer is used on some masks representing that animal, and sometimes deer antlers are attached (Fig. 177). Animal hide is also used occasionally to make ears, as shown in Fig. 79.

An unpainted wooden mask from the state of Oaxaca, shown in Fig. 178, has a snakeskin covering the nose area. Wooden snakes are commonly attached as noses, as are carvings of other animals and human figures. Elaborately carved noses are often attached and are an important symbolic feature of masks. A long, thin nose, as shown in Fig. 163, may have an erotic significance, as is common in masks from Japan and other parts of the world.

174. Characters and dances unknown. On the left (*a*) is a turtle-shell mask from the Ranchería Moluco in San Juan Guichicovi, Oaxaca. The brown face is augmented by a wooden nose and mouth, and the eyes are merely round cut-outs. Mask *b* is from San Mateo del Mar, Oaxaca, a unique village located on a strip of sand between *el mar vivo y el mar muerto* ("the living sea and the dead sea," i.e., the Pacific Ocean and a lagoon). The delicate carving, the simple spacing, and the shapes of eye and mouth combine to make this a true work of art, reminiscent of the work of Paul Klee. Mask *a* property of the University of Arizona. *(a) San Juan Guichicovi, Oaxaca (Zapotec); (b) San Mateo del Mar, Oaxaca (Huave); (a) 30 cm.; (b) 31 cm.; turtle shell, wood (a).* I.B.C.

175. Comic mask, character and dance unknown. This very crude mask from San Luis Potosí is shown with its two hats flapped back from the face. Trimmed in strips of leather, fur, and metal and with only stark eyeholes, it does not resemble the styles seen in Oaxaca and Guerrero. *Tanlajas, San Luis Potosí; 32 cm., not including hat; wood, paint, leather, metal, animal fur, two straw hats.* I.A.C.

174   175

176. Tigre mask, Tecuani Dance. The exceptionally rich quality of this heavy old Tigre is seen in its rough surface texture, which exhibits hard use. The painted wooden eyes are covered with hand-curved glass, and the tongue is made of leather. Tecuani Dance Tigres generally do not have eyeholes; the dancer looks out through the mouth. *Region of Apango, Guerrero (Nahua); height: 34 cm.; depth: 19 cm.; wood, paint, wild boar bristle, leather, glass.* IV.A.C.

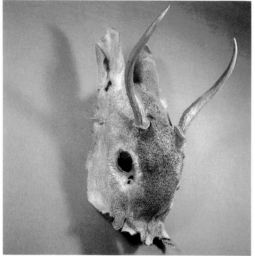

177   178

177. Deer mask. This mask was probably used as a decoy to aid in good hunting. I know of very few masks made from the actual head of an animal, as is this one, although the Mayo/Yaqui dancers do use an entire deer's head as a headdress. Here the animal's eyes have been removed to allow the wearer to look out, and the antlers have been left intact. Collections of the International Folk Art Foundation in the Museum of International Folk Art, Santa Fe, New Mexico. *Place of origin unknown; 33 cm., including antlers; deer head, deer antlers.* IV.A.C.

178. Character and dance unknown. Although this mask was not carved by a skilled craftsman, the unusual use of the stuffed snakeskin dividing the stark face makes it unique and powerful. Collections of the International Folk Art Foundation in the Museum of International Folk Art, Santa Fe, New Mexico. *State of Oaxaca; 26 cm.; wood, snakeskin.* II.A.C.

179. Devil mask, Devil Dance. This very well made Devil, with animal ears and goat horns, has a movable tongue with a serpent resting on it. The design of the nose is derived from representations of the bat. Eye slits are seen above the eyes. The bold carving and design of this mask are the work of a predecessor of the young Chapa, Guerrero, carver Santiago Martínez Delgado (see Fig. 28), whose work has not yet attained the sculptural understanding seen in this Devil. *Apetlanca, Guerrero (Nahua); 49 cm., including horns; wood, paint, goat horns.* II.B.C.

A movable mouth and jaw is integrated into the Moor Mask shown in Fig. 280. Wooden mouths, attached to masks made of gourds and other materials, often show extraordinarily expressive imagination on the part of the carver (Fig. 174*a*). Movable tongues, made of wood or leather, may be seen in Figs. 14 and 179. For symbolic purposes, tongues are sometimes carved in the shape of animals, such as the frog shown in Fig. 251. One unique mask has a glass tongue (Fig. 301).

Teeth from animals or humans may be attached to add realism to masks. In Fig. 231, tiny animal teeth are used. Pieces of bone (Fig. 306) or large boar tusks (Fig. 79) may also be used.

Animal fur of various kinds is sometimes employed for mask decoration (Fig. 2), and many types of animal horns may be seen, such as the goat horns in Figs. 14 and 179.

GLUES

Commercial glues are commonly used in mask-making today. However, vegetable glues have been popular throughout the history of Mexico* and continue to be used in some areas. Vegetable glues are derived from a number of plants, including mesquite (*Prosopis juliflora*), cañuela (*Equisetum ramosissum* Desf.), and *ixcapante* (*Illicium floridum*). Oil of chia is also used in combination with other substances.

Glues derived from various species of orchid are common not only in mask-making but also in the making of other wooden items, such as the violin. Three varieties of orchids employed are Coatzontecoxóchitl (*Stanhopea tigrina nigra*, Batem); *Laelia autumnalis*, Lld.; and *Cyrtodium* (cigar orchid). The bulb of this third orchid serves as an adhesive called *jilotillo*. While soft and fresh, the bulb is scraped with a knife or piece of obsidian, yielding a sticky mass which is the basis of *jilotillo*. When combined with sawdust, this adhesive is used in mending cracks and knotholes in unpainted wooden masks. The mixture is also used to join separate pieces of wood, as in the case of helmet masks too large to be made from a single tree trunk (Fig. 277). *Jilotillo* is extremely strong and is also used to fasten the pochote spines to the masks and to the manta cloth of the costume for the Caimán Dance (Fig. 187).

---

*Adhesives made from orchid plants were used in Pre-Hispanic times, as described by Francisco Hernández: "The *Chichiltictepetza-cuxóchitl* grows roots similar to those of the asphodel, white and fibrous. . . . The root is cold, damp and sticky; an excellent and very adhesive glue which the Indians use is prepared with it, and principally the painters use it to adhere the colors more firmly, so that the figures do not rub out easily. The root is cut in small pieces, dried in the sun and ground, and with the powder this remarkable glue is prepared" (1959, pp. 117–119).

Bernal Díaz del Castillo also mentions an adhesive used by Cortes's army: "And later Cortes ordered . . . that he distribute them, arrows as well as metal arrowheads of copper, among all the crossbowmen, and that he order them always to polish and feather them with paste, which sticks better than that of Castilla, that is made of something like roots that is called zacotle" (1939*b*, 2: 205).

180

181

PAINTS AND LACQUERS

Paints. As with tools and adhesives, paints used in mask-making range from simple ones made from natural materials of the earth to commercially available products. Since the latter are difficult, and sometimes impossible, to come by and are invariably expensive, they are usually used sparingly. A single color may be applied to the whole mask, or an accent of color, such as a touch of white on leather or a red mouth on wood, may be the only painted design.

The dyes used in paint-making have traditionally come from colored earth, minerals, or plants. Earth colors and red tones are often derived from minerals. A yellow paint used by the Huichols for hundreds of years comes from a yellow root which they grind on a flat stone and mix with saliva. This paint has traditionally been used for face painting; on their present masks, which are made for sale, it is being supplanted by commercial paint.

Plant binders are an important ingredient in paints. They are usually added to the dyes made from earth, minerals, or plants and are often mixed with com-

180. Owl mask, Apache Dance. This large, expressive Owl is very well conceived and executed. The reverse side is deeply carved and cleanly finished. I have seen very few masks painted with water-base paint, much of which is here worn off. *Copanatoyac, Guerrero (Nahua); height: 32 cm.; depth: 33 cm.; wood (zompantle), paint (water base).* IV.A.C.

181. Bat mask. This large late-nineteenth-century male Bat mask is from Xataltitlán, Guerrero, near the historic Bat Dance center of Tlacozotitlán (see Fig. 230). On the Bat's arms one can see the cloth showing through where the paint has worn off. This mask appears to be one of a pair of very rare Bat masks. The female mask (not pictured) is larger and similar in features, color, and style, but without a moustache. I have seen other pairs of animal masks, with male and female Turtles and Armadillos, but this is the only pair of Bats I have seen. These mask pairs are one important expression of the concept of duality (see Chapter 9). *Xataltitlán, Guerrero; 55 cm.; wood, paint, cloth.* II.B.C.

182. Apache mask, Apache Dance. Made in the famous lacquer village of Olinalá, Guerrero, for use in Huehuetono, this fine old Apache mask shows heavy use, as the chin is slightly damaged. In this Olinalá lacquer technique, called *rayado* ("scraped" or "marked"), the lacquer was applied in layers (in this case red over green) and then scraped or cut out to reveal the design in the underlying color. Thus animals, flowers, and borders emerge in clearly defined color patterns. *Huehuetono, Guerrero (Nahua); 30 cm.; wood, lacquer.* I.B.C.

183. Tigre mask, Tecuani Dance (*a*); Old Man Carnival mask (*b*). Very careful workmanship is combined with an unusual spirit of fun and entertainment in these two lacquer masks. They were made by mask-maker José Antonio Gabriel (see Appendix). Mask *a* property of the Smithsonian Institution; mask *b* property of the University of Arizona. *Temalacatzingo, Guerrero (Nahua); (a) 27 cm.; (b) 26 cm., including beard; wood, lacquer. (a)* IV.A.C.; *(b)* I.B.C.

mercial powdered paints as well. A plant widely used as a binder in Guerrero is *suelda consuelda,* possibly a species of *Anredera scandens,* Mag., from the family Chenepodiums (Martínez 1937, p. 442). This vine yields a juice which has properties similar to egg white. Used in paint, it proves to be an excellent binding material.

The importance of binders in paint is illustrated in Fig. 180, which shows a fine old Owl mask with only traces of its once colorful designs remaining. Colored water paint was used on this mask and over the years has almost completely washed off. Similarly, I have a number of large, old helmet masks with only the barest traces of the white undercoating known as "Spanish whiting" (*blanco de España*). No color remains whatsoever.

Before painting, an undercoat of Spanish whiting was formerly applied to many of the better masks. Also, some old wooden masks were first covered with a piece of natural-colored, handwoven cloth, carefully glued, coated with Spanish whiting, and then painted. Late-nineteenth-century masks with cloth beneath the paint are shown in Figs. 105 and 181.

An additional ingredient sometimes added to paint is oil of chia. The water-repellent qualities of this oil were known in Pre-Hispanic times,* and it is still used today to produce long-lasting, waterproof paints and lacquers.

---

* "... and even their paint, water does not ruin or damage it, nor do they smear it with chiyan oil"
(Gómara 1966, 2: 437).

Lacquers. Lacquers are also used to impart color and brilliance to masks in some areas. The process of making lacquer is similar to that of making paint; minerals or commercial pigments are used for color and texture, and, in some parts, oil of chia is added for durability. Occasionally, oil of chia is replaced by commercial linseed oil, but this decreases the resistance and the durability of the lacquer.

The lacquering process is far more complicated than painting. First, a colorless paste is applied, and the piece is polished by rubbing with a coarse abrasive, sometimes an agate or a piece of a glass bottle. Then the coloring pigment is rubbed over the surface. The color being used determines the number of coats needed to achieve depth and brilliance. For example, red requires more coats than other colors. Finally, a high polish is obtained by rubbing the piece with a cloth. After eight or ten days, the lacquer is completely dry, and decorations are added, using pigmented lacquer applied with a paintbrush.* Fig. 182 shows a lacquer mask made in Olinalá, Guerrero, a town which specializes in decorated lacquer gourds and masks. Some very interesting lacquer masks are made in Michoacán, where lacquering has been popular for many years (Fig. 87a, b, d, e,

---

* The following information provided by Eduardo Dagach of the Fondo Nacional del Fomento de las Artesanías is an explanation of the lacquer process. Although this information does not apply specifically to mask production, the technique is presumably the same.

"DATA OBTAINED ABOUT THE PROCESS OF LACQUER OR SHELLAC IN TEMALACATZINGO AND OLINALA, GUERRERO

"*Local materials that are used.*

"*Tizacalte.* It is a natural product that is ground in its native state and which can be replaced by calcium carbonate.

"*Tecoxtle.* The tecoxtle is another carbonate probably of magnesia which is also ground in its native state. It serves to harden and dry rapidly.

"*Tolte.* This is a double carbonate of magnesia and calcium that is gathered from the area. It is calcined in the fireplace for four to five days, then ground.

"*Oil of chia.* It is obtained by toasting the chia in a comal, grinding it while hot and kneading it with tepid water. Later it is squeezed out through a linen cloth to obtain the oil. The oil of chia is used in two forms:

"1. Tolte and tecoxtle are stirred on the metate and mixed with oil of chia, giving rise to a paste called chamatl or chamate which is just to begin the process.

"2. Tecoxtle and commercial red lead oxide are mixed with the oil of chia and boiled until the preparation becomes black. This oil is used for the final decoration with a paintbrush. The oldest artisans add whole garlic, because they say that in this way maximum brilliance is obtained. Lately in this part of the process oil of chia is being replaced by commercial linseed oil—but the resistance and durability are diminished.

"*Description of the process.*

"The chamatl is smeared with the finger on the gourd (*jícara*) trying to smooth it while putting it on; later with the tail of a deer the tizacalte or calcium carbonate is taken from a washtub and is dusted over the piece until the oil is absorbed by the carbonate powder. Immediately the piece is polished rubbing it with an agate or a small glass bottle. Once polished, a mixture is made of tolte with the coloring pigment that is going to be used, previously rubbed several times in order to form a consistent coating over the piece. When it does not show signs of being damp, or rather when all the greasiness of the oil has been absorbed, the piece is left. The pigments that are used will determine the number of coats needed to give brilliance to the piece. For example, the color red needs more coats than other colors. The brilliance is obtained by rubbing the piece with a cotton cloth that is stiff and tight. This shine is given to it the first time five hours after the lacquer has been applied; the following time will be the next day when it has dried a little more. Once the piece dries (four or five days) it is impossible to shine. After eight or ten days the decoration begins by means of paintbrushes made in the region, and using pigment which comes from Mexico City and only mixing it with sizing, a different color is applied each day. The paintbrushes are made with cat hair tied and put in the point of a turkey feather. The hairs from the back of a cat are used because they are firmer."

Table 2. Paints and Lacquers Used in Mask-making

Chiapas	oil paint combined with mineral paint (lacquer technique)
Guerrero	oil paints, enamel, paints made from mineral powders, mixtures with *mermeyon chino*, lacquer made with tecoxtle and tolte, [a] extracts from leaves and tree bark, mineral and earth paints, oil of chia
Hidalgo	varnish, zapolin, oil paints
Michoacán	oil paints, enamel, gesso, varnish, plaster combined with oil and paint
Oaxaca	enamel, aniline, *puchino*
Puebla	vinyl
Querétaro	analine, oil paints
Zacatecas	vinyl, oil paints

[a] See note on p. 133.

268). In the small lacquer center of Temalacatzingo, Guerrero, Tigre and other masks continue to be carved and painted according to the traditional lacquer technique (Fig. 183).

In the manufacture of lacquer masks for the Parachicos Dance, according to one mask-maker, the esophagus of a bull is used to smooth the lacquer paint. The esophagus undergoes an elaborate series of preparations before being used in mask-making.[*] It is possible that this was originally done as a symbolic procedure to make the mask and the mask wearer more eloquent and the voice louder.

Information about the paints and lacquers currently used by mask-makers, derived from our survey of these craftsmen, is given in Table 2.

TOOLS

The following section is based on our survey of modern mask-makers who work predominantly with wood (see Appendix). Tools for other materials are mentioned in the description of mask materials and processes elsewhere in this chapter.

Tools employed today for the making of wooden masks are largely improvised from machetes, knives, and other metal implements, which are cut and

---

[*] The preparation of the esophagus was described by Antonio López Hernández, a mask-maker from Chiapa de Corzo, Chiapas (see Appendix): "It must be male, killed during the full moon. First separate the meat, take the member and put it in a bottle of water. Leave the bottle in the sun for twenty-four hours until it floats in the water. (Then it is rotten.) Take out the small member inside and wash it with *jabón de pan*. Afterward put in lime and knead it. Wash it again with clean water. Cut in twelve-to-fifteen-cm. pieces and knead it on a paint brush. Use it when the varnish is fresh (about twenty minutes after application).

Table 3. Tools Used in Mask-making

Chiapas	machete, saw, compass, gouge, chisel, polishers, esophagus of bull (used to smooth paint)
Guerrero	machete, knife, gouge, chisel, saw, adz, sickle, homemade tools
Hidalgo	gouge, chisel, knife, sandpaper
Michoacán	handsaw, rasp, knife, gouge, plane, sandpaper, machete, chisel, brush (*angarito*)
Oaxaca	chisel, knife, gouge, machete, handsaw, plane, sandpaper, *barbequi* (saw), ax, *moso de medra*
Puebla	hammer, knife, wooden mallet, mold
Querétaro	gouge
Zacatecas	knife, adz, gouge, chisel, improvised tools

184. Mask-making tools. Juan Godinillo demonstrates the tools used in making a heavy cow leather Tigre mask, similar to the one shown in Fig. 55. *Zitlala, Guerrero, 1975.*

185. Mask-maker preparing zompantle wood. He prepares the block of wood with rapid blows of his machete. *Apango, Guerrero, 1974.*

186. Mask-maker Miguel Cruz López. He is shown carving a Twins mask for the Mascaritas Dance. See Fig. 209 for other Twins masks by this mask-maker. Photo by Martha Turok. *Pinotepa de Don Luis, Oaxaca (Mixtec).*

shaped to suit the type of wood being used. Commercially manufactured tools are used but are not obtainable in some areas and, when available, may not be within the economic means of the mask-maker. One tool which is used is the *charrasco*, a short curved knife usually used by shoemakers; another is the *gurbia*, a short, wide gouge.

Fig. 144 shows the tools used by Nalberto Abrahán in Tixtla, Guerrero, in 1945. With his left foot acting as a vise, he is pounding with a wooden object. A chisel and a broken machete lie nearby. Fig. 185 shows another Guerrero carver, whom I saw in 1974, doing the preliminary cutting of a piece of zompantle with free swings of a machete, the same tool used in the fields. The tools used by Miguel Cruz López of Pinotepa de Don Luis, Oaxaca, consist of a straight machete and homemade carving tools, as seen in Fig. 186. This artisan specializes in carving masks from hard *parota* (conacaste) wood.

Many types of abrasives are used in mask-making. A simple implement such as a rough piece of glass may be used for finishing wood. An excellent sandpaper is made by grinding glass into a powder and sprinkling it on glue-covered paper. In Chiapas, coarse plant leaves have traditionally been utilized for sanding wood. In certain coastal regions, such as the Isthmus of Tehuantepec and the Yucatán, small squares of very hard, dried shark skin were used. Commercial sandpaper is also used by many mask-makers.

Table 3, based on our survey of mask-makers, gives the tools currently in use by mask-makers in eight states of Mexico.

187. Caimán mask and costume, Caimán Dance. The Caimán Dance with this type of mask and costume was formerly performed in the towns of Ostotitlán, Zimatel, Cuajitlotla, and El Mirador, Guerrero, but these performances ceased fifteen to twenty years ago. Several years ago, I heard that two such costumes still existed in Cuajitlotla, and this is one of them. The masks, which at one time were produced in some quantity, are also no longer available. (For other masks of this type, see Figs. 199 and 247. See pp. 198–201 for a discussion of the significance of the Caimán.) Collections of the International Folk Art Foundation in the Museum of International Folk Art, Santa Fe, New Mexico. *Cuajitlotla, Guerrero (Nahua); 50 cm. (mask only); mask: wood, paint, pochote spines; costume: cotton cloth, pochote spines.* II.B.C.

PART III: THE SIGNIFICANCE AND FUNCTION OF THE MEXICAN MASK

Interpreting ritual is a maddening intellectual challenge when the members of a society are not so articulate as Victor Turner's Ndembu, or the Navaho among whom I worked before starting field research in Zinacantán. Native exegesis on the meaning of rituals . . . is the most revealing source of information. . . . But when, as any Mesoamerica field worker knows all too well, the most common response of an informant asked why or what about a ritual is "it's the custom," then the discovery and interpretive procedures are long and involved indeed.

(Vogt 1976, p. 1)

188. Dwarf masks, Dance of the Dwarves (Enanos) (May 3). This dance was first performed, so they say, in 1804 (see note on p. 152). The two masks seen here are part of a set of twelve replacements, several times removed from the earliest ones. These large masks were worn by small boys some seventy to eighty years ago in a rain dance held in a cave at the beginning of each rainy season. The boys carried yellow canes etched with animal designs and, wearing the huge masks, they appeared to be dwarves. The rain gods, such as Tlaloques, were believed to be dwarves who lived in caves. On the masks, water symbols can be seen in the blue-green eyes, the blue rippling beards and hair, and the snakes curling down the sides of the mask on the right. This set of masks is said to have been carved by a member of the Bahena family who was reputed to have been a master carver at the age of fifteen. In recent times, the masks are said to have come into the possession of Pedro Bahena, who later sold them to various collectors. Such large, intricate masks will probably not be seen in Mexico again due to the amount of wood, time, and talent needed to produce them. Distinctive is the undercoat of black pigment rather than the usual Spanish whiting. These masks are reminiscent of the fine Barbones masks from nearby Ostotitlán (Fig. 32), which may have been carved by a related school of sculptors. *La Parota, Guerrero; (a) 85 cm.; (b) 94 cm.; wood (zompantle), paint. (a)* I.A.C. *(b)* II.A.C.

IN CONTRAST to most articles of ethnic art, masks do not have an obvious practical function; they do not plow fields, keep anyone warm, carry water, or feed families. They are, rather, manifestations of the invisible world of the religious, psychological, and social systems of their cultures. Masks are designed, constructed, and used as symbolic expressions of these systems of beliefs. To understand masks and their symbols, we must first understand the beliefs that gave rise to masks, beliefs that to some degree are still in evidence today.

In Mexico, masks developed as a part of the shamanistic basis of the Pre-Hispanic Indian religions. Masks were used to transform the wearers spiritually and psychologically into gods, supernatural forces, another level of existence. Masks were instruments that allowed the wearers to contact and to exert some control over the forces that were believed to affect their lives and their community.

While shamanism per se is slowly disappearing in Mexico today, many contemporary masks are an expression of a shamanistic element within Indian cultures which has survived the Conquest of Mexico by both the Spaniards and the Catholic Church. If we are to understand the symbols contained in these masks, we must view them within the context of their religious traditions. The objective of Part III, therefore, is to provide a brief explanation of the shamanistic role of masks (Chapter 8), the more important mask symbols (Chapter 9), and the social uses of masks (Chapter 10).

8. Shamanism

IT IS DIFFICULT for most modern readers to regard the concept of the world in which supernatural powers are responsible for rain, diseases, death by "soul loss," and abundance or starvation as anything more than the superstition of a "primitive" people. We see our world as real and rational; we have an appropriate scientific answer for everything that happens. Each night, we can retreat into the protection of our safe, warm houses, secure in our knowledge and logic. But the world was not always like this. To understand how masks have functioned, we must once again enter the world where man was alone with the elements, the world from which modern man is a very recent refugee.

While the great civilizations of Pre-Hispanic Mexico were based on agriculture, their heritage, their world view, and their religious systems were in large part shaped by a hunting and gathering culture. The hunting and gathering culture was never far in the past for these civilizations; indeed, there was a direct and continuing influence exerted by invading groups of less civilized peoples, such as the Chichimecs. However, the difference between agrarian societies and hunting and gathering ones is far more than just a matter of economics, for, as noted by Andreas Lommel: "The world-view or feeling for life of the two cultures is fundamentally different. The planter has a certain idea of how he can render his environment useful. He carries on a productive economy, and his aim is to multiply his possessions. The hunter hunts and seizes what he finds. He feels himself one with nature and does not wish to dominate it in the modern sense; but as a hunter he kills the animal, and this murder which is necessary to his existence gradually comes to weigh heavily upon him" (Lommel 1967, p. 15).

In a hunting society, man was ferocious and cruel in order to survive, and, at the same time, he was timid and weak in comparison to the forces of nature and the animals that stalked him for food. He depended on the elements and the animals for his food, his shelter, and his very existence, and in this aspect, nature was good, his benefactor. On the other hand, the same elements and animals oppressed, frightened, and destroyed him. Further, "in the mind of early

189. **Devil mask.** This extraordinary mask is one of many having two lizards, one on each cheek. It was described as a Devil but obviously once pertained to the shamanistic belief regarding the close relationship of man and animals. *Tlacozotitlán, Guerrero (Nahua); 26 cm.; wood, paint.* II.A.C.

man, the border line between the concrete and the symbolic was blurred; he could not conceive of a life clearly demarcated by any determining facts of reality. He could not separate the natural from the supernatural. For him, the latter was a living force with which he needed to identify" (Turner 1967, pp. 104–105).

In order to gain control over the natural (this dualistic giver and destroyer of life), man tried to become one with the elements and to be like his natural environment: without beginning, without end. He became the worshipper and the worshipped, the killer and the victim, where the life force of blood was given and received. Nothing was what it seemed; men were animals and animals were gods.

The identity between men and animals has existed among people in different places throughout the world, particularly among American Indian groups. Almost all of these groups have myths, stories, and/or songs in which their gods are transformed into animals and animals into men. One good example of this is an Eskimo hunting song:

> In the very earliest time,
> when both people and animals lived on earth,
> a person could become an animal if he wanted to
> and an animal could become a human being.
> Sometimes they were people
> and sometimes animals
> and there was no difference.
> All spoke the same language.
>
> (Rothenberg, ed., 1972, p. 45)

In ancient Mexico, the idea of the mystic unity of man with animals was widespread and formed an important element in the religions of all classical Indian civilizations. The importance of this identity was retained even after these societies became agrarian and ceased to depend on hunting. The Olmecs, for example, associated themselves with the jaguar and were "able" to transform themselves into men-jaguars and jaguar-men.

Given man's need to become one with nature and his invention of the soul as a method of doing so, these views evolved toward two poles: the Lord of the Animals, who is the concentration of these spiritual forces (discussed in further detail in Chapter 9); and the shaman, a spiritual technician whose soul could travel to the spirit world and cause animal spirits to return to earth so that hunger and want could be averted. The shaman must be differentiated from the medicine man and the magician, not only because of his unique practices (which included flying, being killed and brought back to life, the use of crowns, masks, and bones, etc.), but also because the shaman, by benefit of his training, could directly contact the supernatural world at will and served as a guide for the other members of his tribe. As Mircea Eliade states, the shaman is differen-

190. Mask for Fox Dance. The ancient unity of man and animal is well demonstrated in this inventive old composite mask, as the jaguar and the human face become part of one another. The jaguar holds the human eyes in its mouth, while its tongue becomes the human nose. Jaguar paws encircle the strong jaw and chin. In this mask a *nagual, tonal,* or protective meaning seems obvious. (See p. 174 for a discussion of the *nagual* or *tonal.*) *San Luis San Pedro, Guerrero (Nahua); height: 30 cm.; depth: 17 cm.; wood, paint, animal teeth.* II.B.C.

191. Azteca masks, Azteca Dance. Mounted on top of each of these masks is a jaguar protector similar to feline protectors that have been found on helmets in both Mexico and China (see Fig. 192). There is a difference of opinion as to whether these jaguar/tiger images above the human face are malevolent or benevolent (see Fraser, ed., 1968, pp. 82–84). Mask *a* property of the University of Arizona. *(a) Chalpa (near Tlapa), Guerrero (Tlapanec); (b) Ajuchitlán, Guerrero (Nahua); (a) 47 cm.; (b) 37 cm.; wood, paint.* II.A.C.

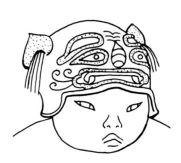

tiated from both medicine men and the lay population "by the intensity of his own magico-religious experiences" and by the fact that "he alone succeeds in acquiring a technique that enables him to undertake ecstatic journeys at will" to the supernatural world (Eliade 1964, pp. 297–298).

Yet it is not shamans themselves who are important in relationship to contemporary masks, but the system of shamanistic beliefs which formed an integral part of Mexican Indian cultures and survived the attempts at suppression by the Catholic Church. Shamanism, which Eliade defines as a "technique of ecstasy" (1964, p. 4) for merging and communicating with the spiritual world, was used by all the members of the tribe. The shaman was the technician of the sacred but not its sole possessor. It was believed that each Indian had a tutelary spirit or spiritual "power" that made him capable of "visions" and augmented his reserves of the sacred (ibid., p. 298). Shamanism was the technique of communicating with the spirit world that was shared by all of the members of the community.

The shamanistic use of masks to facilitate that journey to the spirit world is made clear by Eliade: "There is always some instrument that, in one way or another, is able to establish contact with the 'world of the spirits'.... This...falls under a 'law' well known to the history of religions: *one becomes what one displays.* The wearers of masks *are* really the mythical ancestors [as well as the gods, spirits, and animals] portrayed by their masks" (Eliade 1964, p. 179). Therefore, the use of masks by the members of the tribe is far more than just a ritual performance in homage to the gods or the supernatural powers; it is a method for establishing direct, mystical contact that is used by a large segment of the village.

192. Feline helmets and headdresses from Mexico and China. At upper left is the great Mixtec conqueror Eight Deer, from the Codex Nuttall; at upper center, a human face surmounted by an enormous jaguar headdress, from a clay urn of the Monte Albán III area from Oaxaca. At upper right is a bronze pole-end from early China, Shang period—a human face with a tiger on top; at lower right, a tiger cap of cloth worn by modern Chinese children as an amulet. After Covarrubias 1954, p. 50.

194. Characters and dances unknown. I have known only six masks in Mexico like these with small human faces superimposed on the forehead. Similar masks are used by the Eskimo in shamanistic ceremonies; the small faces represent shaman helpers (Ray 1967, plate following p. 96). Mask *a* depicts a tarantula with human features and is from Xalpatláhuac, Guerrero. Mask *b* is a human face with bat ears. *Guerrero (Nahua); (a) 22 cm.; (b) 30 cm.; wood, paint, bone teeth (a). (a)* II.B.C. *(b)* I.A.D.

193. Devil masks, various dances. On the left is a beautifully carved Crow, whose rather fierce aspect warns of danger to crops. A death head is carved on the brow. This mask was said to have been used for the Crow Dance and the Devil Dance. On the right is a Zopilote (Vulture), possibly used in the Tecuani Dance. On the forehead is a spirit helper of the sort that appears in many forms on Eskimo masks; see, for instance, the shaman helper dog spirits in Dorothy Jean Ray's *Eskimo Masks* (1967, Plate I). Both of these are now termed Devil masks, but they undoubtedly had an esoteric, shamanistic meaning at one time. *(a) Tlanixpatlán, Guerrero; (b) Huitziltepec, Guerrero; (a) 37 cm.; (b) 26 cm.; wood, paint.* V.A.C.

THE MASK AS AN INSTRUMENT OF TRANSFORMATION

Given the need for man in primitive conditions to merge with the animal and natural forces of the world, the invention and use of masks as a catalyst for that transformation was not only logical but probably inevitable. Masks could be made to closely represent the animal or natural force that man wanted to control. In the case of animal deities, masks were (and still are, although rarely) made from parts of that animal, such as the bone or hide, and thus more directly shared the spiritual power of the animal itself.

It is not surprising that the earliest Stone Age masks are of animals. As Walter Sorell notes, "Animal masks were the most important symbols in the totemistic culture; they were among the first and most logical images and disguises for man, whose major and immediate experiences were with the animal world. The mask was undoubtedly preceded by the painting of the body, the first realization of man's sense of decoration which greatly inspired and finally led to the creation of masks. Curt Sachs has pointed out that 'masked culture, one of whose roots lies in the physical, conceives its spirits in perceptible, often in animal form'" (Sorell 1973, p. 9).

Yet the function of masks is not limited to the simple representation of the animal or natural force. In Mexico, as in other areas, Indian groups regarded the face as the representation and the center of an individual's personality. Thus, donning a mask was more than just adopting a disguise; it was the equivalent to temporarily eliminating the personality of the wearer and replacing it with a being from the other world. It was a profound, mysterious, and magical transformation.

In writing about masks in *A Dictionary of Symbols* J. E. Cirlot states: "All transformations are invested with something at once of profound mystery and of the shameful, since anything that is so modified as to become 'something else' while still remaining the thing it was, must inevitably be productive of ambiguity and equivocation. Therefore, metamorphoses must be hidden from view—and hence the need for the mask. Secrecy tends towards transfiguration: it helps what-one-is to become what-one-would-like-to-be; and this is what constitutes its magic character. . . . The mask is equivalent to the chrysalis" (Cirlot 1962, pp. 195–196).

While this transformation is of necessity an individual one for the wearer, it serves a social and collective need and can only exist on the basis of an agreement of the members of that society. In discussing masks as a means of changing personality, C. G. Jung says that through the use of the mask, "the outstanding individual is apparently removed from the sphere of the collective psyche, and to the degree that he succeeds in identifying himself with his persona, he is actually removed. This removal means magical prestige. . . . The building up of prestige is always a product of collective compromise: not only must there be one who wants prestige, there must also be a public seeking somebody on whom to confer prestige. . . . Since society as a whole needs the magically effective

195. Mask for Armadillo Dance and Tlacololero Dance. Users of this mask sought to evoke with sympathetic magic the spirit of the armadillo. The tough armadillo hide is applied with unusual precision for this material and is tinted over with thin paint on the cheek and chin areas. Across the brow are a number of bands of the nine-banded armadillo, the only species found in Mexico. Property of the University of Arizona. *Ayutla, Guerrero (Nahua); 33 cm.; wood, armadillo hide, paint.* I.B.C.

figure, it uses the needful will to power in the individual, and the will to submit in the mass, as a vehicle" (Jung 1956, p. 160). While Jung's insights illustrate the basic psychological mechanisms of the mask as an instrument of transformation, I would say from an anthropological viewpoint that the transformation takes place and that the shaman or masked dancer recognizes this transformation not as a personality change, but as a taking over of the personality by a higher power or god. In essence, "The spiritual act of taking possession of, or rather assimilating, the spirit represented by the mask—to the point of becoming possessed by it or becoming it—was the goal of such a masked man" (Sorell 1973, p. 8).

SHAMANISM AND THE MASK TODAY

The central question remains: to what extent (if any) does the shamanistic use of masks survive in the design and use of contemporary Mexican masks? As I have pointed out, many elements of shamanism have been destroyed or lost or have gone underground during over 450 years of domination by the Spanish and by the Catholic Church. The shaman as an institution has almost totally disappeared from Mexico, except in peripheral groups like the Huichol and Yaqui Indians. For example, one of the primary tasks of the shaman, in which masks often played an important role, was the curing of the sick, whether from soul loss or from broken bones. To my knowledge, this association with the mask has disappeared, and no curing ceremonies in which masks are used exist today. Yet it is my feeling, based on my years of direct observation in small Mexican villages, not only that shamanistic elements still exist, but that they are specifically manifested in the design of modern masks and their use in a large number of contemporary dances. This is true not only of those groups like the Huichols and the Yaquis, whose systems of religious beliefs are still relatively intact, but also of peoples like the Nahuas, who have had extensive contact with Christianity from the beginning.

One good example of the survival of this type of system of beliefs is shown in Timothy Knab's study of San Miguel Tzinacapan, a small Nahuatl-speaking village in the Sierra de Puebla. He states: "The religious phenomena of San Miguel Tzinacapan comprise two distinct and independent systems of religious thought and symbols, that of the public syncretic cult of the saints and the private yet not covert animistic beliefs: the cult of the earth. Individuals may participate in and hold concepts of either or both systems without seeing any conflict or paradox in either" (Knab 1976, p. 3).

Specifically, the belief of the people of San Miguel Tzinacapan in the cult of the earth is the belief in Talocan, which means the earth itself in the Nahuatl of the Sierra de Puebla and also refers to a complete cosmogony. This system of beliefs (and the word *Talocan* itself) most certainly originated directly from classical Aztec religion and its Tlalocan, which was the paradisiacal underworld of the Aztecs. Thus, Talocan and its supernatural beings represent a direct survival of a Pre-Hispanic religion through oral tradition alone, despite Christian contact and efforts to suppress such pagan beliefs.

The people of San Miguel Tzinacapan classify these supernatural beings as *amo tokinwan*, which means "not our brothers," although this is not to say that they are thought of as being totally malevolent. These beings have charge over the natural phenomena with which each is associated. A man must ask the appropriate supernatural being for permission to grow his crops, for personal protection, for rain, and for protection from thunderstorms. While these beliefs are somewhat more agrarian than those we have discussed previously, the transformation of these beings to animals and to humans is well known to these people. I believe these personages are the Lords of the Animals or vestiges thereof. They are said to appear like villagers, in indigenous dress and speaking Nahuatl. They are considered to be dangerous should they enter the village, as is shown in the following prayer:

> *"THEY EAT US!*
> *They are—not—our brother (firmly)*
> *They are worms, wild beasts   yes"*
> *(Knab 1976, p. 6)*

Belief in such supernatural beings is not confined to such groups as the Nahuas. In our field work with the Zoque Indians in Tuxtla Gutiérrez, Chiapas, we recorded a tale that illustrates these Indians' belief in the interaction of the supernatural being and humans:

> *The Moyó are the thunderbolts that live in caves in the mountains. They are very old but look like little boys of about ten years of age. They carry whips which are really serpents.*
>
> *Once there was a little boy who was returning from his cornfield. Someone called to him. When he looked up, he saw a Moyó sitting in a tree, who said to him, "Give me my whip!" He asked the little boy to do that for him because he could not fly away without the whip and it is forbidden for a Moyó to touch the ground, so he could not get it himself.*
>
> *The little boy looked, but instead of a whip he saw a big snake. He was very much frightened and told the Moyó, "That is not a whip; that is a serpent." The Moyó replied, "That is my whip," and he begged and supplicated, "If you will give me the whip, I will clean your field. I shall clean it very well, only don't go there tomorrow, because I will be working."*
>
> *The little boy procured a long stick, carefully put it under the serpent, and lifted it up to the Moyó. When the Moyó took it in his hand, he disappeared so quickly that the little boy did not know what had happened. When the boy returned to his field, he found that the Moyó had cleaned it thoroughly for him.*
>
> *(Cordry and Cordry 1941, pp. 8–10).*

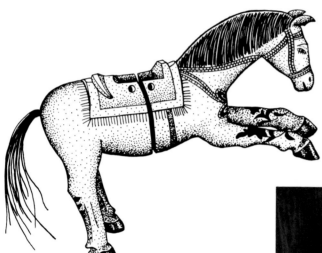

196. Wooden horse used in the Santiago Dance. After a drawing by Donald Cordry. From Cordry 1940, p. 17, Fig. 6.

197. Santiago mask; Santiago horse. Two musicians, one with a bamboo flute, the other with a drum, flank a masked Santiago, who wears a small Santiago horse attached to the front of his body. *Mochitlán, Guerrero, 1970.*

The most direct survival of shamanism is to be found among the Huichol Indians. Each year, Huichol villages send groups of pilgrims from the mountains of Nayarit and Jalisco to Wirikota in the high desert of San Luis Potosí. Led by their village shaman, the pilgrims walk over thirty days and cover over six hundred miles in many cases before they return. During the trip, they fast, drink very little water, and ritually purify their souls. In part, the journey to Wirikota is made to collect peyote, a hallucinogenic cactus that is sacred to the Huichol because the visions it produces allow them to directly see and interact with their gods. In part, it is also a spiritual journey to the center of the Huichol universe, to the place where creation began, to a state of mind in which each pilgrim experiences a direct, personal communication with the gods. This ecstatic, mystical relationship with the gods, which forms the basis of shamanism, is best described by the Huichols themselves:

> . . . *And there on the Earth of the Gods they hear singing*
> > *The gods are singing*
> > *The mountains the hills are singing*
> > *& the roses are singing*
> *The song of life in Wirikota   only heard in Wirikota*
> > *Eternal song of Life*
> > *Only there*
> > *Only there & heard in Wirikota*
> > > *("For the God of Peyote" [Huichol];*
> > > *Rothenberg, ed., 1972, p. 362)*

Belief in the supernatural is not restricted to Indian cultures but is widespread throughout all of Mexico. *Curanderos* (curers or healers) and *brujos* (witches) can be found in almost every village, town, and major city in the country. While they do not, to my knowledge, use masks in their rituals, they do share many functional characteristics with shamans, such as having direct personal experiences with supernatural beings and curing individuals who have suffered soul loss, *susto* or magical terror, or evil winds at the hands of these supernaturals.

One example of the power of these *curanderos* and the depth of people's belief in them occurred recently to a friend of mine who lives in a small but thoroughly acculturated, Spanish-speaking town in the state of Morelos. As a poet, he was particularly grieved to wake up one morning and find that both of his typewriters had been stolen. After hearing about what had happened, two of his friends of the village went directly to a *curandera*, who not only had a vision as to where the typewriters were but also placed a curse on the thief unless they were returned. Two days later and after the word of the curse got around town, the stolen typewriters were miraculously found.

While the preceding examples have sought to document the survival of a number of general shamanistic beliefs in contemporary Mexico, there are also many instances where the use of masks constitutes a specific expression of belief in magic. One such case involves the small, wooden horse of Santiago (St. James) in Cuetzalan, Puebla, used in the Santiago Dance (see Fig. 196). Although this dance was introduced by the Spanish soon after the Conquest, the treatment and veneration given the horse is certainly not part of the Christian tradition.

As we noted in our original field work:

> . . . *in Cuetzalan we encountered a superstition concerning the wooden horse of the Santiago Caballero which we had not observed in the beliefs of Indians elsewhere. The toy animal is deeply venerated and is believed to be endowed with life—possibly a survival of the superstitious awe with which the Indians first viewed the horses of the Spanish conquerors.*
>
> *The principal dancer each year, who has the honor of impersonating the Santiago Caballero, takes the horse from his predecessor and keeps it until the day of his fiesta arrives. During this time he is under obligation to the community to give the horse a bowl of maize and a bowl of water each day. It is believed that, if this is not done, that if the horse is not treated well, it will run away to another village. The people of San Miguel near Cuetzalan, we were told, are firmly convinced that they lost their horse to another village in 1937 owing to this neglect. During the time the horse is in the dancer's house, it is kept either on the household altar or in a small stable or box especially for the purpose.*
>
> *(Cordry and Cordry 1940, pp. 12–15).*

A more direct Pre-Hispanic survival is to be found in the use of the Dwarf masks of La Parota, Guerrero. These large masks may exceed one metre in height and depict a bearded Zeus-like character (see Fig. 188). They are worn by children to imitate dwarves in a rain-petitioning ceremony that is often performed in caves.* The Aztec rain gods, the Tlaloques, were thought to be dwarves and to live under mountains; caves were entrances to their underworld

---

* A copy of the original 1902 description of the Dance of the Dwarves from Campo Morado, Guerrero, and its translation are as follows:

"Campo Morado Gro 4 de Junio 1902 Danza Los Enanos esta Danza fue nacida en 1804 y Esta compuesta por 12 Danzantes Las Mascaras que Ocupaban esta compuesta con culebras Esta Danza La utilisaban para adorar al Dios del agua cuando era tiempo de lluvias y no llovia principalmente el 3 de mayo van a visitarlo a la cueva del tizhuehue Van a danzante y le llevavan el huntle Esta danza fue propiedad de la familia Bahena y ultimamente quedo En Manos del Sr. Pedro Bahena y hasta Esta fecha La conserbo como Mayordomo de la Iglesia de San Sebastian

"Atentamente

"Pedro Bahena"

("Campo Morado, Guerrero, June 4, 1902. Dance of the Dwarves. This dance was born in 1804 and is composed of 12 dancers. The masks which they use are made up of snakes. This Dance was used to adore the God of water when it was time for the rains and it did not rain—principally on the 3rd of May they go to visit the cave of Tizhuehue—they go dancing and they carry the "huntle(?)." This Dance was the property of the family Bahena and of late has remained in the hands of Sr. Pedro Bahena. Until this date he has conserved it as mayordomo of the Church of San Sebastian.

"Attentively

"Pedro Bahena")

198. Cuaxolotl, the goddess of duality. Cuaxolotl, the female counterpart of Xolotl, gave birth to twins, shown at the bottom of the drawing. She wears a mask on the back of her head, probably of Xolotl or Quetzalcoatl. After the Codex Borgia, plate 60.

abodes. Thus, the masked children are transformed into the image of the Tlaloques as a method of attempting to control nature, a transformational process which is the heart of the shamanistic use of masks.

In passing, it should be noted that the masks from La Parota do not appear indigenous, with their long wavy beards and blue eyes. However, as will be discussed in Chapter 9, such beards were known in Pre-Hispanic times and were used as water symbols.

An example of the coexistence of European and Indian traditions (like that of San Miguel Tzinacapan) in mask use appears among the Yaqui and the Mayo Indians today. When Indian musical instruments, such as the flute and the drum, are being played, dancers wear their masks fully over their faces. When European musical instruments (the violin and the harp) are being used, the mask is worn on the side or back of the head. While neither group gives any explanation for this practice, it may well be that this custom began from the recognition that the transformation produced by being fully masked did not fit within the European/Christian framework. Thus, when European instruments are used, the mask is moved to one side to function only as a decoration. There is also a Pre-Hispanic precedent for the wearing of masks on the back of the head, however: Fig. 198, from the Codex Borgia, shows a mask that may represent Xolotl worn on the back of the head of Cuaxolotl. This plate in the Borgia signifies duality, certain directions, and astronomy.

Whereas the examples discussed above demonstrate survivals of specific Pre-Hispanic religious practices, there is a second, more pervasive reason for concluding that many contemporary uses of masks continue to incorporate shamanistic elements, as can readily be seen through the analysis of some of the masked dances and their corresponding fiestas. While dances will be explored in further detail later, it should be noted that there still are a large number of masked dances whose function can only be described as an appeal to supernatural forces in an attempt to control nature.

These "nature" dances abound with masks representing animal figures. Not only are such animal representations one of the main concerns of shamanism, but the animal motifs utilized have a highly developed symbolism that dates directly back to ancient Indian Mexico. Further, the presence of these animals does not seem to be just a continuance of traditional motifs that have lost their original meanings, as the action within these dances closely parallels and reinforces the traditional symbolic meanings that have been associated with these motifs.

Although the individual meanings of these mask symbols are dealt with in Chapter 9, one example of this phenomenon is to be found in the Caimán Dance performed until fairly recently in the Balsas River area in Guerrero. The central figure of this dance is the Caimán (see Figs. 187, 199, 213, 247, 303c), who, like the shamanistic hunting gods, is both the destroyer and the giver of life. His role as menace derives, at least in part, from real life, in that he eats the fish that these people depend upon. He is transformed into a symbol of abundance through the Caimán Dance, in which he is "caught" by the village fishermen and thus assures good fishing for the year to come (see Chapter 9).

A second dance and fiesta characteristic that in my opinion indicates a pervasive survival of Pre-Hispanic religious elements is the large number of fiestas in which the participants get ceremonially "blind drunk" and in which blood is shed as a matter of course. Many people are inclined to believe that this bloodshed is due to the alcohol and the violence that it produces. Having ob-

199. Caimán mask, Caimán Dance. A Caimán mask featuring an unusually large, notched triple nose and pochote spines. Like the masks in Fig. 247, this probably is a representation of a Pre-Columbian figure. It was used in a dance to insure good fishing. Property of the University of Arizona. *Area of Ostotitlán, Guerrero (Nahua); 41 cm.; wood, paint, pochote spines, leather.* III.B.C.

served these fiestas for years, I believe that this question must be answered by considering other elements that we know existed in Pre-Conquest times and the meaning of bloodshed at that time. Human blood was the most sacred thing that was offered to the gods in ancient Mexico. In the Codex Vaticano-Rios we read, ". . . and therefore he clutches the precious thorn: *chalchihuiztli*, instrument for extracting blood from the ear lobes, from the tongue and from the male member, necessary penance . . ." (Kingsborough 1964, 3:54).

Alfonso Caso further explains the significance of the offering of human blood in ancient times: "Since man was created by the sacrifice of the gods, he must reciprocate by offering them his blood in sacrifice. Human sacrifice was essential in Aztec religion, for if a man could not exist except through the creative force of the gods, the latter in turn needed man to sustain them with human sacrifice. Man must nourish the gods with the magic sustenance of life itself, found in human blood and in the human heart" (Caso 1958, p. 12).

The Guerrero village of Zitlala comes to mind in this respect. During the fiesta held there in early May, there is a battle between two types of Tigres, green ones and yellow ones, which I believe have some reference to green and yellow corn. The entire fiesta is a petition for rain. There is great competition and resentment between the three districts of the village. Whether this resentment is artificially produced in order to cause bloodshed I do not know. However, even at the present time, it is necessary to bring policemen from the larger

200. Devil masks, various dances. These masks may derive from Pre-Cortesian human sacrifice, as each Devil holds a child in its mouth. The black mask at upper left (*a*) is from Comala, Guerrero, and was used in the Dance of the Tres Potencias. The child in its mouth is shown being pierced with the sharp fangs and bleeding. The large mask in the center (*b*) has the very prominent animal-type ears so often seen in Devil masks. The upper right mask (*c*) is a horsehair-trimmed Devil with teeth made from the claws of a hawk. It comes from Tlalchapa, Guerrero. The lower mask (*d*) is a Bat Devil mask from Totozintla, Guerrero. Mask *c* property of the University of Arizona. *Guerrero (Nahua); 21.5–56 cm.; wood, paint, animal claws, horsehair. (a, b, d)* II.A.D. *(c)* I.A.D.

village of Chilapa to see that people are not badly hurt. The Tigres carry long ropes containing huge knots, and with these they beat each other over the head and body. The head is protected by extremely heavy, painted leather Tigre masks (Fig. 55). In former times people were killed during the fiesta, and blood is still shed each year. Whether or not this bloodshed is intentional is a matter for conjecture.

At this same fiesta, people walk miles up a very difficult, rocky path to a shrine at the top of the mountain. Near the shrine is a cave where animals such as goats, turkeys, and chickens are sacrificed. The path, which could be cleared out during the year, is left rocky, thereby causing the feet to bleed.

In the fiestas that I have attended in Mecapalapa, a Totonac town in the state of Puebla, the Indians were bloody and very drunk. They have a saying, "The fiesta is not a good one unless there are seven dead." I was told by María Teresa Pomar that a man cut his finger badly during a fiesta in Chicontepec, Veracruz. An outsider wanted to wrap it up, but all the people came around and said, "No, let it bleed.'

There are many masks that are extremely large and heavy, and people are inclined to doubt their use because they are so uncomfortable to wear, but in my opinion this is a part of the ancient heritage of the Indians. They still remember that discomfort in their fiestas and bloodshed were the most important offerings to the gods. Now they offer fruit, vegetables, animals, flowers, and incense, but I do not think that they have forgotten that the most important sacrifice was human blood.

As was mentioned in Chapter 3, the eye openings of some masks are extremely inadequate, so much so that one would think the dancers could not see at all, especially when one considers that drunkenness is part of the ritual aspect of the ceremony. Lommel speaks of a similar situation with the masks of the Altai peoples, the Lapps, and the Samayeds (who were shamanistic hunting peoples): "The eye holes, if there are any at all, greatly restrict the mask-wearer's field of vision. He is entirely concentrated upon his inner world of images, so he waits passively for the coming of the spirits—as is well known, one can best prepare oneself for an inner experience with one's eyes closed" (Lommel 1967, p. 109).

Masks from the region of Ostotitlán previously had very, very narrow eye slits (Fig. 32). Today, as ritual drunkenness or being "blind drunk" has largely supplanted the blind mask, there are more ample provisions for seeing out through the masks, as shown by the Caimán masks with pochote adornment (Figs. 199, 247).

Today, as "progress" reaches more and more of the remote Indian villages, belief in this type of shamanistic use of masks is rapidly fading. Yet, as has been pointed out, there still are a number of villages where the need to identify with and to control supernatural forces forms part of the system of religious beliefs. It should come as no surprise that these are the villages where the most masks are made and used in dances.

201. Devil mask, Devil Dance. Now termed a Devil, this engaging mask shows a frog with two very lifelike, supple *tigres* clinging to the top. The animal interaction here is an equation: the bat and the frog are associated; the bat and the *tigre* are associated; therefore, due to fertility beliefs and the oneness of all things, the frog and the *tigre* should also be associated. Unfortunately, these old meanings and interrelationships hardly hold even in oral traditions today. *El Palmar, Guerrero (Nahua); 29 cm.; wood, paint.* IV.A.D.

202. Tigre masks and costumes with small Tigres. These splendid Tigre costumes display a feature seldom seen today. Besides the large facial masks, each costume has smaller Tigre masks sewn on. Costume *a* has two small masks applied at the lower chest level. On costume *b,* small Tigres are applied on the chest, the elbows, and the knees. The addition of the small Tigres on the costume is a custom also found in very early Chinese art (see Fig. 224). *Tenanquillo, Guerrero; (a) head mask: 37 cm.; small chest masks: 14 cm.; (b) head mask: 40 cm.; small masks on costume: 6.5 cm.; wood, paint, leather, cotton cloth.* V.A.C.

9. Symbolism

THE FOLLOWING ANALYSIS of the major symbols in contemporary Mexican masks is, of necessity, a general one. Its purpose is to identify the designs, treatments, and other variables commonly found in modern masks and to discuss their general meanings, so that the reader can gain insight into the symbolism. It must be stressed that these values are not absolute and cannot be extended to all of the various mask-making groups throughout Mexico today any more than they could have been during Pre-Hispanic times. Although I have tried to use examples that I feel to be representative, the reader is cautioned against arbitrarily applying my conclusions to other Indian groups.

In large part, the generalness of this analysis stems from the fact that there are simply too many indigenous groups in Mexico to permit a detailed analysis of the symbols of each group. Nor does the problem stop here, since the meaning of a particular motif can change from one village to another within the same ethnic group. Also, there are many motifs whose meanings have been lost in recent years. When I arrived in Mexico in the early 1930's, there were many old mask-makers who still knew the meanings of the symbols of their masks but kept them secret. Before you could get any information from them, they had to know and trust you, a process that often required many years. Unfortunately the young men of the villages were often not interested in learning this information; so, as the old mask-makers died, much of their knowledge died with them. Consequently, there are a large number of villages that still continue to produce or use traditional masks without understanding their symbolic meanings.

Further, the process of determining such values is an imprecise one because of the nature of symbolism. A symbol is not necessarily a direct representation that can be readily recognized and identified even by the people for whom it has significance. From an anthropological point of view, symbols do not have to be consciously understood to have meaning or value; in fact, most symbols are not so understood. Much of their basic power springs directly from emotional, non-rational meanings of which people are not even aware.

203. Life/Death clay mask. Middle Pre-Classic culture, ca. 900–300 B.C. Courtesy of the Museo Nacional de Antropología, I.N.A.H., S.E.P., Archivo Fotográfico. I.B.D.

The interpretation of the meaning of a particular mask or symbol involves determining the implicit meanings defined by how it is used, correlating the folklore about the various animals and figures with the masks, and referring to other materials where applicable. In addition, many design features have an intrinsic psychological value because they mimic body parts, as in the case of the phallic, long-nosed masks, but even these must be viewed in relationship to their culture if they are to have any real meaning. As a result, any symbolic analysis is subject to varying interpretations. The following analysis should serve as a beginning, not as the final word.

DUALITY

The concept of duality is central to the indigenous cultures of Mexico. It pervades the remnants of the various Indian religions, as it was a major element in Pre-Hispanic religious beliefs. Duality is manifested both directly in the design of masks and indirectly in their basic function. Because of the importance of this concept, it is vital to define *duality* before proceeding with an exploration of its representation in masks.

Duality can be most simply defined as the condition or state of having two parts which represent two aspects of a whole. No matter how dissimilar or how opposed the two parts seem, they combine to make a single entity, a single concept, or a single god. All cultures are full of examples: male and female (human), mind and matter (reality), good and evil (morality), day and night (twenty-four hours), life and death (the process of life), etc. Thus, a mask can be said to be dualistic if there is an underlying unity of two aspects, as in the Life/Death mask shown in Fig. 203. Without that unity, a mask is not dualistic even if it has two faces or two separate representations of forces, animals, gods, etc.

Almost all of the gods and supernatural forces of Mexican Indian religions were and are dualistic. Generally, this duality is manifested in two basic forms: sexual duality, in that most gods are both male and female at the same time, and attribute duality, in that they are both good and evil, representing both the destroyer and the bringer of fertility. As pointed out in Chapter 8, this duality sprang directly from the perceptions of nature by a hunting society and remained one of the basic characteristics of the religions of the agrarian civilizations of ancient Mexico.

One modern example of this type of religious duality is to be found in the First Fruits rite of the Huichol Indians. Performed after the first rain of the rainy season, this ceremony uses the mask of Tate Nakawé (Grandmother Growth). In a procession around a ceremonial fire, the person representing Tate Nakawé follows behind the person playing the part of Tatewari (Grandfather Fire). When the ceremonial fire is dowsed, the Tate Nakawé mask is removed, and the sex of both gods is reversed as part of the symbolic plea for crop fertility. The smoke from the fire acts as a prayer to the sky for rain, along with the birds that are released at the same time. Fig. 78 shows the Tate Nakawé mask and some of the participants of this ceremony when I witnessed it in 1937.

In addition to the basic duality of Indian gods, there is also an implicit duality in the use of masks, particularly when they serve as an instrument allowing man to identify with and to "become" a supernatural force. In this case, the wearer becomes both the god and the man at the same time. This unification creates a single dualistic entity which permits man some control over the forces of the spirit world. This intrinsic duality is also present in nonshamanistic mask use: by simply wearing a mask, the wearer is assuming another role, taking on a different personality or persona than his normal one. In reality, of course, this different persona is only another aspect of the individual himself, an aspect created through the use of the mask.

Representations of Duality in Masks
The most common method of representing a dualistic entity is through dual-faced masks, similar to representations of the Roman god Janus or the set of Greek theatrical persona masks depicting comedy and tragedy. As noted by Miguel León-Portilla, the ancient Indian cultures felt that, "Beyond doubt, 'face' referred to that which most intimately characterized the intrinsic nature of each

individual" (1963, p. 114). It is logical, therefore, that these people developed this type of configuration as a graphic statement of the two sides of an entity.

This "two-faced" configuration can be manifested in several ways: the inclusion of two separate faces as parts of the main or predominant face, the use of two half-faces to form a split face that appears almost schizophrenic, or the more subtle incorporation of negative and positive symbols on opposing sides of a single-faced mask. Such symbols may vary from the blatantly obvious to a single accepted convention like the "twisted mouth" of Eskimo and other American Indian masks. The use of these types of conventions to represent duality has a long history in Mexico and other parts of the world, as can be seen in the twin figurines from Guerrero and the Marquesas Islands shown in Fig. 204. See also Fig. 205.

As mentioned previously, not all multiple-faced masks are necessarily dualistic. In the extraordinary double-face mask from Jaleaca, Guerrero, shown in Fig. 206c, the two faces are not symbolically differentiated from one another and, therefore, must be considered to represent a single theme. In what is perhaps the most spectacular of all the Jaleaca masks, shown in Figs. 1 and 206b, the paired faces do have different symbols. On the left face, the frog, serpent, beard, and moustache are traditional rain-petitioning symbols. The protruding tongue of the right face of this mask is usually associated with other meanings (such as wisdom, defiance, etc.); however, in this case, the flowing rendition of the tongue suggests that it too is a water symbol, representing thirst. This interpretation is further reinforced by the inclusion of the serpent and the fact that this face also has blue eyes, yet another water symbol. Consequently, it must be concluded that this mask is a representation of a single idea and is not a dualistic mask. It is possible that the double-faced masks shown in Figs. 206b and c were carved with two faces simply to mean greater power, especially if, as suspected, they were used in prayers for rain and good crops. Similarly, it is likely that more significant magic forces are represented by double-faced Devils than by single-faced ones.

In regard to duality, I note here thoughts by Wiltraud Zehnder, who believes that the two-headed and two-faced figures of Pre-Classic Tlatilco represent double rarities found in nature, such as "the double leaves of the mageplant [maguey plant], the double stalk of maize, twins, etc., as well as curious phenomena such as the image which appears while contemplating the surface of water or the intimate relation between one's body and shadow, or the strange case of echo" (1973, p. 87).

Striking examples of contemporary dualistic masks are the extremely rare masks from the Atenxoxola-Xiloxuchicán area of Guerrero pictured in Fig. 207. Fig. 208 shows one of these masks, in which two smaller faces have been carved into the cheeks of the overall mask face. While this type of mask must be considered an example of the "two-faced" method of signifying duality, it can be termed a "three-faced mask" to aid identification and discussion. I believe that the mask in question (Fig. 208) represents Xolotl, the god of duality and mon-

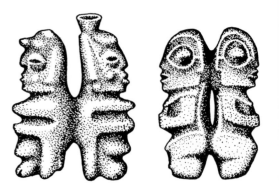

204. Twin figurines. (*a*) Twin figurine of metadiorite and green granite from Guerrero (Collection Miguel Covarrubias); (*b*) Double tiki figurine of black basalt from the Marquesas Islands (Collection of Georges Salles). After Covarrubias 1954, p. 64.

205. Pre-Hispanic double mask figure. This figure, as seen in the Codex Laud, plate 43(28), is described as follows: "we see a sinner seated in the place of the two faces, which, without doubt, represents Omeyocan: the place of duality, or sky, where the creator gods reside" (Kingsborough 1964, 3: 402). There is another reference to what appears to be a double or helmet type of mask in the Florentine Codex: "And they put upon him a mask looking in two directions. It had huge lips and large eyes" (Sahagún 1951, p. 144).

206. Possible Devil masks. The upper center and right masks (*b* and *c*), with their possible dual implications, are the finest of the rare old Jaleaca, Guerrero, masks, other examples of which are shown in Figs. 38 and 242. (Mask *b* is shown in color in Fig. 1.) Their devils, snakes, bats, protruding tongues, and frog are both symbols of evil and a supplication for water. They represent the epitome of academic know-how and perfection of craftsmanship, as well as an earlier carving style. Both the detailed carving and the rich paints used are reminiscent of the work of early church carvers, who had access to the best of tools and materials. Masks *a* and *d* are early-twentieth-century masks by

José Rodríguez and are also made of very hard wood. Although during his adult life he worked a great distance away, it is possible that Rodríguez may have been a grandson or great-grandson of the earlier carver, as there are marked similarities of style, craftsmanship, symbolism, and facial features between the masks seen here and those in Figs. 17 and 37.

Undoubtedly, Rodríguez lacked access to such sophisticated tools as were used on the earlier carvings, and he generally used thinly applied earth pigments, reserving the expensive commercial paints for embellishments on his masks. Although the exact relationship of Rodríguez and this earlier carver may never be known, it appears that Rodríguez's art was nurtured by a fine tradition, to which he brought his own freedom of expression and exaggerated sense of design. Photo by Ferruccio Asta. *(a, d) area of Tlapa, Guerrero; (b, c) Jaleaca, Guerrero (Nahua); (a) 38 cm.; (b) 42 cm.; (c) 46 cm.; (d) 35 cm.; wood, earth paints, commercial paints. (a, d)* II.B.C. *(b, c)* II.B.D.

sters. The two smaller faces on the cheeks are, I believe, the twins born to Xolotl's female counterpart, Cuaxolotl (see Fig. 198). These twins represent duality. It is unclear whether this meaning was consciously intended by the Indians or whether it was an unconscious belief handed down without being understood.

A characteristic of such "three-faced" masks is that the main face retains its own chin, mouth, nose, and forehead, but its eyes are replaced by the two sets of eyes from the smaller masks, creating an almost Picasso-like image. The duality is heightened by the use of color symbolism, as these masks frequently have a line dividing the face into two parts, with each side painted a different color. Usually the two smaller, cheek faces have contrasting features, showing such oppositions as smiling/frowning, male/female, and sleeping (night)/awake (day). It is also important to note the prevalence in these masks of notched noses, which will be discussed below. Another type of dual-faced masks can be found in the Twins (Gemelos) masks of San Juan Colorado, Oaxaca (Fig. 209).

A second method of portraying duality can also be found in the Atenxoxola-Xiloxuchicán-area masks: the use of "split-faces" in which two half-faces combine to form a whole (Fig. 207). In many of the "split-faced" masks, each half-face retains its own nose, mouth, chin, etc., and at least one eye. Again, both the features and the painting of these masks emphasize contrasting elements of pain/joy, male/female, night/day, etc.

According to an Indian informant, both the "three-faced" and the "split-faced" masks were used in the Quilinique Dance, which to my knowledge was performed only in the small, remote *ranchos* in the Atenxoxola-Xiloxuchicán area. Some years ago, the priest of this area decided that this dance was too pagan and ordered the villagers to get rid of all of these masks; so today the dance is no longer practiced, nor are these masks being made. The curious part about the actions of the priest is that the written text (the "Relaciones") for the dance contains no obvious or even discernible pagan references or action, nor were there any in the description of the performance. In fact, the dance is suspiciously bland, as it involves the selling of a mule. The only direct reference to the two-faced masks worn by the participants is the mention of someone's "two-faced" dealings. There seems to be nothing in the dance itself to justify the priest's accusation of paganism; yet, at the same time, there does not seem to be anything that justifies the multitude of split-faced and three-faced masks.

This led me to wonder if there was something behind both the dance and the designs of the masks, some pagan survival. Traditionally, another method of depicting duality is by using a characterizing aspect or sign of a god who is specifically linked to duality. Now let us return to the notched noses that are so prevalent in these Quilinique masks. Unlike the other traits in these masks, whose probable meanings can be discerned by direct observation, the meaning of the notched nose is not readily apparent, even though its repeated usage strongly suggests that it has a symbolic function. The most probable conclusion is that the notched nose is a Pre-Hispanic survival.

207. Double- and triple-face masks, Quilinique Dance. Unfortunately little is known about these rare masks, although their dualistic nature is certainly of ancient origin. They were last used in a dance pertaining to the sale of a mule (perhaps to underscore the "two-faced" nature of bargaining), but their use was eventually banned as pagan by the local priest. Although all bear the style of unskilled carvers, their mystery and fascination is beyond question and is actually accented by their crude execution. Several of these faces have the notched Xolotl nose (as seen in mask *e*, second row from the top, far left), which reinforces their dualistic nature, as Xolotl was the god of dualism and monsters. In the second row from the top on the right (*h*) is a mask with dog faces on each cheek, another Xolotl characteristic. The double beards (top row) are reminiscent of Quetzalcoatl, the double of Xolotl. Masks *a*, *c*, and *p* property of the University of Arizona; mask *e* from the collection of Larry Walsh; mask *f* from Collections of the International Folk Art Foundation in the Museum of International Folk Art, Santa Fe, New Mexico. *Atenxoxola or Xiloxuchicán, Guerrero (Nahua); 23 cm. (approx.); wood, paint.* I.B.D.

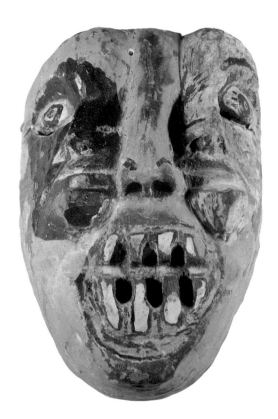

208. Triple-face mask, Quilinique Dance. This detail from Fig. 207 shows the crude yet forceful execution of the rare multiple-face masks. The merging, yet distinct faces of these masks create an interesting optical effect for the viewer. Property of the University of Arizona. *Atenxoxola or Xiloxuchicán, Guerrero (Nahua); 23 cm.; wood, paint.* I.B.D.

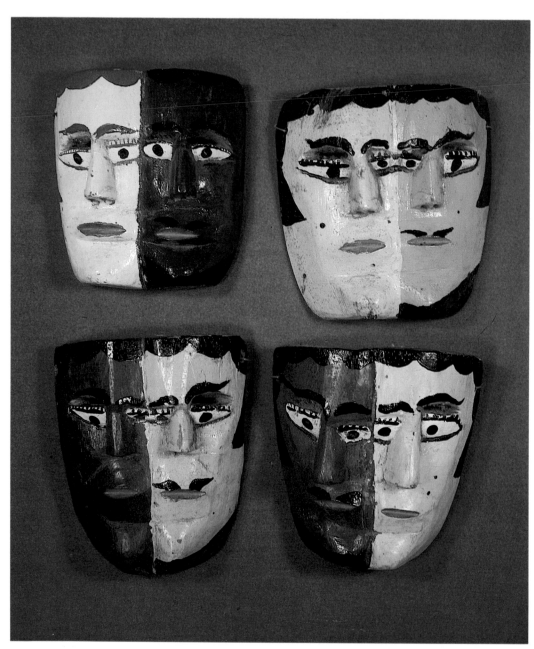

209. Twins masks, Dance of the Twins. These interesting masks were carved by Miguel Cruz López of Pinotepa de Don Luis in the Mixteca Baja of Oaxaca for use in San Juan Colorado. (See also Fig. 186.) Masks *a* and *b* property of the University of Arizona. *San Juan Colorado, Oaxaca (Mixtec); 15 cm. (approx.); wood, paint.* I.A.D.

210. *Itzcuintli*, **"dog."** Symbol of Xolotl, the god of twins and of the deformed. As seen in the Codex Vaticanus 3773, pl. 29 (*left*) and pl. 93 (*right*). After *Comentarios al Codice Borgia* (Seler 1963), vol. 1, Figs. 368–369.

According to the Codex Vaticano-Ríos (Kingsborough 1964, Plate 73, pp. 168–169), the Aztecs associated the notched nose with the dog, which is called *xolotl* in Nahuatl. Xolotl was also an Aztec god, who, as the twin brother of Quetzalcoatl, was more closely associated with the concept of duality than the other gods of the Aztec pantheon (although many of these gods had dualistic characteristics). The god was commonly represented and can be identified by his deformed (very often, notched) nose or by his familiar disguise as a dog with a deformed nose (see Fig. 210). Quetzalcoatl as his twin is also shown with a deformed nose (Durán 1971, plate 1). While this shared characteristic makes identification somewhat more difficult, it does not invalidate the recognition of a characteristic trait of Xolotl or Quetzalcoatl as an indication of duality.

In my opinion, the notched noses of Quilinique masks are Xolotl noses and are specifically used as a convention to indicate duality. I believe that the notched-nose convention has a wider distribution in contemporary Mexican masks than just the small area of Atenxoxola or Xiloxuchicán, Guerrero. In Fig. 247*b*, for instance, we see a long-faced mask of a man who has such a deformed nose and whose cheeks, beard, eyebrows, and top of the head are covered with wooden spines from the pochote tree (those spines are also connected with Xolotl, as discussed later in this chapter). In all likelihood, this deformed nose is that of Xolotl, and this mask must be classified as a Pre-Hispanic survival. A deformed nose suggesting an elephant trunk (Fig. 247*a*) and a nose consisting of three downward-sweeping, curved elements reminiscent of plant forms, one atop the next (Fig. 199) may be other Pre-Hispanic survivals in the same dance. Another possible notched-nose survival of Xolotl is seen in Fig. 207*e*.

There is a valid question, of course, as to whether the mask-makers used the deformed nose consciously to indicate duality and Xolotl, or whether the deformed nose was simply a traditional form used without meaning or understanding. Because of the secrecy of the old mask-makers who carved these masks and the fact that most of them died without passing on their vast stores of knowledge, we will probably never have a definitive answer to this question. However, it is noteworthy that the two smaller cheek faces in the Quilinique mask in Fig. 207*h* have dog ears, another trait specifically associated with Xolotl. These ears are the only zoomorphic forms incorporated in the Quilinique masks. I feel that the dualistic nature of these masks, the prevalent use of the notched nose, and the inclusion of the dog ears are strong indications that at least the makers of these masks consciously used these Pre-Hispanic conventions to depict duality.

Another method of indicating duality is through the use of the twisted mouth, a convention that is found throughout the mask-making cultures of North America, particularly among the Seneca and Eskimo, and in some tribes in Africa. As seen in Fig. 211, one side of the mouth is pulled up in what could be classified as a smile, and the other side is pulled down in a frown or a growl. If one remembers the smiling/frowning opposition of the two-faced masks, the twisted mouth can be seen as a synthesis or refinement of that symbolic convention. Among the Eskimo, for example, the twisted mouth represents a dualistic man-spirit or man-animal relationship (Ray 1967, p. 44). Nevertheless, there are other plausible interpretations for the twisted mouth, including the possibility that it was sometimes used to depict facial paralysis, a fairly common illness. In the Florentine Codex Sahagún reports an Aztec belief as to the origins of this type of facial paralysis: "And of him who secretly tasted it [the sacred wine], who in secret drank some, even tasting only a little, it was said that his mouth would become twisted, it would stretch to one side; to one side his mouth would shift; it would be drawn over" (Sahagún 1950, pp. 21–23).

The interpretation of the twisted-mouth motif in modern Mexican masks is particularly difficult, since there is no direct evidence about its significance. We do know that the twisted mouth has been an important motif for well over two thousand years in Mexico, as a twisted-mouth jaguar mask was found at an Olmec site. Peter T. Furst, in commenting about the Olmec were-jaguar motif, notes that "shamans and jaguars are not merely equivalent, but each is at the same time the other" (1968, pp. 148–149). While Furst does not reach any specific conclusions about the meaning of the twisted-mouth jaguar representations, he does note that hunters who killed this dualistic deity had to undergo ritual purification. In relationship to contemporary Mexican masks, this becomes significant in that the twisted-mouth motif is most commonly found in the masks for the Tlacololero and Tecuani Dances (Figs. 212, 300). The central action of these dances, which are described in more detail in Chapter 10, involves tracking down and finally killing a masked character representing a Tigre (jaguar). Possibly, the twisted-mouth Rastrero character depicts both the hunter and the hunted as a continuance of the Olmec half-man, half-jaguar theme, as the Tigre in these dances also has a dualistic nature. However, it must be admitted that the use of the twisted-mouth convention to indicate duality is only a possibility, and no definitive meaning can yet be assigned to this convention.

211. Viejo mask, Carnival dances. This very well carved mask seems to be a depiction of pain and paralysis. The twisted-mouth feature, which appears with many meanings in various cultures, is nicely balanced against the large eye (at right). The balance is repeated in the planes of the cheeks. (For other twisted-mouth masks, see Figs. 212, 216*d*, and 300.) *San Martín Pachivia, Guerrero.* I.B.C.

Still another method used to symbolize duality is the transformation of one figure to another within the same mask (Fig. 213). These "transformational masks" often show the face of a human being turning into that of an animal. Such masks may represent a man with his animal *nagual* (spiritual alter ego); for further information on *naguales*, see the section on "Form Symbolism" below. Some of the best examples of this type of mask are those made for the Fish Dance and Caimán Dance of Guerrero. They vary from the traditional Mermaid, a woman with the tail of a fish (Fig. 214), to a Caimán step-in figure with the heads of an old man and a woman carved on its body (Fig. 303c). The Mermaid motif may have originated from Spanish influences, but it was readily adapted to fit the needs of the Nahua people. Since the Caimán is a dualistic deity of good and evil like the Tigre, the half-human, half-animal form of the one in Fig. 303c suggests a dualistic force or being that aided people in controlling the environment upon which their lives depended. Quite possibly, the male head on the Caimán figure represents the Lord of the Fish, another shamanistic survival which will be discussed later.

Not all transformational masks symbolize duality. In cases of bats turned into jaguars (Fig. 23), I feel that the masks are portraying the shared characteristics of two entities, rather than showing dual aspects of a single force or being. Then, too, many of these masks may be the result of artistic invention by the mask-maker in an effort to demonstrate his skill and imagination, or they may simply demonstrate the closeness of man and the animals as in Figs. 105 and 190.

COLOR SYMBOLISM

Mexico is a land of colors, ranging from the tropical green and brilliant colors of its flowers during the rainy season to the muted colors and dry browns of its deserts and its dry season. To a large degree, Mexican masks reflect the vivid colors of the environment, particularly as modern commercial paints replace the duller earth tones of traditionally prepared paints. This switch from "natural" paints to commercial ones, by the way, is not always considered a loss by the people who use these masks. I am reminded of a friend who collects Huichol yarn paintings and who was complaining to a Huichol craftsman about a similar conversion from naturally dyed yarn to the extremely bright commercial yarns that are now being used. The Huichol patiently explained that not only were the brighter-colored yarns preferable, they were what the Indians had been searching for all along, since they were much closer to the colors of the peyote visions on which the yarn paintings were based.

Yet, despite the intensity and importance of colors in Mexico, there is no overall system of color symbolism in contemporary masks. There are simply too many diverse groups living in different environments, each with its own unique color setting, for any general system to have developed. Nor is there any inflexible use of a color symbol even in cultures that have associated a meaning with a

212. Rastrero mask, Tlacololero Dance. This is one of the few extant fine wood masks from the state of Morelos. Although the carving is not very well conceived, the twisted mouth (typical of the Rastrero character) and the gross features are comic and strong. In Guerrero, Tlacololero Dance masks characteristically have circles cut into the cheeks for eye openings, but in this Morelos version there are slits under the eyes. (See p. 241 for discussion of the Tlacololero Dance.) From the Raúl Lozano Martini collection. *Region of Jojutla, Morelos (Nahua); 25 cm.; wood, paint.* I.A.C.

color. A red that has a specific significance in one mask may have a completely different meaning or no meaning whatsoever in another mask, even if both are made by the same craftsman. Consequently, color symbolism, where it exists, must be evaluated within the specific context of the mask on which it is used. The following discussion, therefore, is restricted to some of the more generally accepted color symbols in relationship to the masks on which they are used.

Red.   Red is used as the basic face color on some of the Malinche masks (Fig. 44), while others have red-tipped deer antlers instead of a red countenance (Figs. 215, 278). In the Tenochtli Dance, this color usage probably stems from the red of blood, symbolizing the violence and bloodshed that Malinche brought upon her own people with the Conquest and the fall of Tenochtitlán. The red-faced Malinche mask may also be seen in a number of nonhistorical dances as a figure of lust, as Malinche is also the archetypal "wicked woman" of Mexico. Here, the red signifies sexuality and the lasciviousness that led her to become Cortés's mistress, according to various Indian informants. (Prostitutes in Pre-Hispanic times painted their faces red, according to Doris Heyden, personal communication.) In addition, the symbolism of evil in the use of the color red for European Devils may have fused into the red representations of Malinche, providing an example of syncretism.

Blue.   Blue is generally considered a water symbol, as it is found in a large number of rain-petitioning masks, such as the ones from La Parota, Guerrero, shown in Fig. 188. A close examination of these very old masks reveals that both the eyes and the beards were originally painted blue. Despite these seemingly Caucasian features, which appear to be somewhat out of place, these masks were used by children to imitate dwarves who were Aztec rain gods in an almost direct Pre-Hispanic survival. Mermaid masks (Fig. 263) and Mermaid figures worn about the waist (Fig. 303*b*) also have blue eyes. Another rain-petitioning mask with blue eyes can be seen in Fig. 1.

Blue eyes are often given to the Christian religious figures carved by *santeros* (Fig. 270). These masks generally have fair skin tones, light brown or even blond hair, and European features. This is in direct contrast to the possible pagan character of Fig. 146 (also made by a *santero*), who is swarthy and brown-eyed. Reflecting prevailing Mexican prejudice, a fair complexion usually indicates a good character, such as a Christian, a Saint, or Christ, whereas a dark complexion is often used for Moors, pagan Alchileos, and other villains. Blue is also the costume color of the Virgin Mary and the Virgin of Guadalupe.

White.   Most masks representing Death are of the white-skull variety shown in Fig. 47; by association white has come to signify death and the spirit world to some degree. However, black, a more traditional symbol for death, is also used (Fig. 92).

Green.   Green is often used to represent crops and by extension is a fertility symbol, as can be seen in the mask depicting the Corn Spirit pictured in Fig. 313. The mask was made by José Rodríguez of the Tlapanec-Nahua-Popoluca area of Guerrero. Green is sometimes used as a water symbol as well: many of

213. Caimán mask, Fish Dance and Caimán Dance. Symbolic of the unity of man and animal, this fine, very old mask combines a fisherman or river deity with his spiritual brother, the Caimán. Both figures are blue-eyed to symbolize water, and the rippling beard carries the same symbolism. *Alahuistlán, Guerrero (Nahua); 54 cm.; wood, paint.* II.A.C.

214. Mermaid masks, Fish Dance. These two old folk art masks represent mother (*b*) and daughter (*a*) Mermaids, with the daughter calm and the mother full of comic energy, as expressed in her open, see-through mouth, extended tongue, and cheeks with laugh lines. The daughter does not appear to be a mask at all, until one notices the eyeholes at either side of the neck. Mask *a* property of the Smithsonian Institution. *Ayutla, Guerrero (Nahua); (a) 47 cm.; (b) 46 cm.; wood, paint.* II.A.C.

215. Malinche Devil mask, Azteca Dance. This eagle-helmeted Malinche has dyed ixtle hair and horns made of red-tipped deer antlers attached to a base formed by the crown of a native straw hat. See text for discussion of the symbolic meaning of the color red. Property of the University of Arizona. *Tlacozotitlán, Guerrero (Nahua); 39 cm., including horns; wood, paint, deer antlers, ixtle fiber, straw.* II.A.C.

the rain symbols are painted green, and the eyes of a few of the rain-petitioning masks are also green. The green Frog Devil mask in Fig. 248 also demonstrates this type of rain-petitioning symbolism.

Symbolic Patterns. Many of the Tlacololero masks are painted in quadrants or sections of varying colors. While there is no direct evidence as to why this pattern is used, Tlacololeros are the men who clean the fields, and I believe that these painted sections might well be a representation of the fields as seen from a distance (Fig. 216).

Another symbolic pattern that has already been mentioned is the painting of the Quilinique and Twins masks (Figs. 207–208 and 209, respectively). These are two-faced masks, with each face normally painted a different color to emphasize their basic duality.

216. Tlacololero masks, Tlacololero Dance. This set of six Tlacololeros shows far more interesting execution than the masks produced in the same village today. As the *pueblo* and the dancers tire of using the same masks time and time again, new ones are made, perhaps every ten years, but each time with less skill, thought, and craftsmanship. These intense faces are richly carved and painted in sections, most probably to denote the look of the fields and crops during various stages of the slash-and-burn agricultural cycle. Mask *d* (lower left) has a twisted face and represents the Rastrero, who hunts down the Tigre with the help of his dog. Mask *e* (lower center) is a female character with large dimples and no moustache. Mask *b* from Collections of the International Folk Art Foundation in the Museum of International Folk Art, Santa Fe, New Mexico; masks *c* and *f* property of the University of Arizona. *Almolonga, Guerrero (Nahua); 35–38 cm. (approx.); wood, paint. (d)* I.B.C. *(others)* I.A.C.

In addition to these patterns, many groups, including the Huichols, the Mayos, and the Yaquis, have incorporated old face-painting symbols into their masks. As these symbols are extremely complex and their meaning varies with each individual group, it is not practical to explore them within the scope of this book, other than to acknowledge their existence and their source. Some examples of these masks are included in Figs. 72 and 74.

FORM SYMBOLISM

Devil Symbolism

Horned Devil masks are among the most popular masks throughout Mexico. The origins of this type of mask are clearly Christian, for when the Spanish friars came to Mexico, they brought the Devil with them. As I have mentioned in the discussion of duality, Pre-Hispanic deities were thought of as being both good and evil, bringing life and death. Hence, the Indians had no reason or need to concentrate all evil into a single entity, as did the Christians. In terms of iconographic motifs, a review of the surviving codices and masks shows us that there were no two-horned masks in Pre-Hispanic times, although one-horned masks are recognized as a Pre-Hispanic type (Furst 1965, p. 34). When we examine modern Mexican Devil masks, we can readily see that they are divided into two major groups: European Devils and "Devils" with obvious Indian origins.

As we have noted, there were a great number of masks in Mexico when the Spanish arrived. Many of these masks are commonly termed "monster masks." As noted by Esther Pasztory in *Early Chinese Art and the Pacific Basin*, ". . . the monster mask is thought to represent the *nagual* of a man or god. A *nagual* is the guardian spirit of a man and is acquired either by seeking an encounter with an animal or a thing, or more commonly, by consulting the Tonalpohualli, or ritual calendar. In the latter method, a child usually gets as his *nagual* the spirit on whose day he happened to be born. Besides having a close spiritual relationship with the animal, the human is often thought to be able to assume the form of the animal" (Fraser, ed., 1968, pp. 89–90). Another way of identifying and acquiring a *nagual* is by finding the animal's tracks in a ring of ashes or sand put around the house when the child is born.

In their attempts to convert the Indians to Christianity, the Spanish friars found an easy way to denigrate the Indian deities and the individuals' *naguales*. As the Indians often used *nagual* masks in dances in or in front of the churches, the friars simply added two horns to them and renamed them Devils. This adaptation fitted well within the existing Church framework, as the prevailing Christian idea was that it was evil to have animal characteristics or a dual nature. Also, these false gods were obviously the work of the Devil and must have been Devils themselves. Whenever I look at such Indian Devil masks (Figs. 37*b*, 218), I always wonder whether the face is in fact a much older one.

Interestingly enough, the belief that each person has a *nagual* has not totally disappeared. In remote villages, many Indians still believe that a vital aspect of each individual's soul is that person's *tonal*, which is another name for *nagual*. While I know of no cases where the *tonal* is still represented in a mask, these villagers believe that a person's *tonal* can be stolen by a supernatural being, an event that will cause *susto*, or magical fright, resulting in listlessness, inability to sleep, sickness, and death; *susto* can be cured only when the *tonal* is found by a *curandero* and the soul restored to a harmonious balance.

Both types of Devil masks appear in numerous dances throughout Mexico. They are especially associated with Carnival, when a masked Devil often rides down the streets of the town on horseback. Normally, this character is accompanied by a masked man representing Death, another popular and frequently occurring personage in Mexico. Another dance that uses Devil masks is the dance of the Tres Potencias (Three Powers), described in Chapter 10.

217. Devil mask. This is a very old Devil once used for the annual Devil celebration on September 16 in Teloloápan, Guerrero (see Fig. 141), in the days when Devil masks were less elaborate than they are today. This mask has cow horns and the remains of a sheepskin beard and was used long and well; it was abandoned for a newer mask some forty years ago. A hole over the right eye is stuffed with cloth, and a heavy clamp of wire holds pieces together above the nose. This inexpensively produced mask has thin yellow and red water-base paint and ears of heavy leather. *Teloloápan, Guerrero; 31 cm., not including beard; wood, sheepskin, cow horns, cloth, wire clamp, leather, paint.* II.B.C.

218. Devil mask. This mask was probably made around 1920. It represents an exceptionally carved cow or bull head with snakes, a lizard nose, and long wooden tusks, some of which have been broken. The interior of the mask is lined with patches of paper to ease the discomfort of its heavy weight and rough surface on the dancer's face. *Zacuapán, Michoacán (Tarascan); 43 cm., including horns; wood, paint, paper (lining only).* IV.B.D.

219. Mask probably for Lord of the Animals Dance. This twenty-to-thirty-year-old Rodríguez mask combines double images that are transformed into one another. It is carved in a slower tempo than this artist's usual bold masks. The owl on the upper part is a bird of ill omen, as opposed to the rather comical animal below that may be a pig. An unrecognizable animal forms the nose, while the crown is carved into monkeys, a snake, and a deer. *Chapalapa, Guerrero (Tlapanec or Popoloca); 35 cm.; wood, paint (oil).* IV.B.D.

Animal Symbolism

. . . the Tarahumares assert that the dances have been taught them by animals. Like all primitive people, they are close observers of nature. To them the animals are by no means inferior creatures; they understand magic and are possessed of much knowledge, and may assist the Tara-humares in making rain. In spring, the singing of the frog, the chirping of the cricket, all the sounds uttered by the denizens of the greensward, are to the Indian appeals to the deities for rain. For what other reason should they sing or call? For the strange behavior of many animals in the early spring the Tarahumares can find no other explanation but that these creatures, too, are interested in rain. And as the gods grant the prayers of the deer expressed in its antics and dances, and of the turkey in its curi-ous playing, by sending the rain, they easily infer that to please the gods they, too, must dance as the deer and play as the turkey.

(Lumholtz 1902, pp. 330–331)

As noted in Chapter 8, the relationship between man and the animals is one of the most profound and basic elements of Mexican Indian cultures. It is natural and inevitable that masks, as the instrument of unifying man with these forces, utilize animal motifs as their primary source of symbolism. Because of the importance and centrality of the human-animal relationship, an exploration of the symbolic values associated with some of the more important animal motifs is necessary for a complete understanding of contemporary masks.

Lord of the Animals.

. . . he calls "O Mountain dweller   dweller on the tops of mountains"

shaman calls the Lords of Animals . . . one like a jaguar . . . tied with iron chains . . . the iron chains are rattling

the entrails make a noise . . . the entrails roar . . . an animal comes somewhere . . . now the animal comes up . . . it lifts its neck and comes with flashing eyes & lifts its iron throat with terrifying eyes

("Muu's Way or Pictures from the Uterine World" [Cuna];
Rothenberg, ed, 1972, p. 313)

A common belief throughout the shamanistic Indian cultures of Mexico and the rest of the Americas is the belief in a spirit or a number of spirits who take care of the animals and see to their fertility, sustenance, etc. As noted by Andreas Lommel, ". . . the hunters' efforts to animate and dominate nature through the magic of spiritual forces evolves towards two culminating points, two poles. One is the concentration of the spiritual forces in the so-called Lord of the Animals, the other the genesis of the shaman . . . The whole of nature,

220. Jaguar as Lord of the Animals. As seen in the Codex Telleriano-Remensis (Kingsborough 1964, p. 184). After *Comentarios al Códice Borgia*, vol. 2, Fig. 212.

including the animals, belongs to the Lord of the Animals; the welfare of men depends upon him. He disposes of his property, he can at will give it away or barter it, or else gamble or drink it away. But since he is very niggardly, he gives it to men only when he receives offerings from them" (Lommel 1967, p. 27).

In Mexico, the Lord of the Animals is called El Señor de los Animales or El Pastor [Shepherd] de los Animales if there is only one such spirit. Where there are a number of protective spirits for various groups of animals, these spirits are normally named after those animals—the Lord of the Deer, the Lord of the Fish, etc. These spirits are particularly anxious to increase the number of the animals and not let the animal population dwindle.

Gerardo Reichel-Dolmatoff reports a similar set of beliefs among the Desana Indians of South America: "All animals are thought to be subject to an 'owner' (*këgë*), chief (*dorëgë*, from *dorëri*—to give orders), who is their protector and master. This 'Master of Animals' is Vai-mahsë, perhaps the most important divine personification for the Desana hunter. . . . The figure of Vai-mahsë is the personification of the sexual life of the game animals" (Reichel-Dolmatoff 1971, pp. 80–84).

In Mexico, it is believed that the Lord of the Animals lives in wild places and can be somewhat dangerous and malicious to human beings, especially to women. If they walk alone in remote places, he may do them bodily harm or make them pregnant. Even some male informants from Guerrero say that they don't like to walk distances at night for fear of these *duendes* (spirits).

While the belief in a Lord or Lords of the Animals is fairly uniform throughout the indigenous cultures of Mexico, this figure is manifested in diverse forms. In Central and Southern Mexico, he usually is associated with and appears as a jaguar or *tigre*, but he also appears as a bat, a *caimán*, or a human. His manifestation as a *caimán* seems to represent the Lord of the Fish more than the Lord of all the Animals. The emphasis on the jaguar as the Lord of the Animals seems to be a direct Pre-Hispanic survival, as is shown in the Codex Telleriano-Remensis, where we read, in reference to a jaguar (Fig. 220): "This *Tepolotlie* (Tepyolotl) means Lord of the Animals" (Kingsborough 1964, p. 184, pl. 4). The interpreter of this codex says that the jaguar also represents the night: his skin symbolizes the night sky and his spots are the stars. The jaguar is also an echo that reverberates from one mountain to another.

The Huichols of Nayarit have many Lords of the Animals in their religious pantheon. According to Fernando Benítez (1968), Parikuta is the Lord of the Scorpions, and Tatei Uteanaka is the mistress of the river fish. Tatei Uteanaka lives in the wild places of the rivers Chapalangana and Lerma and is considered by the Indians to be a great fish with wings. Through a helper, a fish with a light in his head named Shurakame, she takes care that the fish do not get caught in the nets or on fishhooks. According to Benítez, "There is also a Lord of the Wild Boars, of the Wolves, of the Serpents and possibly all the animals have a lord, which also can be due to the necessity that the Indians felt of relying upon a guide or leader endowed with power apart from the ordinary" (1968, p. 267).

221. Helmet mask, said to have been for Coyote Dance. Here we see a helmet mask with a rather humorous human countenance, which is flanked by an owl and a coyote. Often there was no space in houses for large ceremonial masks such as this one and they were left out in the heavy rains of the season, thus causing all paint but traces of Spanish whiting to wash off. This mask and that of Figs. 30–31 were probably used originally for the Lord of the Animals Dance. *Tulimán, Guerrero (Nahua); 56 cm.; wood, possibly water paints (now washed away).* II.B.C.

We find hundreds and hundreds of very good Mexican masks that represent the Lord of the Animals. Some of these are great wooden *cascos* (helmet masks) which have not been used for many years. Many of the *cascos* have an animal, usually a bat or *tigre*, on one side and, on the other, a bearded human face with a long nose as a representation of the Lord of the Animals (Figs. 30–31, 221). As will be discussed later, the long nose is a phallic symbol and is associated with fertility. In regard to the possible survival of Pre-Conquest motifs in these contemporary masks, the long-nosed helmet masks seem to represent Tezcatlipoca as the Lord of the Animals rather than the jaguar.

Fig. 222 contains examples of masks of both animal figures and human faces, the latter representing the Lord of the Animals. The human faces are usually painted white and often have protruding tongues (as in Fig. 222*b*). In some cases, they also have a small *tigre* on the forehead (Fig. 222*c*). All these masks now tend to be called Devils, since every mask that has an animal on it is thought to be a Devil. Of course, these are not Devils but were used in the Animal Dance, as were the helmet masks mentioned above. This dance has not been performed for many years and may no longer be given except possibly in very remote villages. Several of my informants have mentioned the Lord of the Animals in recent years but only very slightly. I believe it is something too close to the people's hearts to be made public now, but there are probably still ceremonies and beliefs that are kept secret and should be investigated. This is one of the important matters that must be worked upon by young investigators before all traces of it are gone.

Tigre (Jaguar/Tiger).

¡O tigre, animal el más noble y ágil de la antigua Mesoamérica, deificado por los olmecas, zapotecas, teotihuacanos, toltecas y aztecas desde mil años antes del nacimiento de Cristo, no te acobardes en tu lucha brave, sigue muriendo como has muerto miles de veces en los milenarias fiestas pueblerinas!

(O tigre, *the most noble and agile animal of ancient Mesoamerica, deified by the Olmecs, Zapotecs, Teotihuacanos, Toltecs, and Aztecs since a thousand years before the birth of Christ, don't become frightened in your brave struggle, continue to die as you have died thousands of times in the millenary small-town fiestas.)*

(Horcasitas 1971, p. 583)

Undoubtedly, the jaguar (generally called *tigre* in Spanish) was and is the single most important animal to the Indians of Central and Southern Mexico. In the ancient Indian civilizations in these areas, the jaguar was the symbol of war, as was the eagle. These wars were more than just wars of conquest; they were the sacred "flower wars" that were waged to obtain captives to be sacrificed to the gods. In this respect, the symbol of the jaguar was more than a representa-

222. Animal masks and four Lord of the Animals masks, Animal Dance. The style and fine workmanship of the superb masks leads me to believe that they were made by José Rodríguez. In the top row we see four anthropomorphic Pastores (Shepherds) who represent the Lord of the Animals. This fearsome creature was believed to watch over the animals, providing for their food and safety. The animals in the second and third rows include (*e*) a Mule, (*f*) a Rabbit, (*g*) a Rooster, (*h*) an Owl, (*i*) a Donkey, (*j*) a Monkey, (*k*) a Rabbit, and (*l*) a Dog. Many of these animals suddenly came on the market in 1976, then disappeared entirely, indicating that this Animal Dance is no longer in fashion. Mask *d* property of the University of Arizona; mask *g* property of Beth Burstein. *Area and group unknown; 23–44 cm.; wood, paint. (a, c)* II.B.C. *(b, d)* I.A.C. *(e, f, i, k, l)* IV.A.C. *(g, h, j)* IV.B.C.

227

228
229

227. Bat mask, Bat Dance or Lord of the Animals Dance. As in Fig. 226, we see a human face peering out from behind the bat. The mask is intricately carved and painted, with the human brow and jaw supporting the bat. Human eyes appear on the wings. Collections of the International Folk Art Foundation in the Museum of International Folk Art, Santa Fe, New Mexico. *Comala, Guerrero (Nahua); 28 cm. (approx.); wood, paint.* V.A.C.

228. Bat mask, Bat Dance or Lord of the Animals Dance. This is the only Bat mask I have seen showing the bat in its natural resting position, with its head pointed down. The chin indentation on the reverse side shows that the mask is meant to be worn in this manner. Property of the University of Arizona. *Las Sauces, Guerrero (Nahua); 28 cm.; wood, paint.* V.A.C.

229. Bat mask, Bat Dance or Lord of the Animals Dance. This composite of human and bat features includes a third element, the jaguar or *tigre*, as the bat's head closely resembles that of a feline. The bat and the *tigre* are closely associated in the Indian mind (see also Fig. 23). *San Miguel Oapan, Guerrero (Nahua); 31 cm., including ears; wood, paint, animal teeth.* V.B.C.

230. Bat Devil mask, Bat Dance or Lord of the Animals Dance. The remote, historically important town of Tlacozotitlán, Guerrero, may well have been the birthplace of the Bat Dance, as it is the source of the widest variety of artistically exciting old Bat masks. This mask, termed a Bat Devil, is entirely original in conception. *Tlacozotitlán, Guerrero (Nahua); height: 33 cm.; width: 36 cm.; wood, paint.* IV.B.C.

231. Bat mask, Bat Dance or Lord of the Animals Dance. The proportions of this small, charming mask are exaggerated, yet blend well with the simplicity and movement of the carving. In the Bat Dance, there were many other animals, such as Butterflies, Coyotes, Owls, etc. All gathered in dance with the Bats to give homage to the Christ Child on December 23 each year. *Tlacozotitlán, Guerrero (Nahua); 23 cm.; wood, paint, animal teeth (possibly from a bat).* IV.B.C.

Bat (Murciélago, Tzinacan).

> *. . . There came Killer Bats*
>   *And snatched off their heads*
> *There came Lurking Jaguar*
>   *And ate their flesh.*

> (The Popol Vuh *[Maya]; English version by Munro Edmonson;*
>   *Rothenberg, ed., 1972, p. 79)*

232. Helmet mask, Bat Dance. This very old helmet mask was used in the Bat Dance held on December 23 in Tlacozotitlán, Guerrero, and shows many of the dance's characters: the Christ Child (with movable arms), the Three Kings, an Angel, a Dove, a Squirrel, a Fish, a Coyote, a Bat, and other animals. Because of its weight and height (which in part can be judged by the placement of the eyeholes near the bottom, just above the figure of the Bat), this mask was worn only at the beginning of the dance and then placed on the ground and danced around. It is obvious that it was made with great care and love. Property of the University of Arizona. *Tlacozotitlán, Guerrero (Nahua); 90 cm. (approx.); wood, traces of Spanish whiting.* II.A.D.

The bat is a powerful image within the Indian psyche. It has fired the plastic imagination of mask carvers more than any other subject except the jaguar, with which it is closely associated. Even masks whose principal subjects are other animals or people are often associated with bats through the smooth flow of the mask-makers' artistry and are thus linked to the dark symbolism of the bat (Fig. 178).

The symbolic meanings of the bat and the reasons for its ascendancy as a design motif are relatively easy to understand, particularly if one remembers that even in European cultures the bat has always represented witchcraft and darkness. It is a creature of the night and of caves. To the Indian, night is the time of the underworld, the time when supernatural beings emerge onto the earth, a time of danger.

Because bats often dwell in caves, most cultures have associated the two; however, this association takes on special meaning to Mexican Indian groups. Traditionally, caves have been and still are thought of as entrances to the underworld. Supernatural beings are thought to live in these caves and use them for their own purposes. Caves are also associated with water, not only because they are usually wet and damp, but also because it was believed that springs originated in caves and that, therefore, the rain gods either lived in these caves or used them as exits from their underworld homes. Thus, the bat also came to be associated with water, rain, and crop fertility. As noted by Doris Heyden (1976, pp. 1–2), the cave was thought of as the earth's vagina, a concept which further reinforces the fertility aspect of the bat, the jaguar, and the snake.

There is another, perhaps even more compelling, reason for the bat's prominence: Mexico is the home of the vampire bat. These bats, which helped create the legends of Europe, are a reality in the tropical areas of the Americas. Belonging to the family Desmodontidae, vampire bats live solely on the blood of vertebrate animals (including humans) and often transmit fatal diseases such as rabies. Blood has a great religious significance in shamanistic societies, as it is directly equated with life and the life force. As noted earlier, blood sacrifice was one of the major elements of Pre-Hispanic religions, and even today the Huichol Indians sacrifice a bull and offer a cup of its blood to the sun to renew its force before they set off on their annual peyote pilgrimage. Thus, in addition to its other connotations, the bat came to symbolize death and blood sacrifice as well as fertility.

The symbolism of the bat derives from Pre-Hispanic traditions, as is suggested in the quotation from the *Popol Vuh* at the beginning of this section. Throughout almost all of the surviving codices, the bat is depicted as a deity connected with death and sacrifice. The death bat in the *Popol Vuh* cuts off people's heads, including the head of the story's hero, Hunahpu. As Eric Thompson notes, "In modern folklore, the same story exists, but now the victim is Christ, who, like Hunahpu, is in prison awaiting his fate" (1962, pp. 348–349). Thompson also mentions that the bat is still regarded as a sorcerer and is associated with sorcery by the Mayans in present-day Guatemala. In the Codex

Magliabecchiano we read, "They say that this demon that is painted here (Quetzalcoatl) committed a horrible, despicable, ugly act, that when Quetzalcoatl was washing himself, he touched his male member with his hands and caused to come forth. He cast it onto a rock, and there was born the bat" (Nuttall 1903, p. 62).

Like most other animals, the bat has a dualistic nature and is also a fertility symbol—in part because of the already mentioned association with water, and in part through a transformation similar to that of the jaguar. The bat, like the jaguar, is viewed as a destroyer of life; the masked dances using the bat motif, then, are an attempt to control and reverse this characteristic, so that in the end, the bat becomes a positive symbol as well. We must also remember that the sacrificial aspect of the bat was considered positive and life-giving within Indian cultures.

The dualistic nature of the bat can be seen by examining some of the Bat masks. Very often, the bat is carved in such a manner that its short tail between its hind legs can be taken for a penis (Fig. 227), which is one method of indicating a fertility symbol. In addition, a great many of the dances in which Bat masks were used were rain-petitioning dances. Many of the rain-petitioning masks by José Rodríguez are surmounted by bats (Figs. 17a, d, g).

Another positive account of the bat is found in a Cora legend recorded by Carl Lumholtz:

> In the beginning the earth was flat and full of water, and therefore the corn rotted. The ancient people had to think and work and fast much to get the world in shape. The birds came together to see what they could do to bring about order in the world, so that it would be possible to plant corn. First they asked the red-headed vulture, the principal of all the birds, to set things right, but he said he could not. They sent for all the birds in the world, one after another, to induce them to perform the deed, but none would undertake it. At last came the bat, very old and much wrinkled. His hair and his beard were white with age, and there was plenty of dirt on his face, as he never bathes. He was supporting himself with a stick, because he was so old he could hardly walk. He also said that he was no equal to the task, but at last he agreed to try what he could do. That same night he darted violently through the air, cutting outlets for the waters; but he made the valleys so deep that it was impossible to walk about, and the principal men reproached him for this. "Then I will put everything back as it was before," he said.
>
> "No, no!" they all said. "What we want is to make the slopes of a lower incline, and to leave some level land, and do not make all the country mountains."
>
> This the bat did, and the principal men thanked him for it. Thus the world has remained up to this day.
>
> (Lumholtz 1902, 1: 513–514)

The bat has always been closely associated with dance. This, I believe, stems from mimicry of the see-saw motion of the bat's flight, but for whatever reason, this association is quite ancient, as is demonstrated by a quote from the Florentine Codex: "And one [in the likeness of a] bat was there, [also] doing a dance; indeed [in an array] like a bat was he adorned. He had two gourd rattles which, one in each hand, he went rattling" (Sahagún 1951, p. 120).

To my knowledge, the Bat Dance (Danza de los Murciélagos) is no longer being performed. In the villages of San Miguel Oapan (Fig. 229), Totozintla (Figs. 23–25, 30–31), San Francisco (Figs. 116–117), and Tlacozotitlán (Figs. 120–121, 230, 231, 232) in the state of Guerrero, this dance used to be performed, and, as a result, these villages produced some of the finest Bat masks ever seen. All of these villages are within thirty-five air-kilometers of one another. The other major area that produced Bat masks is some fifty kilometers from Totozintla in the triangle made by the towns of Apaxtla, Cuetzala, and Ostotitlán.

The Bat Dance was performed on December 23 in Tlacozotitlán, which is said to be its birthplace. This dance involved all of the animals, except the Devil Bat, paying homage to the Christ Child. The amazing, very old helmet mask in Fig. 232 shows many of the characters in the Bat Dance: the Christ Child, the Three Kings, an Angel, and the various animals who pay homage to the infant Jesus. Note that the Bat, as opposed to the Devil Bat, is also included in the group of worshipping animals. Some Devil Bat masks show a bat with a baby in its mouth (Fig. 200*d*).

Armadillo (Ayo-tochtli). The armadillo is identified with the earth by most of the Indian groups in Mexico. This stems from the fact that it is a burrowing animal and has the ability to disappear rapidly into the earth. Seler, for instance, notes that the Huichol Indians associate the armadillo with the earth, which is ruled by Tate Nakawé (Grandmother Growth), thus making the animal a fertility symbol (Seler n.d., 2, part 3: 20). While there is very little information on the armadillo from ancient sources, its name in Nahuatl, *ayo-tochtli*, literally means "tortoise-rabbit" (Robelo 1904, p. 65), implying that the Aztecs may have held similar beliefs, as the rabbit was closely associated with the moon and thereby the gods of vegetation and harvest, and the tortoise was a water symbol.

The use of the armadillo as a fertility symbol continued in some parts of Mexico until very recent times. Old helmet masks such as the one pictured in Figs. 236–237 were used in the Armadillo Dance, which took place in small *ranchos* near El Limón, Guerrero, in the early spring. The Armadillo figures in these old helmet masks were covered with real armadillo skin, and the men who took part in the dance also wore masks with patches of armadillo skin on their cheeks and foreheads (Fig. 233). The dance began on May 6 and continued every Sunday in May, the month in which corn was planted. In this case, the armadillo was believed to represent the earth or earth deity and its presence in the dance was designed to guarantee the fertility of the just-planted corn. Other Armadillo masks, for use in the Rabbit Dance, can be seen in Figs. 83 and 84.

233. Armadillo masks, Armadillo Dance. The armadillo, with its ability to disappear by burrowing, was closely identified with the earth by most of the Indians of Mexico. The Aztecs called it *ayo-tochtli,* "tortoise-rabbit." The rabbit is closely associated with the moon and is thus a fertility symbol, while the tortoise is a water symbol. The Armadillo Dance, performed in El Limón, Guerrero, on May 6 and each Sunday in May thereafter, was a plea for good crops and the needed rain. These masks are from a set of six used in the dance; also used were a Pig mask, a Coyote mask, and a large Armadillo figure to be worn about the waist of a man or boy (Figs. 234, 235). At the end of the dance the Coyote eats the Pig. Also made for this dance was the helmet mask shown in Figs. 236–237. The delightful small, squatting armadillos from Northwestern Guerrero shown in Figs. 83 and 84 were used not in the Armadillo Dance but rather in the Rabbit Dance. Masks *b* and *d* property of the Smithsonian Institution. *El Limón (near Ayutla), Guerrero (Nahua); 30 cm. (approx.); wood, paint, armadillo hide.* I.A.C.

235

234. Armadillo figure, Armadillo Dance. This carefully carved old Armadillo is made to be worn about the dancer's waist. Made of unpainted wood, it may easily be over thirty years old. *El Limón, Guerrero (Nahua); 1942.* IV.A.C.

235. Armadillo figure, Armadillo Dance. A more recent Armadillo, made in the same village and for the same dance as the one in Fig. 234, this one does not have the step-in feature seen there but is carved from two pieces of wood that are tied to the dancer's waist in front and back. The two Armadillos contrast sharply in style and show the individuality allowed the Mexican mask-makers and the lack of rigid traditional styles. It is not known how much time elapsed between the carving of the first Armadillo and that of the second. Property of the University of Arizona. *El Limón, Guerrero (Nahua).* IV.A.C.

While it is obvious that the armadillo is not as important as the symbols previously discussed, one indication of its power (and by implication, the power of all the animal symbols) is given by Carl Lumholtz: "In Cocucho, Michoacán (cocucho—earthenware jar), another robbers' nest about fifteen miles west of Cherán, the people until recently adored the Devil. He was represented by an armadillo decked out with horns and claws, and his worshippers sacrificed part of their booty to the 'Cocucho Saint,' El Santo Cocucho, as the image was called. So strong was the belief in its potency that once during a revolution, the Mexicans abducted it in order to use it against their enemies. It was kept in a secret place, and once a year carried around at night in a torch-light procession, until it finally fell into the hands of a priest, who burned it and thus ended its worship" (Lumholtz 1902, 2:411). Once again, it should be noted that this type of "Devil" was not really a Devil at all but an animal deity with horns added to satisfy the requirement of the Church. The robbers probably worshipped the armadillo because they buried their treasure in the earth and the armadillo was noted for taking care of earth things.

The Dog (Itzcuintli). Of all the animal figures, the dog is clearly the friendliest and most beneficial to the Indians. Today, the use of the Dog mask (Figs. 238–239) is predominantly restricted to the various Tigre dances (Tlacololero, Tecuani, and Tigre), in which the Dog plays a central role in helping to capture the Tigre and thus, on the symbolic level, transforming it from the destroyer to the bringer of fertility.

In these dances (described in further detail in Chapter 10), one of the central heroes is a comic Dog character by the name of Maravilla (Marvel). After much fruitless searching for the Tigre, the human characters form a column behind Maravilla, who then flushes it out so that it can be captured and killed. Despite

236–237. Helmet mask, Armadillo Dance. These two views of a beautifully executed helmet mask depict a fertility deity or Lord of the Animals in close association with the armadillo, an animal which has fertility and agricultural significance. Both sides show human faces of similar color and expression that are obviously meant to be personages of importance. Fig. 236 shows an intent human with two finely crafted, long-tailed armadillos on the brow and armadillo hide applied down the side of the face and on the chin to evoke sympathetic magic. Fig. 237 has two carved armadillos in place of a beard and armadillo hide on top of the head and as sideburns. *El Limón, Guerrero (Nahua); height: 50 cm.; circumference: 128 cm.; wood, paint, armadillo hide. (Each face)* II.A.C.

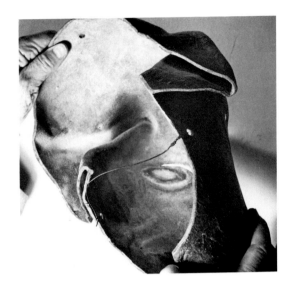

238–239. Maravilla (Dog) mask, Tecuani Dance. This ingeniously cut and folded Dog mask is fashioned from a single piece of leather and used in the Tecuani Dance. As Maravilla, or Marvel, the Dog leads the men in hunting and capturing the Tigre, who has been menacing the village. Note the skill which went into folding and forming the ears, seen in the photograph of the inner side of the mask (Fig. 239). Property of the University of Arizona. *Region of Ayutla, Guerrero (Nahua); leather.* IV.A.C.

the wide variations in the dances, the Dog is always assigned the crucial role of leading the humans to the Tigre. The Dog, then, can be seen as an important agent by which the Tigre is transformed into a symbol of fertility.

In part, the function of the Dog in these dances obviously derives from the actual use of dogs within a hunting society. The domestication of these animals provided hunting societies a superior method of controlling their hostile environments. However, just as the Tigre is more than a simple animal menace to the Indian, the Dog also has great symbolic significance. I believe that this symbolic meaning is partly due to the survival of elements of Pre-Hispanic religions.

A review of the Aztec and the Mayan codices shows that both of these peoples believed that the dog guided the dead to the underworld. Tozzer and Allen say of the Mayans, "At the time when the Spaniards made their acquaintance, it was the constant practice of the Mexicans to commit to the grave with the dead a dog. . . . The Mexicans believed that four years after death, when the soul had already passed through many dangers on its way to the underworld, it came at last to the bank of a great river, the Chicunauhapan, which encircled the underworld proper. The souls could get across this river only when they were awaited by their little dog, who, recognizing his master on the opposite side, rushed into the water to bring him over" (Tozzer and Allen 1910, p. 360). The Aztecs specifically associated the dog with Xolotl, the god of twins, deformity, monsters, and duality. As noted by Laurette Séjourné, "It is, in effect, Xolotl appearing as a dog who is in charge of guiding the souls of the dead through the bends of the underworld that only he knows; since nobody, except him, has ever returned" (1962, pp. 90–108).

Seler states that the Mayans also associated the dog with lightning: "The lightning, however, which cleaves the earth, seems to have been considered by these old tribes as the opener of roads in the underworld, and therefore the idea existed that one could travel safely in the underworld only with the help of a dog" (n.d., 3, part 4:8). It may be through this identification with lightning that the dog came to be used in connection with a prayer for rain, as pointed out by Tozzer and Allen (1910, p. 363).

There is yet one more important aspect of the dog in Pre-Conquest Mexico. The dog and the turkey were the only domesticated animals in Central America, where both served the same purpose: to be eaten (Seler n.d., 3, part 4:8), although the eating of dogs was primarily restricted to ceremonial and religious occasions. Therefore, the dog was not only the protector and the aid to hunting but food itself.

On a symbolic level, there was clearly a dualistic aspect to the dog in Pre-Hispanic religions, particularly that of the Aztecs, whose god of duality, Xolotl, was normally represented in the guise of a dog. But the duality involved was not the normal "evil-good" duality of most of the ancient gods. The dog served as a bridge between such negative and positive aspects, a helpful spirit that allowed man protection by turning threatening forces into beneficial ones.

The question now must be to what degree (if any) contemporary mask designs and usages are influenced by these ancient religious values. As late as 1907, Alfred M. Tozzer (1907, p. 47) noted that the Lacandones still made a small figure of a dog to place on the grave, a direct survival of the Pre-Conquest religious practices. But, what is more important, I feel that the implicit symbolism of the dog as it is revealed in the Tigre dances directly parallels the beliefs held by Pre-Hispanic Indians. Undoubtedly, not all of the beliefs about dogs have survived, but I believe the central symbolic role of the dog—that of a beneficial agent transforming negative values to positive ones—is such a survival.

Lizard (Chintete, Cuetzpalin). To the Indians of Central and Southern Mexico, the lizard represents sexuality, lust, and hence abundance. Probably this association stems from its size and shape, since the Indians equate the lizard with the penis, an equation that has existed from Pre-Conquest times, as is recorded in the Codex Borgia (Seler 1963, *Comentarios,* 1:77). Most Mexican Indians, of course, do not have a puritanical heritage and generally regard this figure as a source of fun and amusement. Both the lizard's meaning and the Indians' attitude toward it are illustrated by a toy (used in the Tecuani Dance) that I collected in the state of Morelos. It consists of a pole with three lizards climbing it; at the top of this pole is the figure of a nude woman sitting with her legs spread apart, obviously ready for intercourse. Just below the woman, there is a bed made of pieces of bamboo in a sort of hammock arrangement. When a string is pulled, the lizards thrust their bodies up towards the woman, and at the same time the bamboo bed springs out to hit the viewer in the eye. The spectators think this is extremely humorous and a great source of excitement.

The most common use of the lizard or *chintete* on masks is on the Malinche masks. As noted above, Malinche masks are often painted red to signify sexual passion and lust. They sometimes have a small lizard on each cheek, with a similar connotation (Fig. 44).

240. Mask for Coyote Dance (*a*); Dog mask for Tlacololero Dance (*b*). These two masks exhibit a similar symbolism, the exact meaning of which is now lost. One suspects that the multiple canine heads may represent a family or pack of animals, but the actual meaning was probably far more complicated and significant. In the Tlacololero Dance there is usually a single dog, Maravilla, who hunts the Tigre. This Maravilla has four extra eyes to help in the search. Mask *b* property of the University of Arizona. *(a) Michoacán; (b) Apango, Guerrero; (a) 28 cm.; (b) height: 29 cm.; width: 29 cm.; wood, paint.* IV.A.D.

In commenting on the lizard's significance in Pre-Conquest Mexico, Seler states, ". . . the sign *cuetzpalin* (lizard) corresponds to the penis" (1963, *Comentarios,* 1:77). He adds, "There is no doubt that we must suppose the original meaning of the sign *cuetzpalin* to be lust or the stimulus of lust, the sexual instinct and that from this original meaning was derived the other meaning, the idea of the fecundating force attributed to this sign" (ibid., p. 78). The small lizard called the *chintete* (*tzinteti* in Nahuatl) has the same erotic significance as the *cuetzpalin,* according to the Nahuatl scholar Fernando Horcasitas. While the lizard is predominantly a sexual symbol, there is yet another meaning: divinatory. One Guerreran informant told me that the lizards whisper secrets to the wearer of the masks. A similar meaning has also been reported among the Yaquis. In the Yaqui mask in Fig. 74*b,* the painted lizards are probably used in this divinatory sense. In other masks with lizards, from Guerrero, Michoacán, and Puebla, the carved lizards on each cheek or side of the face could be sexual, divinatory, or both, a situation that probably would have made Freud very happy (see Figs. 17*e,* 189).

The lizard is often confused with the *cipactli,* the earth monster that the Aztecs believed to hold the earth on its back. The *cipactli* was a huge *caimán* differentiated from the regular *caimán* (*acuetzpalin* in Nahuatl) in that it was depicted with spines growing from its back. The similarity in form of these

241. Horned Serpent mask and step-in figure, rain-petitioning dance. These extraordinary, well-preserved carvings were executed during the first few years of the twentieth century and have not been used for twenty years or more. *La Parota, Guerrero.* IV.B.C.

242. Devil masks with rain-petitioning implications. Two more extraordinary old masks from Jaleaca, Guerrero (see also Figs. 1, 38, and 206). At left (*a*) is a mask which was carved for a child. Including the beard and animal figure on the head, it is 34 cm. high. The amazing adult mask at right (*b*), painted in tones of red and gold, is more massive but has the same height as the child's mask. Mask *a* property of the University of Arizona. Photograph by Ferruccio Asta. *Jaleaca, Guerrero; (a) 34 cm.; (b) 34 cm.; hardwood, paint.* II.A.C.

three reptiles makes it difficult to differentiate them. The relationship of the *cipactli* to modern masks will be explored in the Caimán section of this chapter.

Serpent (Coatl [Nahuatl]; Kan [Yucatecan Mayan]). The serpent has a long, convoluted history in Mexico. Serpent motifs pervade both ancient and modern architecture, statuary, legends, religions, and masks, as well as forming part of the national symbol of Mexico. It is impossible to provide the lengthy discussion that this subject merits within the scope of this book; indeed, many books have already been written on the serpent in Mexico without exhausting the topic. Yet, because of the importance of the snake in modern masks, I feel it necessary to provide a brief overview of its historical values before exploring its contemporary symbolism.

Although Mexican Indians recognized and used many different species of snakes in their art and mythology, there is one underlying aspect of the serpent which dominates all others: the serpent as an agricultural symbol. As Lommel points out in *Prehistoric and Primitive Man*, "Agriculture requires a completely different relationship between man and his environment. His interest in game and the procreation of animals gradually lessens and he becomes more and more preoccupied with the fertility of the soil on which he depends for his livelihood. An entirely new kind of symbolism in art develops from this new relationship. The snake is the symbol of the soil, and it is snake motifs, with their phallic associations, which frequently predominate in art all the way from Mesopotamia, where they originate, to India, China and Central America" (Lommel 1966, p. 65).

It is important to note that the animal symbols that we have discussed so far originated within the context of a hunting society, the wellspring of shamanism. While the use of these animal deities was transmuted to serve the needs of the predominantly agrarian Mexican Indian cultures, these animals must be regarded as "older gods." The advent of the serpent as an expression of an agricultural society with its differing system of values sets the scene for a struggle for supremacy between the two religious concepts.

This conflict was still in progress when the Spaniards arrived and was manifest in the struggle between Quetzalcoatl (the plumed serpent) and Tezcatlipoca, one of whose common guises was that of the jaguar. Quetzalcoatl was a legendary figure who arose during the Toltec period and who came to represent fertility, art, technology, agriculture, religious science, and wizardry. Tezcatlipoca was the wizard god of the night and shadows who was associated with war and sacrifice through his guise as a jaguar. Mythologically, the fall of Tollan (Tula) and the flight of Quetzalcoatl, which is the source of most of the Quetzalcoatl legends, was the direct result of Tezcatlipoca's jealousy. This myth mirrors the historical reality of Tollan being overwhelmed by barbarian tribes who still held their beliefs in older, hunting-related gods like Tezcatlipoca.

As John Bierhorst points out in his commentary on the Quetzalcoatl poem/songs, this struggle can be viewed as the result of "the entrenched dualism of what might be styled, on one hand, a cult of the serpent, emphasizing fertility, wisdom, and the peaceful pursuit of the arts; on the other, a 'jaguar' cult, marked by militarism and morbidity. By Aztec times the former had come to be represented essentially, though not wholly, by the spirit of Quetzalcoatl; the latter by Tezcatlipoca, the particular deity of the Nahuatl-speaking peoples and, specifically, a god of darkness and shadows. It was during the rule of the Aztecs that human sacrifice began to be practiced on a grand scale; but the 'serpent' and 'jaguar' alternatives had always coexisted in the Mexican mind and undoubtedly continued to do so even if the 'jaguar' had temporarily gained the ascendancy" (Bierhorst, ed., 1974, p. 79). It is interesting to note that the symbol of the Aztecs, which became the national symbol of Mexico, is that of an eagle conquering a serpent. As the eagle is closely allied with the jaguar, this symbol is a graphic statement of the Aztec value system: the ascendancy of warlike values over more peaceful agrarian ones.

The myth of Quetzalcoatl and of his conflict with the more militaristic deities was by no means confined to the Nahuas. Quetzalcoatl corresponds directly to the Mayan god Kukulcan, whose name also translates as "plumed serpent." Similar myths can be found throughout the Indian tribes of Mexico, reflecting their transition from hunting to agriculture.

Modern symbolic values of the snake, then, are an outgrowth of this tradition and must be viewed within this basic framework if they are to be fully understood. Today, there are three major "meanings" of the snake that can be identified: sexuality, water, and wizardry. These are separate, yet related, manifestations of the Quetzalcoatl and allied myths.

As a sexual symbol, the snake functions in much the same way as the lizard. Without doubt, this meaning stems in large part from its phallic shape. However, one should remember that sexuality is equated with fertility in the Indian mind and thus has more positive connotations than in the more compartmentalized European view. Naturally, sexuality has its negative connotations as well, as is manifested in the Malinche masks; but whether this is due to the mores of the Indians or to European influences, it is impossible to say. Generally, though, the snake is viewed as a sexual fertility symbol.

One good example of the sexual-fertility connotations of the snake can be found in the Dance of the Negritos (Little Negroes) as it is normally performed in the states of Veracruz and Puebla. (For a more complete description of this dance, see Chapter 10.) As noted by Frances Toor (1947, pp. 354–355), the central characters of this dance include Field Workers, Clowns, and a white "Woman" named Maringuilla, who holds either a live but harmless Snake or a wooden one. The principal action of the dance involves the Workers and Clowns receiving mock bites from the Snake, only to be cured magically by a Sorcerer who invokes the four winds. The dance ends with the Snake temporarily escaping and all of the dancers killing it.

The Dance of the Negritos is a mixture of both Christian and Indian elements. In many areas of Veracruz and Puebla, there are large numbers of poisonous snakes which endanger the field workers. Thus, as with the Tigre, the symbolic death of the Snake insures safety and abundance. However, the sexual comments and Maringuilla's role in the dance add an extra dimension of fertility-sexuality to the symbolism of the serpent. Toor adds that in many villages, the figure of Maringuilla is also likened to that of Malinche, and the dance is said to kill "evil" sexual instincts in women. There is, as well, a Christian overlay of the serpent in the garden of Eden.

Another example of the serpent's connection to sexuality is also given by Toor: "In Yucatan the wicked woman is the *x-tabai*, a demon of the woods. She appears at times young, beautiful, finely clad, with loose flowing hair, to lure a man into the bush. If he cannot get away from her after she has revealed her true self, she chokes him to death. . . . She may also become a green and yellow snake with markings on its back, and stop up a man's nostrils with the tip of her tail. There is no use trying to shoot the snake because it cannot be killed and will only return to do harm" (Toor 1947, p. 531).

The serpent is also widely accepted as a water sign throughout Mexico. It is in this aspect that snakes are more often used in contemporary masks. The masks created by José Rodríguez for the rain-petitioning Diablo Macho and Diablo Sapo dances (Figs. 15, 17, and 248) consist of human faces adorned with snakes and other water signs, such as bats and frogs. In many masks, the connection between serpents and water is made not directly but through a symbolic representation of the snake. As noted below in "The Symbolism of the Human Face," the most common equation is that of the snake with the hair. In part, the use of snakes to represent hair derives from the shared physical characteristics of the snake, hair, and water, as all three have the same flowing, twisting qualities. The use of this design convention can be seen in the La Parota mask in Fig. 188*b* and in the Jaleaca mask in Fig. 242*b*. Snakes are also represented by whips by many different Indian groups. One example of the snake-whip convention and its connection to water is given in the description of the Tlaxcala Carnival dances in Chapter 4.

The Yaquis and Mayos of Sonora also think of the snake as a water sign. They "believe horned serpents live in mountain springs, for which reason they never go dry. When the serpents leave them, they go to the sea, causing floods which are necessary to their crops" (Toor 1947, p. 508). There are also similar beliefs among almost all of the Oaxacan groups. "The Mixe around Zempaltepec also believe in a horned water serpent that lives in the springs and is associated with heavy rains and floods. . . . [They] make offerings, at the serpent springs, of tamales and tepache; also of the blood of turkeys and hens when they gather the first ears of corn" (ibid.). For a unique example of a large Horned Serpent mask and a step-in Horned Serpent figure from La Parota, Guerrero, see Fig. 241.

In our own field work with the Zoque Indians in Tuxtla Gutiérrez, Chiapas, we collected a tale that again illustrates the serpent's connection with water:

> *The Tsahuatsan is a huge serpent with seven heads that lives in the mountain tops. It does not have a fixed abode, but is driven from place to place by the Moyó or thunderbolts with their serpent whips. When it is in the air, it travels with big clouds and makes a whishing sound. Wherever it falls down, a lake is formed. It usually travels back and forth from Mactumatsa to the Sumidero. When the Moyó drive the Tsahuatsan, a big storm arises.*
>
> *(Cordry and Cordry 1941, pp. 16–17)*

The third major aspect of the serpent today is the association with wizardry (a continuation of the myth of Quetzalcoatl). Another Zoque serpent tale which has already been quoted in Chapter 8 illustrates the Zoque belief that serpents are directly connected with sorcery and magical powers. While the snake as a sign for witchcraft is not normally isolated from its other connotations in masks, it forms a magical undercurrent that is always present when serpents are incorporated in mask designs. Indeed, it is correct to say that the serpent still represents a magical fertility symbol whose power is equaled only by that of the menacing *tigre*.

Caimanes, Fish, and Mermaids. While the *caimán* (a term used for caimans, alligators, and crocodiles) was once found in many rivers in Mexico, Caimán masks and the Caimán Dance are found almost exclusively in the Nahua villages along the Balsas River and the other rivers in the state of Guerrero. To my knowledge, the only other place that uses the Caimán mask and costume is a small, isolated Nahuatl-speaking village called Tempoal in the Huastec region in the state of Veracruz. The river people of Guerrero view the *caimán* as a threat to their survival, as it eats fish, one of the main sources of

243. Caimán figure, Fish Dance. Made in the poorer Indian fashion with simple carving, pochote spines, and a thin wash of paint, this Caimán (half of which is pictured here) was made to be worn about the dancer's waist. (For a more elaborate Caimán from Tula, Guerrero, on the Balsas River, see Fig. 303.) *Totozintla, Guerrero (Nahua); length: 60 cm. (approx.); wood, paint, pochote spines, animal teeth.* IV.A.C.

244. Dog mask. This wooden Dog mask is in the best tradition of paper-thin, delicately carved Puebla masks from before 1900. The painting is detailed and skillfully executed. The god Xolotl in his guise of a dog was believed to lead the dead across the river to the underworld, an idea that has persisted for centuries. This Dog has *caimán* ears which associated it with rivers and water. I have seen another crudely fashioned Dog with *caimán* ears from the state of Guerrero, which leads me to believe that the symbolism here is traditional and may cover a wide area. *State of Puebla; 20 cm.; wood, paint.* IV.A.D.

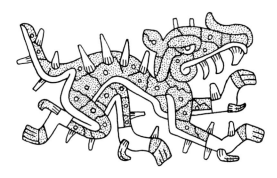

245. *Cipactli*, "*caimán*." As seen in the Codex Borgia. After *Comentarios al Códice Borgia* (Seler 1963), vol. 1, Fig. 1.

food of these villages. A certain amount of the awe accorded to this reptile may also be attributed to its potential direct menace to human life. However, it should be stressed that *caimanes* are now quite rare and do not constitute any real danger to the populace or their food supply. In fact, *caimanes* have not been seen for many years in the great Balsas River, except for a single report three years ago when the river was very high and villagers from the important mask-making village of Tlacozotitlán claimed they saw two *caimanes* eating a burro that had drowned in the river.

Therefore, like the *tigre*, the *caimán* represents a destructive force of nature. Similarly, this force is transformed into one of abundance through the masked dance. The Caimán Dance, described in Chapter 10, involves the symbolic "netting" of the Caimán figure by Fishermen, so that the menace not only is neutralized but turns into a power that assures good fishing. Again, this closely parallels the central plot of the Tigre dances. The Caimán Dance (along with the Fish Dance) uses long Caimán or Fish figures which the dancers step into and wear about the waist (Fig. 243). Malinche and the head of an Old Man of the River occur on some of the large Caimán and Fish figures used in these dances (Fig. 303c).

Yet the *caimán* motif is also used in masks outside of these river areas where its function and meaning have an obvious correlation to daily life. One good example of this phenomenon can be seen in a fine old Dog mask from Puebla that has *caimán* heads for ears (Fig. 244). This suggests to me that another, older meaning of the *caimán* motif has survived.

In attempting to identify this other meaning of the *caimán*, we note, "On the Mexican plateau, the belief was widely held that the earth rested on the back of a crocodile which, in turn, floated in a huge lake or sea. Representations of these saurian earth monsters are common in Mexican art. In the Codex Borgia, page 27, maize plants complete with ears of corn—almost a field of them—grow from the creature's back. Sometimes a human skull rests in the monster's open jaws (Codex Borgia: 3) and at times the nostrils of the beast are stopped with tubular plugs" (Thompson 1970, pp. 216–217).

The belief in a crocodile–earth monster was not confined to the Mexican plateau, but, like so many other beliefs, spread to Yucatán and Oaxaca as well as other areas. According to Seler (n.d., 3, part 4:63), the earth monster was called *cipactli* ("the spiny one") in Nahuatl to differentiate it from the regular *caimán*, which was called *acuetzpalin* ("water lizard"). Yet, even today, the Zapotec Indians call the *caimán* the *pichijlla*, which also means "the spiny one." The Indian names for the earth monster assume great importance in relationship to modern Caimán masks when one notices that the Caimán step-in figures in the Caimán Dance in Guerrero have spines from the pochote tree on their backs that are remarkably similar to the representation of the spines growing from the back of the *cipactli*, and Caimán masks also have pochote spines. From certain drawings in the codices, one wonders whether effigies in Pre-Hispanic times were made using pochote spines as now. (See Fig. 245.)

246. Pochote tree. The pochote tree is widely distributed in Mexico, and the spines on its bark have been used and depicted symbolically from Pre-Conquest clay pots to the present. Representations of the Aztec earth monster *cipactli* (Fig. 245) are often adorned with pochote spines. The pochote tree has more than symbolic significance, as the fruit gives a cottonlike fiber used by country people and the seeds yield oil. *Region of Mayanalán, Guerrero.*

247. Caimán masks, Caimán Dance. The Caimán Dance was performed in Ostotitlán, El Mirador, Zimatil, and Cuajitlotla, Guerrero. Mask *b* here has a notched nose which probably represents Xolotl, the god of duality and monsters (see pp. 167–168). The nose of mask *a* probably derives from another Pre-Columbian tradition about which we do not know. Although their meaning may not have been clear to those who made and used them some fifteen to forty years ago, these masks demonstrate a remarkable word-of-mouth survival from Pre-Conquest times. Mask *a* has reptile skin behind the pochote spines. In this area, imitation reptile skins were often used. Mask *a* property of the Smithsonian Institution. *(a) El Mirador, Guerrero (Nahua); (b) Ostotitlán, Guerrero (Nahua); (a) 40 cm.; (b) 46 cm.; wood, paint, pochote spines, reptile skin.* III.B.C.

Yet another facet of the *caimán* symbol is brought out by this line of reasoning. The spines of the pochote tree (also known as the "silk-cotton" or ceiba tree; see Fig. 246) had an important religious significance in Pre-Hispanic times and were copied on clay vessels and figures in Pre-Conquest sculpture. Given the importance of these pochote spines, it seems significant that they also occur on the masks that we have previously identified as Xolotl masks in discussing the symbolism of the dog motif. Therefore, the question must arise as to the connection between Xolotl and the *caimán*.

Xolotl, in addition to being associated with duality, was also the god of monsters and deformity. Then too, in his guise as a dog, Xolotl took the dead across the river to the underworld, an underworld that must in part be associated with the earth monster if for no other reason than their proximity. As can be seen in Fig. 210, Xolotl was often represented as a dog with tufts of hair that look remarkably like the pochote spines on the Caimán masks and figures. Further, since Xolotl was also associated with a small salamander called the axolotl,* and since in Pre-Conquest Mexico there was often much confusion between *caimanes* and lizards, Xolotl may have become associated with the *caimán* by extension.

Returning to the Puebla Dog mask with *caimán* ears, I believe that this is a direct, contemporary manifestation of the relationship between the *caimán*–earth monster and Xolotl. Xolotl is represented by the dog, which is his normal guise; the *caimán* heads symbolize the earth monster *cipactli*. Thus, I am led to believe that the *caimán* as used in many modern masks (Fig. 247*b*) is associated with and symbolizes Xolotl to some degree. (This belief is reinforced by the notched nose of the Caimán in Fig. 247*b*—another common symbol for Xolotl.)

In regard to the significance of the fish motif, when used in masks for dances like the Fish Dance, it clearly functions as a prayer for good fishing. When used in masks for other types of dances, it signifies water, as is shown in the rain-petitioning masks from the Diablo Macho Dance in Fig. 17. The mermaid motif also has the same dual function of being a prayer for good fishing and a water sign. This interpretation of the mermaid is also supported by my experi-

---

*Xolotl's connection to the axolotl, a small salamander, illustrates both his dualistic nature and his linkage to the *caimán* and to the *cipactli*, or earth monster:

"In this myth concerning the creation of the sun and the moon, the gods were going to sacrifice themselves to give strength to the sun and Xolotl wished not to die.

"And when he felt death was to overtake him, he fled from his presence; he ran; he quickly entered a field of green maize, and took the form of, and quickly turned into, two young maize stalks [growing] from a single root, which the workers in the field have named *Xolotl*. But there, in the field of green maize, he was seen. Then once again he fled from him; once more he quickly entered a maguey field. There also he quickly changed himself into a maguey plant [consisting of] two [parts] called *mexolotl*. Once more he was seen, and once more he quickly entered into the water and went to take the shape of [an amphibious animal called] *axolotl*. There they could go to seize him, that they might slay him" (Sahagún 1953, p. 8).

The small water creature axolotl exists today and carries the name inherited from the god Xolotl. The axolotl can live on land or water and is noted for its monstrous looks. Hence, Xolotl is connected to water, monstrosity, and, through the common cosmological shifts, to the *caimán* and *cipactli*.

248. Diablo Sapo (Frog Devil) masks, Diablo Sapo Dance (a rain-petitioning dance). Three masks by José Rodríguez featuring the water symbol of frogs. They give equal importance to human and animal features, with each face and frog being highly individualistic in both carving and painting. In such earth monster masks, the emerging face may be that of the animal spirit, an earth god, or the spirit of the earth itself. (See Fig. 249 for a similar conception from the Codex Borgia.) Mask *c* property of the University of Arizona. *Guerrero (Tlapanec or Popoloca); 28–33 cm.; wood, paint (oil).* II.A.C.

250. Devil mask. The area of Copanatoyac, Guerrero, produced very fine masks some twenty to fifty years ago, and this Devil is in its best tradition. The monsterlike human face has bat ears and a frog in the mouth (possibly related to the ritual eating of frogs and snakes; see Fig. 133). Ample openings for sight are provided under the eyes, while the dancer could breathe through holes in the mouth on either side of the frog. Property of the University of Arizona. *Copanatoyac, Guerrero (Nahua); height: 25 cm.; depth: 16 cm.; wood, paint, animal teeth.* II.B.C.

249. Head of Tlaltecuhtli, goddess of earth, looking out of the open mouth of a *cipactli*. As seen in the Codex Borgia. After *Comentarios al Códice Borgia* (Seler 1963), vol. 2, Fig. 1.

251. Devil mask. Termed a Devil mask today, this snub-nosed creature once probably had another, deeper significance. The tongue has a frog sitting on it, perhaps a holdover from the ritual eating of snakes and frogs. *Tlanixpatlán, Guerrero (Nahua); 22 cm.; wood, paint.* IV.B.D.

ences among the Huichol Indians of Nayarit in 1938. I was shown a lake in the mountains where dwelt a water deity described as being part fish and part woman—similar to a mermaid. On a high ledge above the lake, there were many small sculptures of clay, which were offered to this deity as prayers for rain.

Mermaids are supposedly Post-Hispanic in origin, but I am of the opinion that, inasmuch as the codices are so filled with pictures of fish with heads of birds and animals, some student may someday discover a drawing or a photograph of a fish with a human head, proving that there were Pre-Hispanic mermaids. Eric Thompson says that, according to the Chorti Maya of Guatemala, the water goddess Chicchan was a mermaid, the upper part being a woman and the lower part a fish (1970, pp. 262–264). There is no conclusive proof of a Pre-Conquest mermaid motif, however.

Frogs and Toads. Frogs and toads are water animals and are commonly used in rain-petitioning masks. These animals were identified with water and rain by both the Mayans and the Aztecs. The Mayans, according to Thompson (1970, pp. 239, 265), believed that the croaking of frogs was a rain charm. Frogs and toads are quite common in all of the extant pictorial codices and are often shown swimming or spouting water. In Fig. 248, we see a fine set of Frog Devil masks, each consisting of a frog body surrounding a human head, perhaps referring to a deity long ago forgotten. In Fig. 249 we see the head of the goddess Tlaltecuhtli looking out from the jaws of a *cipactli*. The Frog Devil masks may have had a similar meaning originally: an earth or water deity looking out from the back of a frog.

By extension of the water symbolism, frogs also have a crop-fertility connotation. An extremely large Frog mask (Fig. 256) was used in a harvest dance in the area of Campo Morado, Guerrero, along with an Iguana mask (Fig. 252) and a number of other animal masks, including several insects and other invertebrates.

In Fig. 15, we see a mask made by José Rodríguez with a particular type of frog motif: two frogs in the mouth of a human figure. This may relate to the Aztec ceremonies in which live frogs and serpents were swallowed during the feasts of Atamalqualiztli (Sahagún 1951, pp. 163–164, 188; see also Fig. 133 of this volume). It might also relate to the fact that mouths were associated with caves and water, which are the natural habitats of frogs and/or toads. Other masks with frogs in their mouths are shown in Figs. 250 and 251.

Frogs also have an association with the bat. According to *The World of Bats* by Alvin Novick and Nina Leen, vampire bats "can jump like frogs—the only bats able to do it" (1969, p. 165). As the Mexican Indians were such close observers of nature, I am sure that they were aware of this and it was one of the reasons that these animals were linked together (see Fig. 24).

Birds. Although bird motifs formed an important element of Pre-Conquest art and mythology, birds are not a common or major design in modern masks. The most important bird currently used in masks is the eagle. As mentioned in the section dealing with the jaguar, the Aztecs used the eagle as a sym-

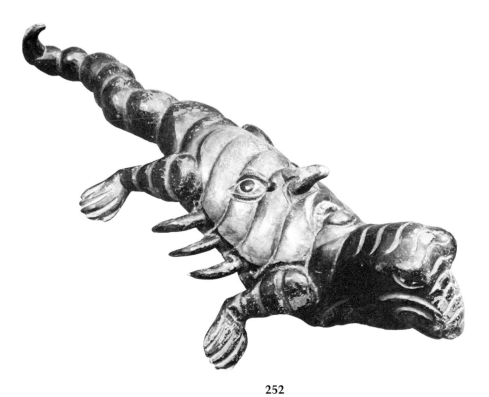

252

253

252–256. Harvest celebration masks. These five animal masks with joyous human faces are from a set of extraordinary masks made around 1900 and worn by dancers who went into the fields to celebrate after the crops were harvested in October. They were probably carved by members of the Bahena family (see Fig. 188). A number of invertebrate masks are included. Masks of this subject and size have not been seen previously, to my knowledge. The masks shown here are an Iguana (Fig. 252), an unidentified Insect (Fig. 253), a Scorpion (Fig. 254), a Crab (Fig. 255), and a Frog (Fig. 256). Other masks from the same set, not shown, include a Grasshopper, a Beetle, a Tarantula, an Armadillo, a Dog, and a Spider. Photographs of Figs. 252–253 by Ferruccio Asta; photographs of Figs. 254–256 by Carlos López Campos. Fig. 252 property of Beth Burstein; Fig. 253 property of Mr. and Mrs. Robert Lauter. *Area of Campo Morado–La Parota, Guerrero (Nahua); (Fig. 252) 64 cm.; (Fig. 253) 50 cm.; (Fig. 254) 79 cm.; (Fig. 255) 85 cm.; (Fig. 256) 67 cm.; wood, paint.* V.A.C.

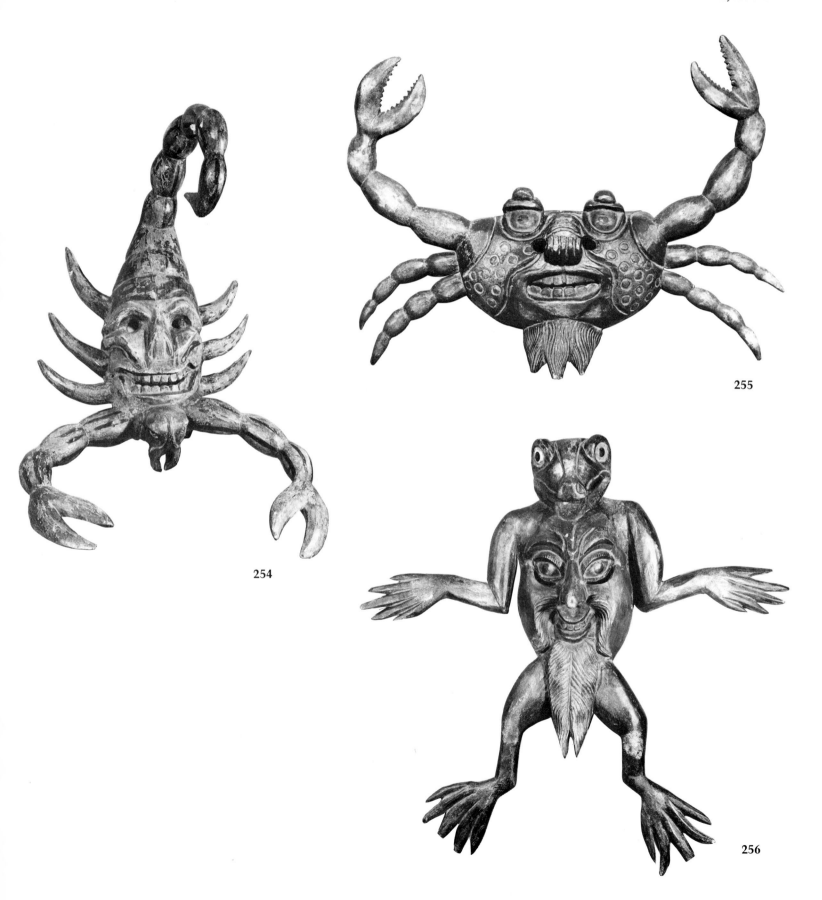

254

255

256

bol for and as a god of war. Today, the eagle is not an active symbol but is restricted to a historical re-enactment of the warfare of the Conquest in the Azteca and Tenochtli dances performed in Central and Southern Mexico. These Eagle Knight masks depict Pre-Conquest Indian knights with great headdresses carved of wood (Fig. 131). Other birds depicted in contemporary masks include the Owl, which was greatly feared as a bringer of bad luck (see Fig. 150), the Vulture (*zopilote*) (Fig. 193*b*), and the Crow (Fig. 193*a*).

Invertebrates.

Thus, it was named the dance of the gods.
    And all came forth [as] humming birds, butterflies, honeybees, flies, birds, giant horned beetles, black beetles—those forms men took; in these guises they came dancing.

(*Sahagún 1951, p. 163*)

257. Pig Devil mask. This sympathetic Pig Devil is simply carved, with a few gouges and incised scorpions on either cheek. The scorpions function as signs reinforcing the "dirty" aspect of the pig. The eyeholes are open and expressive. Crude teeth fill the mouth opening. *Xalpatláhuac, Guerrero; height: 23 cm.; depth at snout: 17 cm.; wood, paint (water base), animal teeth.* IV.A.C.

258. Butterfly mask, Bat Dance. The butterfly has not been a common mask subject in the recent past but is frequently seen in Pre-Hispanic recordings of all kinds. This beautiful Butterfly mask from the Balsas River area was used in the Guerrero Bat Dance. It combines the freedom and the originality displayed in the very best masks by carvers who created their images entirely free from outside influences. This Butterfly has a spirit in the form of a small head at the base of the tail. The butterfly, symbol of the planet Venus and of the dead warrior, is also a symbol of fire and the fire god. Eulalia Guzmán writes, "The quivering of a bright flame reminded them of the agitation of a butterfly's wings" (cited in Westheim 1965, p. 74). *San Francisco, Guerrero (Nahua); height: 29 cm.; width: 37 cm.; wood, paint.* V.A.C.

259. Malinche mask, Pastorela Dance. This rare old mask is a representation of Malinche. The antennae and the outward-splayed semi-triangular sections seen about the chin, cheeks, and head are an ancient Pre-Hispanic symbol for the butterfly as shown in Fig. 260*c, e, f*). The goddess Xochiquetzal is seen wearing this butterfly symbol as a nose ornament in Fig. 260*d*. Among other meanings, the butterfly symbolized the soul of the warrior. *Area of Axoxuca, Guerrero; height: 42 cm.; width: 42 cm.; wood, paint, ribbons.* II.A.C.

260. Butterfly symbols. (*a*) Flower with butterfly, from the Codex Magliabecchiano. (*b*) Face of the god Xochipilli, from the Codex Borgia. (*c*) Butterfly from the cloak of Macuilxochitl, from the Codex Magliabecchiano. (*d*) Head of the goddess Xochiquetzal, from the Codex Borgia. (*e*) Gold nose pendant, from the National Museum of Mexico. (*f*) Butterfly ornament for a *quechquemitl*, from a private collection. After *El México Antiguo*, 10 (1965): 460.

Like birds, insects and other invertebrates do not have a major role in modern masks. Nevertheless, as this book was being prepared for publication, several extraordinary masks came to me from Campo Morado, Guerrero, an area which has produced many divergent types of masks. As shown in Figs. 252–256, these are large wooden masks of invertebrates and other animals with human faces carved into their backs in much the same manner as the Frog Devil masks of José Rodríguez (Fig. 248). In addition to the Insect, Scorpion, and Crab shown in Figs. 253–255, this group of masks includes a Grasshopper, a Beetle, and a Tarantula, all creatures very rarely seen in Mexican masks.

There are only four invertebrates that have any widespread usage on masks, the bee, the butterfly, the grasshopper, and the scorpion. Generally, the use of bee and grasshopper motifs is restricted to Malinche masks (see Fig. 44b). Within this context, both of these insects take on negative connotations. I believe that the bee must be interpreted as a manifestation of the stinging aspect of the Malinche character, both in terms of hostility toward the figure and the fact that she "stung" Mexico. It is interesting to note that Pre-Conquest Indians kept bees for honey and wax and generally viewed them in a positive sense. Consequently, I feel that the bee's negative associations are of recent origin.

In the case of the grasshopper, I can only surmise that its negative connotation in the Malinche masks derives from the locust and its devastation of crops, similar to the Spanish devastation of Mexico. The grasshopper was and still is important as a food source.

The scorpion appears in a carved form on the faces of many masks (Fig. 68c) and as a painted decoration as well (Figs. 70, 257). It usually carries the poisonous, stinging connotation and the meaning of evil. Among the wooden masks from Campo Morado, Guerrero, mentioned above, however, is a large Scorpion (Fig. 254) which does not have these negative connotations.

The Butterfly as a basic mask form was used twenty or more years ago in Bat Dances (Fig. 258). Some Malinche masks also have Pre-Hispanic butterfly symbols (Figs. 259, 278).

Plant Symbolism

Of the enormous number of masks I have seen and recorded since I first came to Mexico in 1931, I have discovered very few that contain representations of plants, other than those with pochote spines. There are, however, two masks by José Rodríguez that depict the Corn Spirit; one of these is shown in Fig. 313. Looking closely at what appear to be horns on these masks, one can see that they are actually cornstalks with the characteristic corn leaves at the base of each plant. As these stalks rise, they are transformed into serpents, which are water and fertility symbols. The Corn Spirit itself is the small figure above the main face of the mask. In the mask shown in Fig. 313, the breasts of the Corn Spirit are comprised of lizards, forming a double image and another fertility symbol. At the bottom of both of these masks, serpents are once again introduced in the marvelous plastic and imaginative transformations wrought by this

261. Characters and dance unknown. These highly unusual masks from the area of Tlacotepec, Guerrero, are the only ones I have seen with carved figures of snails on the face and forehead, as well as some type of kernels or small fruits carved into the cheeks. One of Quetzalcoatl's symbols was the snail; Quetzalcoatl was also the bringer of corn and of agriculture. *El Coral, Guerrero; (a) 23 cm.; (b) 24 cm.; wood, paint.* VII.A.C.

master craftsman. In Fig. 261 we see two masks with corn or some other type of kernels or fruits on their cheeks; this is an extremely rare example of a plant motif on masks.

The plant most commonly associated with masks is the pochote or ceiba tree, whose spines are often used on Caimán figures and masks and Xolotl masks, as noted earlier in this chapter, as well as on the Chameleon masks shown in Fig. 9. The pochote tree was commonly regarded throughout Mexico as the Tree of Life. In one myth, Quetzalcoatl is vanquished by Tezcatlipoca and flees west, where "the hero passes through the ceiba [pochote] tree . . . , which becomes a portal to the realm of the dead (with the implication of rebirth . . .)" (Bierhorst, ed., 1974, p. 72). This is, of course, another link of the pochote tree with Xolotl as the double of Quetzalcoatl. It would seem that pochote spines were used in order to incorporate the magic properties of the tree into the masks.

The relative absence of plant motifs in modern masks is extremely significant. It is not that the Mexican Indians are unconcerned with agriculture. Indeed, the vast majority of animal masks are specifically designed and used to ensure crop fertility. Nor does this lack stem from a shortage of vegetation myths or deities, for there are a large number of such myths and gods, since agriculture has played a central role in creating and maintaining classical Indian civilizations for thousands of years. These civilizations first cultivated corn, changing it from a weed to a major source of food (another achievement ascribed to Quetzalcoatl, by the way).

No, the answer to the apparent neglect of plants in masks lies in the very function of the mask itself. Masks were and are designed to transform the wearer, to allow him to identify with and control the forces of nature that threaten him. Plants, crops, and agriculture are not threats, but other forces (the lack of rain, wild beasts, spirits of the night) are. Masks are an integral part of a shamanistic tradition that grew out of the needs of a hunting society and was adapted to fit the emerging needs of an agrarian society. Even though such masks were used to ensure the fertility of both animals and plants, the most important figures remained animals.

Plants were important, however, in the process of making masks. Mask-makers commonly took hallucinogenic drugs as a part of the mask-making process to allow their imaginations freer range and to initiate a personal, mystical contact with the supernatural forces. One Indian informant recently described the preparations that mask-makers underwent before starting to work: "When they would begin making masks, they would fast. Yes, they would fast because they would take advantage of the morning freshness to begin their wooden masks. And since they were also influenced by or drugged with [hallucinogenic] mushrooms, so it [mask design] can be better understood. Those mushrooms were cut from some tree or the land on the twenty-fourth of June, the day of San Juan Bautista. This was done at sunrise, and they were stored in clay jars which they made; some substances were extracted from plants they knew and were added to the mushrooms. The mushroom, I repeat, helped in many forms. They would use the liquid only when they had to make many masks." The use of hallucinogens seems to have been a fairly standard practice, although this custom now seems to be dying due to the Mexican government's crackdown on drugs.

The wood that was used in masks was also thought to have special significance, as it was commonly believed that powerful spirits resided in or protected various types of trees. Consequently, rituals were devised so that these spirits would not be offended and/or would be harnessed within the mask itself.

Finally, many different plant fibers are used in masks for hair and beards. (See Chapter 7 for a more detailed discussion of mask-making materials.)

Symbolism of the Human Face

Mexico abounds with a great number of masks representing human characters: Cortés, Santiago (St. James), Pre-Hispanic Indians, Viejitos, Moors, assorted

Christian saints, and many, many more. Most of these human masks, however, cannot be said to be symbolic in and of themselves. Rather, they are representational in that they seek to depict individuals, even though the depiction may be stylized. In many cases, facial distortion does constitute symbolism, as it has intrinsic meanings that are not readily apparent on the surface; this type of symbolism will be discussed below. But, although figures like Cortés and Santiago have symbolic values as a result of their historical roles, these values are not manifested in the masks themselves. Consequently these human figures will not be discussed here.

In my opinion, one human mask that does evidence symbolism is the Malinche mask. As mentioned on pp. 34 and 170, the Malinche figure has come to mean far more than the actual individual and her historic deeds. Combining with other Mexican myths such as the *x-tabai* and the Llorona (with its parallels to the Greek Medea legend), Malinche masks are used in many nonhistorical dances to represent the threat of female sexuality, although to some degree they have a comic implication as well. The symbolic values attributed to Malinche form an interesting comment on the Mexican mind and the effects of the *machismo* concept.

As discussed on p. 3, most Mexican Indian groups equated the human face with the personality and the identity of an individual (León-Portilla 1963, p. 114). At least some of these Indian groups, however, went one step further; they believed that the face (and the head) was the physical location of one of each person's two souls (Ichon 1973, pp. 175–177). The use of a mask then hides (i.e., temporarily removes) an individual's personality and soul from the world and replaces them with desired attributes, characteristics, and soul. On a shamanistic level, it is believed that the individual is transformed into another being or god. But since "one becomes what one displays" (Eliade 1964, p. 179), the mask offers the wearer the opportunity to select and to control his new face, his new personality, his new soul. It is logical, therefore, that mask-makers have developed a symbolism of the different parts of the human face, a symbolism that is both a language and a method of control. The remainder of this section is an exploration of that language.

Although this discussion centers on facial symbolism in modern masks, I have in the course of my studies discovered a section of the Codex Vaticano-Ríos which I believe sheds some light on the iconology of the human face (Fig. 262). Although this codex is Post-Hispanic, it shows the parts of the body in relationship to their Pre-Conquest day signs, which were determined through complicated astrological computations. The fact that the great centers of learning which produced those calculations have disappeared does not eliminate the possibility that this Pre-Hispanic symbolism of the face may have survived to influence modern masks. Even before the Conquest, the common people were removed from the culture of the great cities and probably established their own correlations of these beliefs to their everyday environment, and in the more remote areas where most masks were made, the relationship of Indians to their environment has remained far more constant than is generally believed.

It has also been recognized that ethnic art forms and symbols change far more slowly than other aspects of a culture (Fraser, ed., 1966, pp. 264–265). Further, many of these symbols are "natural" symbols, that is, the very shapes of some facial parts suggest a meaning, a meaning that has been discovered and used by mask-makers throughout the world. However, far too much time has elapsed since the writing of this codex for me to state that there is any exact correlation between the traits these day signs embody and contemporary mask symbolism. I am including the body parts and day signs given by the Codex Vaticano-Rios so that the reader can decide their relevance.

Hair: Lluvia (Rain, Water).

Hair has magical properties connected with the life force and with weather, crops, and fertility. The Huichols see serpents in their own flowing hair, in one organ of the body . . .

(Lumholtz 1902, 2:235)

To the Huichols and most other Mexican Indian groups, hair is a powerful, multifaceted symbol. The various meanings of this symbol, however, spring from one central core: the identification of hair with water. The ancient day sign for hair is "rain" or "water"; this symbolic equation probably originated from shared physical characteristics of hair and water, as both are fluid and flowing. Hair is most often used as a water symbol in modern masks.

This can be readily seen in the large Dwarf masks from La Parota, Guerrero, pictured in Fig. 188. As noted in Chapter 8, these masks were worn by children to imitate dwarves in a rain-petitioning ceremony. They have long sectional beards which are painted blue and brown to reinforce their identification with the muddy river water of Guerrero. Some have long serpents (another water sign) carved along the sides of their heads. At first glance, these Zeus-like masks appear to be of European origin, as beards are not normally associated with Indians. Indeed, beards are one feature of the face not accounted for in the Codex Vaticano-Ríos. However, the ceremony appears to be a direct Pre-Hispanic survival, with the masked children representing the Aztec rain gods, the Tlaloques, who were thought to be dwarves. Further, as noted by Bernal (1969, p. 78), beards which appear to be false are often seen in Olmec sculpture. In Plate 60 of the Codex Borgia, we can see a mask or double face, probably of Xolotl or Quetzalcoatl, wearing a large, heavy beard (see Fig. 198). Whether the use of beards in modern masks (Fig. 10) is a continuance of this tradition or a European influence is a moot point, since modern mask-makers often use the beard as a water symbol in the same manner as other human hair.

The La Parota masks also underscore the common equation of hair with serpents, also probably due to similar characteristics. As discussed earlier in this chapter, serpents are also a water symbol. Consequently, the hair-serpent iden-

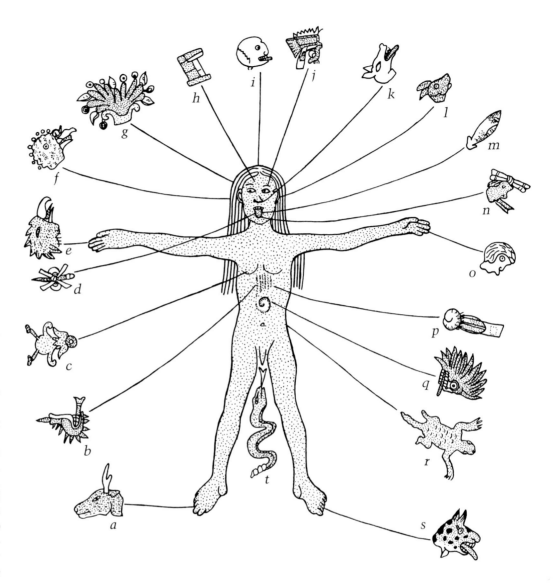

262. Body symbolism. After the Codex Vaticano-Ríos. Each of the twenty "characters" governed one part of the body, as follows: (a) deer (*venado* or *ciervo*), left foot; (b) lizard (*bufeo*, identified by Kingsborough as *cipactli*), liver; (c) rose (*rosa*), nipples; (d) tremor (*temblor*, identified by Kingsborough as *ollin*, earthquake), tongue; (e) eagle (*águila*), right arm; (f) buzzard or vulture (*aura*), right ear; (g) water (*agua*), hair; (h) house (*casa*), brain; (i) death (*muerte*), head; (j) rain (*lluvia*), eyes, tears; (k) dog (*perro*), nose; (l) rabbit (*conejo*), left ear; (m) flint knife (*pedernal*), teeth; (n) wind (*ayre*), breath; (o) little doll-like figure (*mono*), left arm; (p) cane (*caña*), heart; (q) herb or grass (*malinalli*), intestine; (r) lizard (*lagartija*), womb; (s) *tigre*, left foot; (t) snake (*culebra*), penis. (See Kingsborough 1964, 3: 167, pl. 73.)

tity reinforces the basic meaning of hair as water and also expands its connotations to include those of fertility.

The hair-serpent association has a major ramification in the symbolism of mask design. Lumholtz notes that "Girdles and ribbons, inasmuch as they are considered as rain-serpents, are in themselves prayers for rain and the results of rain, namely, good crops, health and life; and the designs on those objects are made in imitation of the markings on the backs of the real reptiles" (1902, 2:214). The use of ribbons and related materials to represent serpents is not restricted to the Huichols but is widespread throughout Mexico.

Hair also is a crop fertility symbol, in that it sometimes represents cornsilk. In the state of Morelos, women still dye their hair yellow or green in imitation of cornsilk (Cordry and Cordry 1968, p. 128). This custom seems to be a Pre-Hispanic survival, as Torquemada (1943, 2:269–270) noted that in ancient

263. Mermaid mask, Fish Dance. A very fine old Mermaid mask designed to show the mermaid face and tail, with the tail forming the headdress. From the Balsas River area, it has cerulean blue eyes that represent water or rain. *Totozintla, Guerrero (Nahua); 38.5 cm.; wood, paint.* II.A.C.

Mexico a festival was held in honor of Xilonen, the goddess of the green corn. During the festival, the women wore their hair unbound, shaking and tossing it in the dances which were the chief feature in the ceremony, in order that the corn might grow in profusion. Durán also notes, "To the hair on the crown of this woman's head was tied a vertical green feather which represented the tassels of the stalks of corn. It was tied with a red ribbon, indicating that at the time of this feast the maize was almost ripe but still green" (1971, p. 223).

Because of the obvious importance of the values associated with hair (water and crop fertility) to these agricultural peoples, it is not surprising that many Indian groups also equated hair with the life force of people. In referring to the Lacandón Indians of Chiapas, Donald Leonard stated, "Immediately upon death a lock of hair from each side of his head was cut and placed in his hands along with the bone of a monkey (which had been saved for this purpose)" (1955, p. 5). In Aztec sacrificial ceremonies, the victim's hair was cut, signifying death itself. This seems to imply that hair is a positive element directly related to the life force.

Eyes: Lluvia (Rain, Water). The eyes can also signify rain, water, and sky. It may seem odd to assign two aspects of the face to symbolize the same thing, but, if one considers the importance of water for these agricultural peoples, whose crops often depend solely upon the scanty rainfall, the dual symbolization is quite logical. The association of eyes with rain could stem from the fact that tears mimic the rain, as well as that the eyes are immersed in liquid. The Aztecs considered tears an augury for rain. In commenting about the sacrifices of women and children, Sahagún states, "And if children went crying, their tears coursing down and bathing their faces, it was said and understood that indeed it would rain. [For] their tears signified rain. Therefore [men] were joyful; thus were their hearts at rest. Hence they said: 'Verily, soon rain will set in; yea, now soon we shall have rain'" (1951, p. 44).

In Fig. 263, we see a Mermaid mask for the Fish Dance from Totozintla, Guerrero. This beautiful example of the imaginative versatility of the Mexican artist represents a prayer for good fishing and is a water sign, as has been noted earlier. She has wonderful cerulean blue eyes to emphasize her connection to the water. The large rain-petitioning La Parota masks that were mentioned above also have blue eyes, as do a large number of other rain- or water-related masks.

Another aspect of the eye that merits exploration can be seen in Fig. 264. This modern Tigre mask has mirror eyes. Since the jaguar or *tigre* is associated with water and underground rivers, it might be that the mirror represents the shimmering of a pool of water or of a river. Yet, it is strange that such mirror eyes are only found in Tigre masks. One clue to this problem was given by Díaz del Castillo (1939*a*, pp. 302–304) when he described the Spaniards visiting the temples of the City of Mexico and seeing the shrine of Huitzilopochtli. There they saw a statue of Tezcatlipoca with a face like a jaguar and bright shining eyes made of obsidian mirror. It may well be that the modern Tigre masks are a

264. Tigre mask. This Tigre with mirror eyes is adorned with wild boar bristles and animal tusks and teeth. *Acatlán, Guerrero.* IV.A.C.

survival of Tezcatlipoca in his jaguar disguise. Still, the exact meaning of the mirror eyes eluded me until one day when an informant was describing a set of masks to me. He got quite excited about one mask in particular, saying that it was alive. When I asked him how he could tell it was alive, he told me that it was because the eyes shone very brightly and followed him around the room. This mask was one of the mirror-eyed Tigre masks. This led me to conclude that the mirrors are inserted in an effort to incorporate the feeling of life in the mask itself. The mask then becomes the living god himself, not just an imitation.

A third kind of eye symbolism is found in the use of the color blue in many masks of religious characters (see discussion in the section on colors above).

Nose: Perro (Dog). One symbolic aspect of the nose already dealt with in the sections on duality and the dog is the probable connection of the deformed nose with Xolotl, the god associated with duality, deformity, and monsters, who was characterized both by a deformed nose and by his guise as a dog, which he assumed to take the dead across the river to the underworld (see Fig. 210). Masks with such deformed noses are, I believe, meant as representations of this god.

A second nose design shows what I think is another Pre-Hispanic survival. The mask shown in Fig. 106 has a very distinctive twisted-snake nose, which looks remarkably like the twisted nose of the type of Tlaloc represented in Fig. 107.

A third type of nose which I believe to be a survival from the Pre-Hispanic is the long, turned-up nose. The nose was characteristic of the Aztec god Yacatecuhtli (Lord of the Nose), who was pictured as the god of travelers, merchants, and commerce (Fig. 265). A modern example of this distinctive nose can be seen in the lacquer mask from Michoacán shown in Fig. 268.

Another aspect of the nose in modern masks (and perhaps a more universal one) is its use as a phallic symbol. Fig. 267 shows a humorous mask from Culapan, Oaxaca, with a very long nose which is ridged to make a noise when a stick is scraped across it. This long nose has a definite sexual connotation that is quite comic to the Indians.

Mouth—Tongue: Ollin (Earthquake); Teeth: Pedernal (Stone Knife); Breath: Viento (Wind). Perhaps the most significant aspect of the mouth is the symbolism of the twisted mouth, which has been mentioned earlier (see Figs. 211, 212). While there are many differing interpretations of the twisted mouth, it may well represent duality in modern Mexican masks, as it does in other American Indian masks. Today, the twisted mouth is used most commonly on the Rastrero (Tracker) figure of the Tlacololero and other Tigre dances.

As the instrument of speech, the tongue is of great importance. In *The Lost Language of Symbolism,* we read: "In Mexico the tongue protruding from the mouth was the symbol of *Wisdom.* It is often thus found in the portraits of priests, kings, and other exalted personages supposed to be endowed with Great Wisdom" (Bayley 1952, 2:127–130). The protruding tongue (Fig. 266) signified power, defiance, and evil, as can be seen in the Devil masks in Figs. 34 and 269. Another meaning for the protruding tongue is death. "Transición" urns pertain-

265. Yacatecuhtli, god of travelers. As seen in the Codex Fejervary-Mayer. After *Comentarios al Códice Borgia* (Seler 1963), vol. 2, Fig. 135.

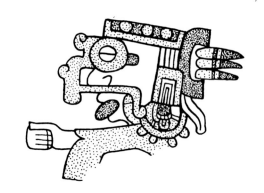

266. Protruding-tongue visage. After the Codex Nuttall. After Nuttall, ed., 1974, p. 33.

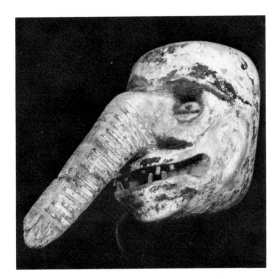

267. Raspador mask. This comic old wooden mask has a long, phallic nose, which serves as a musical instrument called a *raspador*. Noise is produced by scraping the nose with a stick. *Cuilapan, Oaxaca.* I.B.C.

268. Yacatecuhtli mask. The workmanship of this fine lacquer mask is superb, with its strong use of color and movement. Yacatecuhtli, the god of travelers, was depicted in Pre-Conquest times with a prominent upturned nose (see Fig. 265), and this mask is definitely a survival of this god. *Michoacán (Tarascan); height: 20 cm.; width at nose: 19 cm.; wood, lacquer.* I.B.C.

ing to ancient Oaxacan water gods (Paddock 1966, figures 93, 97, 114) show greatly exaggerated protruding tongues. When the Tigre is "killed" in the dance, the performer, in some areas, dons a second mask that represents a dead Tigre with its tongue hanging out.

Other Facial Symbols. Female masks are very often characterized by small, delicate ears, like those in Fig. 270, and by carved or painted dimples. Dimples are used particularly in Malinche masks, where the inner part of the dimples is often painted silver or gold (Fig. 44). The use of the delicate ears and the dimples as conventions to represent woman may stem from an effort to suggest coquettishness and female attractiveness. On female masks, it is necessary to have ears on which to hang earrings, one of the principal adornments of women in ancient times as today.

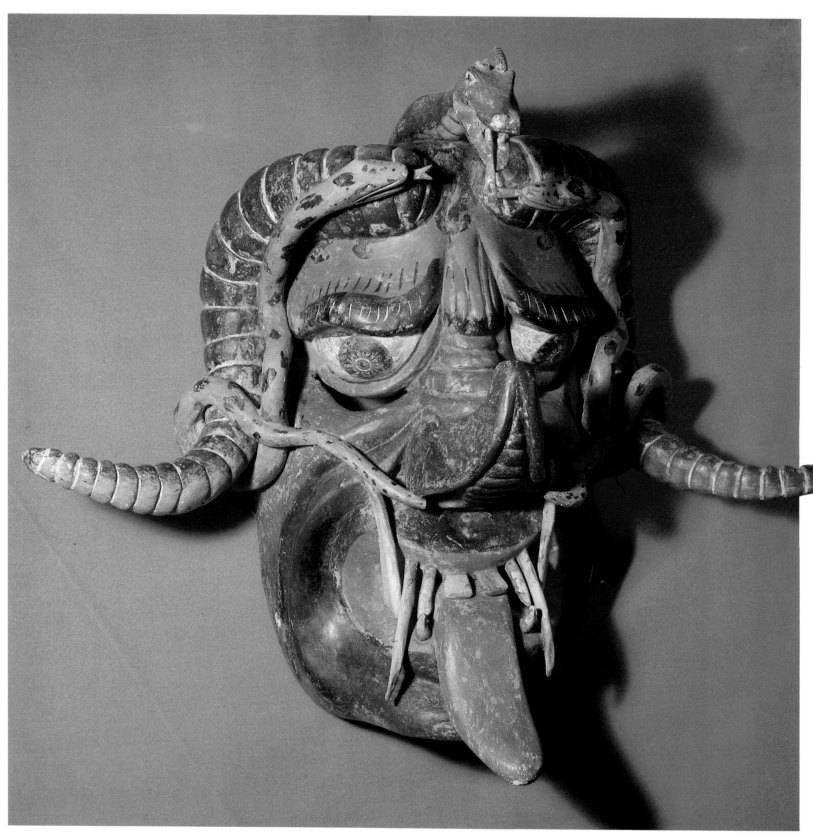

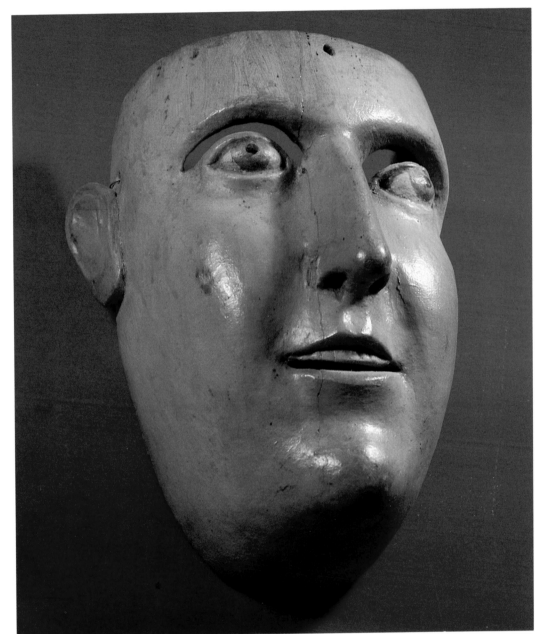

269. Devil mask. Here is an intricate and superb example of the best in Guerrero master carving. Although based on human facial elements, this large Devil almost enters the monster class, with its leather-tongued, coiling serpents, upturned bat nose, and wooden tusks and teeth. The horns curve in a great sweep and have miraculously remained unbroken, despite the obviously heavy use the mask has had. The surface on both sides is chipped and worn, but the paint is still the original. *Tlapexco, Guerrero (Nahua); height: 53 cm.; width: 65 cm.; wood, paint, leather.* II.B.C.

270. Angel mask. This Angel is carved with great delicacy of expression. Noteworthy are the small pink ears, which were carefully attached to the mask and which have holes pierced through for earrings. Such delicate ears are a female characteristic in Mexican masks. The long, shapely nose and the delicately carved teeth show exceptional workmanship. We recognize this as an Angel because of its blue eyes and pale skin tones. The eyes are not drawn as well as one would expect from a mask of this overall quality. The mask is quite thin, ranging from 6 to 7 mm. in thickness. It is an example of the style used in seventeenth- and eighteenth-century *santero* carving. *State of Puebla; 19 cm.; wood, paint (with gesso undercoat).* I.A.C.

10. Social Uses of Masks

CHAPTER 8 discussed some major aspects of the underlying shamanistic basis that gave rise to the development of masks in Mexico and that still exerts a degree of influence in contemporary masks, although its importance is rapidly diminishing. Yet such an emphasis on the religious significance of Mexican masks, no matter how crucial a step in understanding, is of necessity a distortion of the actual role of the mask within the various indigenous cultures, for neither religion nor art can be arbitrarily isolated from the social context. In particular, "the traditional art of the New World . . . has remained a *whole art*" (Bierhorst, ed., 1974, p. xvii), an art that combines all elements of society and that has a definite function in respect to those elements.

If masks are to be understood, they must be viewed as social instruments, as is pointed out by Douglas Fraser in *The Many Faces of Primitive Art*: ". . . partly on analogy with older Western forms, primitive art has often come to be regarded as a sort of congealed religious imagery. Frequently scholars too have supported the religious interpretation of this art, and many of them find in it evidence of 'deeper' spiritual values and 'underlying' metaphysical convictions. What this view of primitive artifacts as fixed religious symbols ignores, however, is the vast *social* domain of the arts, particularly present in primitive societies" (Fraser, ed., n.d., p. 255).

The religious values and processes embodied in masks are not in opposition to or separate from the social domain; they are an integral part of a culture and operate to maintain cultural cohesion. In fact, one of the major roles of a religious system is to act as a method of social control, as Timothy Knab found in his study of a Nahua Indian village in the Sierra de Puebla: "The phenomena specific supernaturals /alpishke/, /kʷawtenchane/, /tepeyolome/ only appear to and castigate those who transgress their particular domains. A man must not cut too much firewood, kill too many fish, slash the hills too brutally if he is to continue life in San Miguel. . . . These and other supernaturals must be satisfied with the way a man lives and propitiates them or they can cause his ruin" (Knab 1976, p. 11).

271. Tenochtli Dance. A village street is the scene of this enactment of the Tenochtli Dance. The dance concerns the battle between the Spanish and the Indian populations of Mexico City at the time of the Conquest and ends with the fall of the great city. The characters include Malinche, Huiquixtle (with snakes), Viejo Bailón or Cortés, Abuela Teresa (Malinche's mother and Cortés's *suegra* [mother-in-law]), and several soldiers. *Acatlán, Guerrero, January 1974.*

272–273. Lenten Fiesta. The special Lenten Fiesta of Las Sauces, Guerrero, takes place each year on the fourth Friday of Lent. When we attended in 1972 (March 10) a group of Tecuani dancers had come to perform from the larger town of Apaxtla. They were led by a *maestro* (leader) named Leobar de Román, who played a bamboo flute and small drum. Fig. 272 shows a group of Tigre Hunters wearing leather masks trimmed with horsehair. An unusual feature of this performance is seen in Fig. 273, which shows a rope stretched high above the plaza by the Tecuani group. The Tigre attempts to escape by climbing along the rope but is pursued by Hunters and Dog alike, despite the dangerous height. In the end the Tigre is captured. The intrepid Apaxtla Tecuanis perform at only

This is not to say that religious systems can be reduced just to forces of social control. Both in parts of Mexico where elements of shamanism still exist, with masks as one of the methods of its expression, and in more acculturated areas, masks are intimately connected with the entire social life of the communities that made them. The mask and the dance are direct manifestations of traditions and culture. The dances and often the masks themselves are handed down from generation to generation and are a matter of pride to the village, the participants and their families. Maintenance of these customs indicates a well-ordered community with respect for traditions and heritage. The mask and the dance signify unity, a plan, a scheme of things. Unfortunately, many of these customs are now being lost.

This correspondence between the mask and social values is more clearly shown through an examination of the symbolic process in and of the mask itself. "In a broad sense, symbolism may be said to exist when some components of the mind's experience elicit activity and values ordinarily associated with other components of experience. . . . A symbol . . . is an object or action that represents another entity in virtue of some arbitrarily assigned conceptual relationship between them," according to Raymond Firth (n.d., p. 28). Since symbols are by their very nature arbitrary (as opposed to being universal), their meaning must be culturally defined and agreed upon if they are to be more than just personally significant. As symbols correlate to other components of experience to have meaning, the symbols must be said to reflect and represent the social and cultural values of a society. Therefore, as stated by Firth, ". . . the system of representations conveyed by objects of art, in particular the system of symbols, corresponds to some system of social relationships" (ibid., p. 18).

The relevance of this type of social agreement and the assignment of values in relationship to the mask has been pointed out in Jung's remarks on masks as a means of changing personality (see p. 147). Not only are the symbols within the masks dependent on social agreement, but the entire transformation process of the mask is as well. As the transformation requires collective agreement, the result must also conform to the needs of the society, that is, its social values.

However, the social functions of the mask in Mexico are not as sharply delineated, prevalent, or crucial as those in other mask-making cultures. In over 450 years of contact, European influences and the hostility of the Church toward indigenous religious practices have eliminated many of the common social uses. Masks are not used in initiation rites, death rites, or curing as they are in other, less acculturated mask-making societies. Nor are they used to buttress the authority of tribal leaders and the cultural mores and laws as is common in Africa. Indeed, the social uses of the mask in Mexico today are loosely defined and overlap into several functional categories at the same time. Nonetheless, they still have a place and definite function within the social system of the indigenous groups of Mexico.

one other time each year, on February 2 at the big Apaxtla Fair. Diego de Durán writes of a feast of ancient times: "All these games and festivities were carried out in an [artificial] forest set up in the courtyard of the temple in front of the image of the god Tlaloc. In the middle of this forest was placed a very large tree. . . . This tree was called Tota, which means Our Father, because around it were placed four smaller [trees], [the main one] seeming to be the father of the others. . . . from each of the small trees emerged a twisted straw rope, attached to the large one in the center" (Durán 1971, pp. 160–162). The arrangement of ropes stretched between four equidistant points as seen in Fig. 273 may be a remnant of this ancient fiesta. *Las Sauces, Guerrero, 1972.*

MAYORDOMOS: THE SOCIAL SYSTEM OF MASK USE

Many people have a surprisingly naïve view of masked dances and fiestas, feeling that they are spontaneous events in which villagers take out their masks and their costumes and get together to perform traditional dances their parents taught them. In fact, most of these dances require large expenditures of time and money. Dancers must be recruited, trained, masked, costumed, rehearsed, and often fed. Since a village usually holds only one major fiesta a year, the fiesta and the dance are often a main source of village pride and status; nothing can be left to chance.

In Mexico, the responsibility for these celebrations is normally given to the mayordomo of the village. "The system of mayordomía is the basic Spanish system for sponsoring sacred images and buildings and for maintaining a yearly cycle of feast-day celebrations. It is a system of hierarchic nature whereby religious and civil activities are integrated" (Foster 1967, p. 195).

The position of mayordomo is one of the four voluntary civil-religious positions in the Mexican village social structure; the holders of these four positions perform the basic duties of the community. While the names may vary from community to community, they are generally called the *alguacil* (constable), *mayordomo* (city steward), *regidor* (alderman), and *alcalde* (mayor, or jus-

274. Boys wearing cardboard masks for the Zoque Indian Fiesta of San Roque. *Tuxtla Gutiérrez, Chiapas, 1940.*

tice of the peace), according to the *Handbook of Middle American Indians* (Wauchope, gen. ed., 1967, 6:285–289).

Thus, the masked dances and the feast-day fiestas are not simple entertainment, nor are they separate from the social structure of the community. Their organization, performance, and sponsorship by the mayordomo directly affect the social status of both the individual and the community. As George M. Foster notes, this system is a way for each citizen to achieve respectability within the community. A man, despite his origins, can achieve status and prestige by serving at each level of the system. Also the system is a source of entertainment and allows the person to feel a part of the community. It also serves as a means of redistribution of wealth and power by continually maintaining social and economic equality. It is a check against any one individual's obtaining too much personal wealth (Foster 1967, pp. 194–211).

While other officials often provide the necessary funds, in most villages it is the mayordomo who is responsible for the masked dances. The mayordomo is charged with storing and maintaining the masks to be used, although the masks are usually stored in a church or municipal building because of problems of space. He is also responsible for the training and recruiting of the dancers. This is a major task. The number of the dancers and the quality of the dance itself are directly dependent on the mayordomo's personality and financial situation. One informant, Santos Tesillo, an ex-mayordomo and teacher of the Dance of the Negritos in Capulhuac, state of Mexico (Fig. 99), told me that the number of dancers can vary from 50 to 125, depending on the mayordomo. He also said that the length of the dance is related to how well the mayordomo provides food and drink for the participants.

In Pinotepa de Don Luis, Oaxaca, the judge of the barrio (equivalent to the mayordomo) keeps the twenty-four to twenty-five masks for one year in the church or the municipal building. He feeds the *topiles* (the constables or alguaciles) and gives them alms pay for the meals they provide during fiestas. He also orders them to repair the roads and clean up the barrio for the fiestas. However, the Mestizos keep their own masks, and, in this village, the musician of each dance manages the Indian dancers.

These positions are not free from the social conflicts that beset many villages in their transition from an Indian culture to the more national Mestizo one. As reported in *Costumes and Weaving of the Zoque Indians of Chiapas, Mexico* (Cordry and Cordry 1941, pp. 50–53), Tuxtla Gutiérrez, Chiapas, was in the midst of such a transition in 1940, having both a large Zoque Indian population and a large Mestizo one. During the time we spent in Tuxtla, there were loud complaints and much criticism of the Mestiza *presidenta* (equivalent to the mayor or alcalde) by the Zoques. She was supposed to sponsor the Zoque dancers and musicians but instead spent the money on a brass band from Chiapa de Corzo and on marimba music. Further, she had failed to provide for the killing of a bull, as was formerly the custom, to furnish meat for the dancers, musicians, and other church officials, using the money instead for a bullfight and dance with marimba music that was principally attended by Mestizos, although the occasion was the Fiesta of San Roque, an important Zoque festival. In fact, the only way that we were able to see the dance was to offer to pay part of the expenses.

This incident typifies the sort of social conflict that has led to the general decline in the use of masks in dances in twentieth-century Mexico. When masks and masked dances no longer have a social value within the community, they are discontinued. Unfortunately, too many Mexicans no longer wish to be reminded of their Indian traditions, customs, and past as they rush to become "modern"; therefore, the masks and the dances that formally symbolized that past and provided continuity are being rapidly left behind.

MASKED DANCES AND THEIR FUNCTION

As mentioned earlier in this chapter, the mask and, by implication, the masked dance in Mexico cannot be said to have the specific social functions (initiation, death rites, curing, etc.) that they have in many other mask-making cultures. We can, however, identify five major themes of these dances: historical, Christian, occupational, nature-related, and entertainment-oriented. The first four themes have a definite social function: they embody and teach community values, history, and religion. Nor should the social value of entertainment be overlooked, as it provides an outlet for the release of tensions and allows people to participate in their community and identify with it.

Of course, most masked dances do not fit neatly into one or the other of the above categories but overlap into several at the same time. Also, many of the dances that must now be categorized as entertainment may have had some other function in the past, a function that has either been forgotten or suppressed by the Church. On the other hand, no dance can really be said to be without entertainment value.

Usually, masked dances are performed on the village's or barrio's saint's day, on general religious holidays (Carnival, Christmas, etc.), on national holidays, or for change of office in some Indian communities. These occasions for the dances should not be confused with the purpose of the dance for the community, as the content of the dance does not usually correlate with the official occasion. The principal exceptions to this situation are the nature dances which are keyed to the ecological calendar and some of the historical dances which are keyed to specific dates.

The following section contains brief descriptions of a few typical masked dances within each of the five categories. These descriptions are only general in nature and should not be considered in any way definitive, as the dances vary widely depending on when and where they are performed.

Historical Dances

The Conquest.   The most popular and most important of the historical dances are a group of related dances dealing with the theme of the Spanish Conquest of Mexico. Known by many different names (Azteca Dance, Tenochtli Dance, Chichimec Dance, Plume Dance, Dance of the Concheros, Dance of the Cuerudos), these are variants on a basic theme, not just different names for the same dance; but they are sufficiently similar to warrant a single discussion. Dances from the Conquest group are performed in villages from Nayarit to Chiapas, usually on the village's saint's day, with the most spectacular performances held in Jalisco and Oaxaca.

The general theme of these dances and the characters are drawn from a historical account of the Conquest, from the Indian point of view. That is to say, the Conquest is presented as a tragedy of the destruction of the Indian civilization by the Spaniards, a tragedy that has its redemption and happy ending through the advent of Christianity. The characters may include: Moctezuma, the king of the Aztecs at the time of the Conquest; Malinche, the Indian woman who became the interpreter and mistress of Cortés; Hernán Cortés, the Spanish conqueror of Mexico; "typical" Indian warriors; and Spanish soldiers.

Depending on where the dance is performed and what version is used, the characters who are masked can range from everyone to no one; Malinche is almost always masked. Fig. 131 shows an Indian personage from the Azteca

275. Chilolo mask (Mixtec combat mask), Chilolo Dance. This distinctively styled combat mask is characteristic only of Juxtlahuaca, Oaxaca, where twelve personages all masked alike dance in the Chilolo Dance, a derivative of the Moors and Christians theme. Unusual features are the protruding eyes and the rather clumsy wooden moustaches. Formerly in the Cayuqui Estage collection. *Juxtlahuaca, Oaxaca (Mixtec); 17 cm.; wood, paint.* I.B.C.

276–277. Malinche and Cortés helmet mask, Tenochtli Dance. The depiction of both Cortés and Malinche on this large helmet mask signifies power. One of the faces has an extended tongue (Fig. 277, left), and both faces are bearded. The reason for putting a beard on Malinche can only be surmised. Both faces have a number of large lizards crawling about; lizards symbolize lust and wantonness, as does the intense pink color. *Atlapecuanapa, Guerrero (Nahua); height: 50 cm.; circumference: 128 cm.; wood, paint. (Each face)* II.A.C.

Dance. Another mask from the Azteca Dance shows Malinche wearing an eagle helmet (Fig. 215). Malinche is one of the most popular mask motifs throughout the country and is subject to wide divergencies in her portrayal, as noted in Chapter 2 (see also Figs. 44, 97, 259).

While the masks and the costumes of the Conquest dances strive to give a somewhat accurate picture of Pre-Hispanic Indian dress, these representations are by no means absolutely authentic, nor do they derive directly from the indigenous culture. As pointed out by Irene and Arturo Warman in *El efímero y eterno del arte popular mexicano* (1971, 2:743), the Conquest dances probably derived from the Dance of the Moors and Christians during the eighteenth and nineteenth centuries.

Despite the lack of authenticity, these dances do provide Mexicans an opportunity to develop a positive image of their Indian past by showing it as a "golden age." Further, they serve as an expression of the hostility that was and is felt toward the Spanish conquerors and rulers, a hostility that can be easily seen by comparing the masks and the costumes of the Indian warriors to those of the Spaniards. Almost invariably, the Indian costumes are beautiful and dignified, while those of the Spaniards are ugly, ill fitting, and without taste. In fact, the only positive aspect of the Spanish that is presented in most of these dances is that they brought Christianity to the New World.

Battle of the Fifth of May. A second important historical "dance" (in this case, actually a re-enactment rather than a dance) is La Batalla del Cinco de Mayo (The Battle of the Fifth of May). May 5 is the anniversary of the Mexican army's victory over the French at Puebla in 1862. The Battle of the Fifth of May is performed in the city of Puebla on this date by the Mexican Ministry of War and in the villages around Puebla by the villagers themselves on various dates. Since 1920, it has also been presented in Peñon, an old Aztec village that is now part of Mexico City, because these villagers saw the performance, liked it, and decided to enact it.

While May 5 is a national holiday, its celebration is especially emphasized in the Puebla area, with the more interesting enactments taking place in the smaller villages, such as Huejotzingo. All of the Battles of the Fifth of May involve semihistoric costumes and masks of the French soldiers (Soldados Zuaves or Franceses), the Mexican Indian forces (Zacapoaxtlas), the regular Mexican army troops (Chinacos), the armed citizens, and numerous historical generals. Particularly in the smaller towns, the participants who represent the Zuaves and the Zacapoaxtlas are masked and have beautiful, imaginative costumes. The performance of the battle itself is a fairly accurate recreation of this famous and well-documented conflict. Masks for this dance are shown in Figs. 64 and 91.

Christian Dances

When the first Spanish friars arrived in Mexico with Cortés, they were confronted with a vast pagan world with its own complex religious system rooted in shamanism and human sacrifice. Theirs was a holy crusade to convert the In-

278. Malinche mask, probably Malinche Dance. This is a particularly lifelike Malinche, especially considering the difficult medium of copper in which it is worked. (See Fig. 157 for another treatment of copper.) The projections with circles in the center below the chin and above the forehead are Pre-Columbian butterfly symbols (see Figs. 259–260). *Region of Altamirano, Guerrero (Nahua); 51 cm., from tip of horns to bottom of chin ornaments; copper, human hair, deer antlers, ribbons.* II.A.C.

280. Moor mask, Dance of the Moors and Christians. This sad-faced Moor dates from 1915–1940 and is in a simple, expressive style no longer seen today. The face is boldly carved, with a movable jaw that contains a stationary tongue attached to the lower lip. Distinctive of the style are the bloody slash wounds and the shape of the eyes and brows. The mask shows great wear, especially in the holes used to attach it to the dancer's head, where the string has worn away the wood. The interior shows some termite damage. At times the Dance of the Moors and Christians is still seen before the great churches of Taxco, the dancers traveling many miles from their settlements to perform and do homage in this way. *Region of Taxco, Guerrero (Nahua); height with jaw open: 43 cm.; depth, from earlobe to tip of nose: 29.2 cm.; wood (zompantle), paint.* I.A.C.

279. Possibly Moor mask, Dance of the Moors and Christians. This mask of very hard wood may be more than two hundred years old. The cord used for securing the mask is of carefully twisted handwoven cloth that was identified by Dr. Junius Bird as work from the eighteenth or nineteenth century. The paint, which was applied without undercoat, is now very thin. *Chiepetepec, Guerrero (Tlapanec); 24.2 cm.; wood, paint.* I.A.C.

281. Dance of the Moors and Christians. The dance pictured here was performed in honor of the Virgin of Guadalupe. The dancer on the left wears a strongly carved Moor mask and a crescent of paper and ribbons. Beside him stands another "pagan" character with a large hat and mask. The Church of Guadalupe, where this scene took place, stands on a high hill overlooking the town of Iguala. *Iguala, Guerrero, December 12, 1970. (Left mask)* I.B.C. *(Right mask)* I.A.C.

282. Moor masks, Dance of the Moors and Christians. The style of these sensitive faces, with their narrow heads, long noses and upper lips, and prominent cheekbones, comprised an entire school of fine Guerrero masks around the turn of this century. The Barbones masks in Fig. 32 also fall into this school. Unusual are the tall leather caps with their leather streamers and the combination of blue eyes and dark complexion seen in mask *b*. Mask *b* from Collections of the International Folk Art Foundation in the Museum of International Folk Art, Santa Fe, New Mexico. *Region of Alahuistlán, Guerrero; 57 cm. (approx.), including cap; wood, paint, leather.* I.A.C.

283. Morismo mask, Dance of the Moors and Christians (variant). This freely conceived Moor mask has great charm in its very human and humorous expression. Unpliable wood has been worked with great talent into repeating and reversing half-moons to form flesh and muscle forms that are very much alive and indicative of the diversity of expression that the talented Mexican mask-makers achieve. Property of the University of Arizona. *Teponzontepec, state of Mexico; 25.4 cm.; wood, paint.* I.A.C.

dians to Christianity and to eliminate "Devil worship." One of the ways that they accomplished this was through the introduction of dances and plays with a Christian theme used as a teaching device. This was already a standard teaching method in Europe for illiterate peasants, but it also had extra advantages in Mexico. As mentioned in the section on Devil masks (Chapter 9), this allowed the friars an opportunity to denigrate the Indian gods by transforming their masks into Devil masks simply by adding two horns. Further, the Indians already had a deep-rooted dance festival tradition; by continuing this tradition with Christian themes rather than trying to suppress it, the Church was more easily able to become the center of community life and to maintain a positive image (Leonard 1959, p. 118).

Dance of the Moors and Christians. Probably, the first Christian dance introduced into Mexico was the Dance of the Moors and Christians. The first record of the dance was in 1524, when it was presented to Cortés in Coatzacoalcos. References to this dance are scattered throughout the early Spanish records. The dance was performed at most of the important civil and religious ceremonies in the first two centuries of the Colonial era (Warman Gryj and Warman 1971, 2: 747).

Part of the reason for the obvious popularity of this dance, both then and now, lies in its central theme: the dramatic confrontation between good, represented by the Christians, and evil, embodied in the heathen Moors. It was through the struggle of good and evil that this dance was raised from just another Church pageant to an involving drama for Spaniards and Indians alike. One must also remember that the Moors had been expelled from Spain a scant thirty years before the Conquest of Mexico after seven centuries of war. The theme was fresh and historically important in the minds of the Spanish priests; moreover, it was duplicated by the situation that they found in Mexico, with only the names of the pagan idolators changed. The Church, particularly the Spanish branch, was once again engaged in a holy crusade that was epitomized by this dance.

Today, the Dance of the Moors and Christians is more than just one dance; it is an entire group of dances that are performed throughout Mexico, Central America, many countries in South America, New Mexico in the United States, and even the Philippines. In Mexico, its variants include the Dances of El Marquez, Los Santiagos, Las Moritas, Los Alchileos, Los Matachines, Los Tastoanes, Los Doce Pares de Francia, and many others. (Many variants are described in Warman Gryj 1972, pp. 138–165.) Its pageantry and dramatic conflict have also influenced a great number of other dances. And, what is most important within the context of this book, the splendor of this dance, with its representations of kings, sultans, nobility, and exotic foreigners, has provided an environment in which the tremendous plastic talent of Mexican craftsmen and artists could blossom into a profusion of beautiful masks and costumes.

There is also a Dance of the Female Moors (Las Moritas) in Axochiapan, Morelos, which we witnessed in January 1974. The Female Moors were dressed in red satin capes and did not wear masks. Only the King of the Moors and the King of the Christians wore masks.

Another radical variation in the Moor masks is in those made for the Dance of Los Alchileos (the archers). These are large, very impressive helmet masks with high, usually elaborate headdresses carved from wood. The style of these masks seems to vary according to the individual mask-maker more than the styles of other types of Moor masks. Fig. 286 shows two Alchileo masks from San Martín Pachivia, Guerrero. There is an enormous difference between these masks and the one from Cacalotepec, Guerrero (Fig. 287), which seems surrealistic by comparison.

The dance normally begins with the encounter between the Moors' army and that of the Christians. Ambassadors from these two armies meet and hold a long discussion about the superiority of the Virgin versus Mohammed. This theological discussion soon results in individual combat with swords or machetes between the ambassadors, ending with one being conquered and seized. The other side sends knights to get back its ambassador, with a general fight between the two armies soon resulting. After these armies have confronted each other once or a number of times, the Christians are victorious, thanks to the intervention of an angel or a saint in the midst of the battle. After this, either the Moors are convinced of their idolatry and convert to Christianity or they are killed by the Christians. Often the grand finale is the burning of the fort of the Moors in a brilliant "fire" made of crepe paper, red paint, etc. In the past, the entire dance was done on horseback, but it is most often done on foot today.

The Santiago or Santiaguero Dance is a variant of the dance of the Moors and Christians that is also closely related to the dances of the Conquest. Santiago (St. James) was the patron saint of Cortés's army, and several visions of him were seen in the sky before decisive battles between the Spanish and the Indians, so that his name became a battle cry that led the Spaniards to victory. One of the most distinctive features of this dance is that Santiago wears a small wooden horse which is attached in front (and sometimes also in the rear) of the dancer's waist, as can be seen in Fig. 197. Santiago carries a lance and is better dressed than the other Christian soldiers. In some cases, Santiago fights the Moors, sometimes the Turks; at other times, he seems to fight all the famous heathens of history, including Cain, Pontius Pilate, etc. The ambassadors play the same role described above. The resulting fight is won by the Christians, and the heathen ruler is made to accept Christianity.

Pastorela Dance.   After the Dance of the Moors and Christians with all of its variations, the second important Christian dance is the Pastorela Dance, or Nativity pastoral. This is one of the few dances in Mexico which is predominantly for girls or women. The Pastorela or Las Pastoras originally came from the popular theater and its concern with the Nativity story. One of the parts of this theatrical presentation was the adoration of the baby Jesus, which was danced. The present Pastorela is either a direct re-enactment of this theatrical scene, or a slight modification of it with different music.

284. Moro Chino mask, Dance of the Moors and Christians. This classic red Moro Chino has the brow and cheek projections seen in all Moro Chino masks (Fig. 42). The face is fierce, as a combat mask should be, with large blue eyes and a mouth over-full of carved white teeth. Property of the University of Arizona. *Mochitlán, Guerrero (Nahua); 17.8 cm.; wood (zompantle), paint.* I.B.C.

285. Moro Pasión (Suffering Moor) mask, Dance of the Moors and Christians (variant). In many cases I have seen masks of clearly traditional form whose original meaning has been lost. This mask has two such elements, the most prominent being the coiled nose. I feel that this type of nose at one time represented the maxillae or proboscis of a butterfly, a form often used in sixteenth- to eighteenth-century Mexico. The butterfly was a common symbol for Xochiquetzal, the goddess of flowers and beauty (see Fig. 260*d*). The gold protrusions seen above the brows and on either cheek remain a mystery, although they continue to appear on the red Moro Chino masks of Guerrero. This mask is old and well executed, with thin eye slits above the painted eyes. Characteristic of Puebla masks are the thin carving and the deep indentation for the dancer's face. *State of Puebla; height: 30 cm.; depth: 25 cm.; wood, paint.* II.A.C.

286. Alchileo (or Archareo) masks, Dance of the Moors and Christians. Although simpler and more primitive in design, these two helmet masks come from the same area that produced the masks in Fig. 138. The Alchileo character represents a pagan soldier who fights on the side of the Moors against the Christians in this ancient dance of Spanish origin (Santamaría 1959, p. 53). Mask *a* property of the Smithsonian Institution. *San Martín Pachivia, Guerrero (Nahua); (a) 57 cm.; (b) 50 cm.; wood, paint, gold leaf.* I.A.C.

287. Alchileo mask, Dance of the Moors and Christians (variant). This interesting Alchileo and a companion mask, not seen here, may be simplified survival versions of the Tigre and the Eagle, two other foes of the Christians in other dances. In this variation of the Dance of the Moors and Christians, the Alchileo characters fight with Pilate and the Moors against the eventually victorious Santiago. This small mask is topped by a headdress with what may be an eagle, while the headdress of the mask not pictured here is surmounted by a *tigre*. This is a very different interpretation from that of the older Alchileo masks from a different area of Guerrero shown in Fig. 286. *Cacalotepec, Guerrero (Nahua); 14–15 cm., not including headdress; 45 cm., including headdress.* II.B.C.

288. Santiago mask, Santiago Dance (Dance of the Moors and Christians variant). An unusually fine old Santiago with a movable jaw attached with wooden pegs. It was made in Guerrero near the border of the state of Mexico, and the distinctive style was copied there for many years. Christians were commonly conceived as blond and blue-eyed, as is this mask, to contrast well with the black-bearded Moors also depicted in these combat dances. *Cacahuamanche, Guerrero (Nahua); 29 cm.; wood, paint (oil).* I.A.C.

289. Hermit mask, Pastorela Dance. This crude Hermit relates in style and materials to the more sophisticated Hermit seen in Fig. 155*b*. The use of crude materials such as undyed fiber and the woeful expression create a similar effect, although the masks were made in different areas. *State of Durango; 27 cm., not including beard; wood, ixtle fiber.* I.A.C.

290. Hermit mask, Pastorela Dance. This charming Hermit shows great individuality of style, with its small, cut-out eyes and open-mouthed smile. The long, pointed nose contrasts with the characteristically low Indian forehead. Designs carved into the beard and facial planes give the mask both movement and character. *Michoacán (Tarascan); 37 cm.; wood, paint.* I.B.C.

292. Devil mask, Dance of the Tres Potencias. Used in an allegorical dance imported from Europe depicting the struggle between the soul and sin, this Devil has a mouth that suggests the idea of a bloodsucking bat. The bat nose and the circular treatment of the mouth and chin are unique to this region, in contrast to the fusion of bat spirit styles found elsewhere. The thin dark red color is accented by the black of the horns and goatee, while yellow is used for the tusks and in small touches on the nose. *Region of Cañón de Gavilán, Guerrero (Nahua); 39 cm.; wood, paint.* II.B.C.

291. Angel mask, Pastorela Dance. This rather saccharine winged Angel is typical of the nineteenth-century church figures and reminiscent of a popular art imitation of the seventeenth-century Spanish artist Murillo. Such delicate, small features are rarely seen today. This mask, from the state of Puebla, probably comes from a rural area, as it is not finely finished or painted and the inside was left quite rough. The Angel has the traditionally small ears and dimples usually found on the few masks of female characters made in Mexico. The state of Puebla, with its magnificent capital city, Puebla de los Angeles, is a traditionally strong center for the Catholic Church in Mexico. Property of the University of Arizona. *State of Puebla; height: 26.7 cm.; width: 26.7 cm.; wood (zompantle), paint (oil base with gesso undercoat).* II.A.C.

In this dance, the girls or women playing the parts of the Shepherds are dressed very simply and generally do not wear masks. Masks are used in some versions but are usually restricted to Devil and Hermit figures, who are generally played by men. Examples of Hermit masks can be found in Figs. 7, 60, 139, 155*b*, 173, 289, and 290. An Angel mask used in the Pastorela in the state of Puebla can be seen in Fig. 291. In Figs. 56 and 57 we see two very rare female Pastorela masks. Devil masks used in this dance are shown in Figs. 307 and 312.

Dance of the Tres Potencias. While the Pastorela is a loose, flowing adaptation of a dance-play, the last major Christian dance to be discussed, that of the Tres Potencias (Three Powers), is far more formal and fixed. This dance has a written text for the spoken passages, as the Dances of the Moors and Christians do in many cases. The Dance of the Tres Potencias is performed predominantly in Guerrero, and the written text, which is called the *relaciones*, is still in Nahuatl in some of the remote mountain villages, since Nahuatl is still the basic language of at least the elders of the community. The dance-play is based on a morality play imported from Europe but has grown to include typical Mexican touches.

The theme of the Tres Potencias is the struggle for supremacy between good and evil. An elaborate version may have many masked participants, such as Christ, the Virgin, the Soul, the Flesh, the World, the Devil, Sin, Lucifer, Death, and one or more comic characters. Lucifer and Sin dance with Death. The speeches are long, and the dance-play ends with a great physical struggle. The Soul is finally victorious and is symbolically lifted toward heaven, as Sin, Lucifer, and the Devil meet defeat and are burned. Fig. 34 shows a Devil mask that was used in this dance in Acapetlahuaya, Guerrero. It should be compared to the Devil mask from the region of Cañón de Gavilán, Guerrero, in Fig. 292. Other masks used in the dance are shown in Figs. 200*a* and 293.

Occupational Dances.

The third category of dance themes is occupational. These dances fulfill a two-pronged social function. First, they show the duties, attitudes, and skills needed for certain jobs, and thus function as teaching aids for the community and its children. Second and more important, they extend social recognition to those who work at these jobs, thereby stressing their importance to the community. Some of the dances that use masks include the Vaquero (see below), Hortelaños (Fig. 165), and Jardineros (Figs. 169, 170) dances. To some degree the Tlacololero Dance must also be considered an occupational dance, but, since its main action centers on the pursuit and capture of the Tigre, it is discussed with the Tigre dances (below).

Vaquero Dance. The Vaquero (Cowboy) Dance is a good example of an occupational dance. While it can vary from pure choreography to a semidramatic structure, there is one scene that is common to all versions: the capture of a bull. Today the bull is a counterfeit one that is carried on the shoulders of one of the dancers, but in the past, some versions used a real bull that was captured and

293. Time-Sin-Death mask, Dance of the Tres Potencias. There is a startling rhythm of form in this carving. The pink center face with its twisted mouth represents Sin, who is flanked on the cheeks by a skull-headed Death and the brown face of Time. Unfortunately, the name of the artist who made this mask is no longer known. From the collection of Larry Walsh. *Copalillo, Guerrero (Nahua); 31 cm.; wood, paint.* I.B.D.

killed. The most widespread version of the dance consists of a group of sixteen dancers who are divided into two groups, each with its own captain. These captains establish a merry dialogue, while at the same time performing tactical movements with their men. Finally, the bull is captured. A more complex version has a number of other characters, including the Mayordomo. These characters perform a short drama in which the quality of animals in various locations is discussed. This version shares the same climax of the capture of the bull. This dance is principally presented in the states of Morelos, Puebla, and Guerrero. Vaquero masks can be seen in Figs. 294 and 295.

Nature-Related Dances

As mentioned in Chapters 8 and 9, the mask and the masked dance were devices that man in primitive conditions used in order to identify with and attempt to control the forces of nature. It is then no surprise that a great number of masked dances still center around the weather, crops, hunting, and fishing, particularly in more remote locations where people still depend on old methods of farming and hunting for their survival. These are the dances whose roots descend into Pre-Hispanic history and in which the ancient gods still survive, however fragmented and incomplete that survival may be.

Some of the more important nature dances include the Tigre dances, which center around the capture and the death of a *tigre*; the Diablo Macho Dance, a rain-petitioning dance (Figs. 15, 17); the Armadillo Dance, a crop-fertility dance that uses masks trimmed with armadillo hide (Figs. 195, 233, 236–237) and a large wooden Armadillo (Figs. 234, 235); the Fish and Caimán dances, both intended to ensure good fishing (see below); and literally hundreds of others.

Many of these dances have been described briefly in various places in the text because their performances shed light on mask symbols. However, those descriptions centered on symbolic relationships and were often incomplete. I am therefore including here a short synopsis of a few of the more important nature dances.

Tigre Dances. This is a set of related dances which are performed throughout Mexico and are known under many different names. One variant is the Tecuani Dance; *tecuani* means "wild beast" in Nahuatl and refers to the Tigre. Fernando Horcasitas informs me that the Tecuani Dance is one of the few Pre-Hispanic "farsas" (as Durán calls them) that have survived. Another important variant is the Tlacololero Dance, in which the Tigre appears as a menace who has been harming the field workers (Tlacololeros). Normally, these dances are fairly complex, with a large number of characters and set speeches; consequently, they are usually run by a "maestro" (teacher, master of the dance), who trains the dancers, gives them cues, and possesses the written script for the dance. The maestro is very often the musician: in the case of the Tecuani Dance, he plays a small drum and bamboo flute. In addition to the Tigre, the cast of characters can include one or more of the following: a Rastrero (Tracker); a Dog, who is named Maravilla or "Marvel" in many of these dances; a Deer; a Medic to

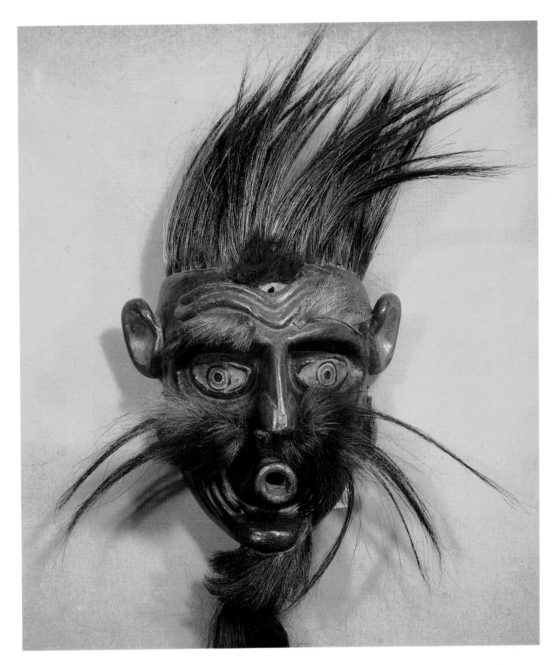

294. Vaquero mask, Vaquero Dance. The round, "whistling" mouth is typical of many Vaquero masks, indicating the Vaquero's calling and whistling for the cattle. A similar round mouth is sometimes found in Pre-Columbian clay figurines; its meaning there is unknown. The deep carving and somber painting of this fine mask are unusual. The eyes are deepset, and there is a see-out opening above the brow. *Zacatlanzillo, Guerrero; 24 cm., not including hair or beard; wood, paint, horsehair.* I.B.C.

296. River Spirit mask, Fish Dance. Used in a plea for good fishing, this old mask combines strong carving and water symbolism in the form of color, symbolic creatures, and facial expression. The fish-shaped eyebrows and beard and the human face are reminiscent of the Greek sea-god Neptune. *San Martín Pachivia, Guerrero (Nahua); 27 cm.; wood, paint.* II.A.C.

295. Vaquero mask, Vaquero Dance. This Vaquero also has the typical round mouth. Lines carved and painted about the face and the trim of black horsehair make a simple yet forceful statement. Property of the Smithsonian Institution. *Tlacuitlapa, Guerrero (Nahua); 24 cm.; wood, paint, horsehair.* I.B.C.

patch up the "wounded"; men who carry spears and cords to tie up the Tigre; and a man who dresses up as a woman and who is regarded as a comic figure. The masks for these characters can be made out of wood, as in Figs. 299 and 300, or leather, as in Figs. 2 and 238–239. There is tremendous freedom in the execution of these masks, as can be seen by comparing the Rastrero of El Portrerillo, Guerrero, in Fig. 2 to the one from Ajuchitlán, Guerrero, in Fig. 300 or to the same figure from Chalpatlahua, Guerrero, in Fig. 299.

The Tlacololero Dance, whose central action (like that of all the tigre dances) involves tracking down and finally "killing" the Tigre, has a direct connection to crop fertility that is often missing in the other dances. Here, the masked Tlacololeros (Field Workers), along with the Rastrero, who sometimes wears a twisted-mouth mask, the Dog Maravilla, and various other characters, start hunting the Tigre. Normally, the Tlacololero dancers wear wide-brimmed straw hats that are adorned with herbage, palms, and flowers. They carry whips (which usually symbolize serpents) or sometimes even chains, and hit each other on their padded left arms to simulate the crackling of burning brush and tree trunks. (The term *tlacololero* specifically refers to a man who prepares the land for cultivation in the slash-and-burn method.) Some of these dancers also hold dried badgers, raccoons, and other animals that symbolize the fertility of the soil. Characteristically, there is quite a bit of horse-play and vulgar humor in which local scandals and peoples' weaknesses are referred to before the Tigre is found. Toward the end of the dance, the whole column of dancers follows the Dog character, which flushes the Tigre out of the bushes. When the Tigre comes into sight, there are wild skirmishes, and one or two people are "wounded" before the Tigre is killed and skinned. Masks for the Tlacololero Dance are shown in Figs. 216 and 301.

Fish Dance, Caimán Dance. The Fish Dance is sometimes done in combination with the Caimán Dance. Both dances use sympathetic magic to ensure good fishing and are performed along the Balsas River and other rivers in Guerrero. In one version, there are from fourteen to twenty Fishermen who carry nets; they also attach bunches of carved wooden fish around their waists or shoulders; these clank together as noisemakers and provide accompaniment (Fig. 303*a*). Two drums are also used: the *teponaztli*, a horizontal two-tone wooden drum, and the *huehuetl*, a vertical drum. In some villages, a small, primitive harp is played along with the violin.

In addition to masked characters, these dances have characters who wear wooden figures fastened to their waists. In Tula, Guerrero, a young boy wears a Caimán figure in this way (Fig. 303*c*); a Caimán figure from Totozintla appears in Fig. 243. In Tetela del Río the Fish Dance also contains a large Mermaid figure (Fig. 303*b*). Other animals are sometimes used as well. These characters, along with other small boys wearing fish around their waists, try to escape the Fishermen and their nets. After a great deal of cavorting about, the fish are caught, and good fishing is assured. Other masks for the Fish and Caimán dances can been seen in Figs. 20*a*, 58, 187, 199, 213, 214, 247, 263, 296, and 302.

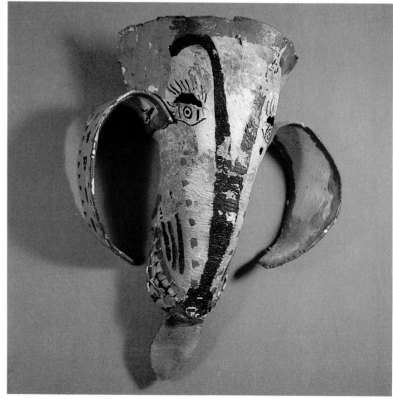

297. Tigre mask, Tigre Dance. This very large old mask has seen long use and has been repainted many times. In spite of the enormous mouth there are slits beneath the eyes for the dancer to see out, as the mouth comes to chin level when the mask is tipped forward to be worn. Collections of the International Folk Art Foundation in the Museum of International Folk Art, Santa Fe, New Mexico. *San Simón (near Acapetlahuaya), Guerrero (Nahua); height: 30 cm.; width: 36 cm.; length: 38 cm. (as positioned in photograph); wood, paint, animal teeth.* IV.B.C.

298. Tigre mask, Tigre Dance. In contrast to the obvious feline in Fig. 297 is this unique conception of a Tigre. The use of leather for a Tigre mask is quite rare, as they are most often fashioned out of wood, copper, or papier mâché. From the collection of Raúl Lozano Martini. *State of Mexico; 25 cm.; leather, paint.* IV.B.C.

299. Rastrero mask, Tecuani Dance. This mask, by a talented but untrained carver, was probably made for his own use. The carving is fairly realistic, but simplified and stylized. The thick white paint is now very worn. The animal hair is attached to the mask under pieces of leather that are nailed to the wood. *Chalpatlahua, Guerrero (Nahua); 16.5 cm.; wood (zompantle), paint (water base), animal hair, leather, nails.* I.B.C.

301. Tlacololero mask, Tlacololero Dance.
The round eyeholes on the cheeks are typical
of masks of this dance. An unusual feature of
this mask is the smooth tongue, made from a
piece of glass that was probably found in a
river and may be the remains of a bottle.
*Ayutla, Guerrero (Nahua); 29 cm.; wood,
paint, glass.* I.A.C.

300. Rastrero mask, Tecuani Dance. This is
another Rastrero from the popular Tecuani
Dance performed widely in Guerrero villages.
Made of heavy wood, this mask has a suitably
wild aspect. The eyes of the mask are quite
inconspicuous, but the eye slits are distinctively carved rectangles that reinforce the purpose of the Rastrero character—tracking and
killing the clever and illusive Tigre. Property
of the University of Arizona. *Ajuchitlán,
Guerrero (Nahua); 26 cm.; wood, paint, animal hair, animal teeth.* I.B.C.

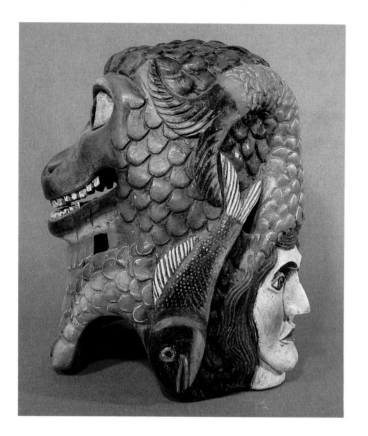

302. Caimán/Mermaid mask, Fish Dance. There is a theory that these very heavy helmet masks served as a motif or inspiration for a given dance. They were placed on the ground or on some elevated area and were worn only briefly during the dance. This fine helmet is thoughtfully carved to fit the dancer's shoulders. There are ample eyeholes on the Mermaid side next to the fish tails. At approximately the same elevation the dancer could look out of the Caimán mouth on the other side. *Tetela del Río, Guerrero; height: 48 cm.; circumference: 115 cm.; wood, paint. (Left)* IV.B.C *(Right)* II.A.D.

303. Accessories for Fish Dance and Caimán Dance. The Mermaid seen here (*b*) was meant to be worn by a small boy in the Fish Dance in Tetela del Río, Guerrero, the only community where these Mermaids are carved. Its arms are movable. The Caimán (*c*) was also made to be worn about the waist of a small boy. Its back is covered with pochote spines, and there are two heads projecting from it. In front of the body opening is an Old Man of the River figure. The third accessory (*a*) is a string of fish which was worn about the dancer's neck and used as a noisemaker during the dance. Fish and Mermaid property of the University of Arizona. *(a) Totozintla, Guerrero (Nahua); (b) Tetela del Río, Guerrero (Nahua); (c) Tula, Guerrero (Nahua); (a) each fish: 27 cm.; (b) 95 cm., from tip of tail to tip of nose; (c) 101 cm.; wood, paint, cloth undercoat (b). (a)* IV.A.C. *(b)* II.A.C. *(c)* V.A.C.

Feria Regional de Corpus

en Papantla, Ver., durante los días del 31 de mayo al 10 de junio de 1945

La H. Junta de Mejoras Materiales de Papantla, Ver., ha organizado para los días del 31 de mayo al 10 de junio próximos un sugestivo programa de festejos que le harán muy grata e inolvidable su visita, y le darán la oportunidad de admirar sus famosas danzas, sus ruinas arqueológicas del Tajín y sus bailes con sabor del trópico.

Programa de los principales atractivos:

DANZAS REGIONALES: Negritos, Moros y Españoles, Santiagos, Tocotines, Guaguas, en el peligroso acto del volteador o sea el Salto de la Muerte, la ya FAMOSA y conocida MUNDIALMENTE del PALO VOLADOR, en la que figura el "AS" de esta Danza JOSÉ GARCIA LOZANO, único en la región que sobre un mástil de 30 metros de altura y cuya coronación mide 30 centímetros de diámetro, ejecuta su atrevido baile, tocando al mismo tiempo un tambor y una flauta, haciendo escalofriantes contorsiones y peligrosos saltos.

Carreras de Caballos, -- TAPADAS DE GALLOS

y toda clase de juegos permitidos por la Ley.

Foot ball, Basket ball y Base ball,

entre los mejores Equipos de Poza Rica, Gutiérrez Zamora, Alamo y de esta localidad, se llevarán a cabo en el "Campo Deportivo Papanteco" y en la Cancha de la Escuela "Melchor Ocampo".

GRANDES Y SUNTUOSOS BAILES

diariamente en el Parque "Constitución" y en el Salón "Recreativo Papanteco", amenizados por Orquestas foráneas y locales.

Diariamente se quemarán vistosos Fuegos Artificiales, sin faltar los típicos Toritos

EL DOMINGO 10 DE JUNIO para cerrar con broche de oro esta Feria, se verificará la

"La Noche Totonaca"

a la que asistirán ataviadas con el Traje Regional Totonaco antiguo y moderno, las más bellas señoritas de la localidad, que se disputarán dos premios:

1o. – Para la que se presente vestida con MAYOR PROPIEDAD a la usanza ANTIGUA.
2o. – Para la que imite mejor a la INDIA TOTONACA ACTUAL.

Nota:–Un Jurado Calificador compuesto por personas bien documentadas, otorgará los premios a quienes lo merezcan.

PAPANTLA, la tierra hospitalaria por excelencia ESPERA SU VISITA.

Papantla, Ver., mayo de 1945   LA COMISION

304. Announcement of Regional Fair of Corpus Christi. *Papantla, Veracruz, 1945.*

Deer Dance (Yaqui and Mayo).   Thanks to the Ballet Folklórico of Mexico, the Deer Dance is probably the best-known of all the nature dances in Mexico. An excellent description has been given by James S. Griffith:

> *In its aboriginal form as performed today, it involves a single deer imper-*
> *sonator and three or four singers. One of these plays the water drum and*
> *the others play rasps. The deer is frequently bare to the waist, and wears*
> *a skirt made from a rebozo (a woman's shawl). Upon his head is strapped*
> *a small deer head, complete with antlers. He has a belt of pendant deer*
> *hooves about his waist and cocoon rattles on his legs, and he holds a*
> *gourd rattle in each hand. His dance is highly imitative of the actions of a*
> *deer, grazing, drinking, pausing to sniff the air, and fleeing. The songs to*
> *which he dances usually contain references to flowers*
> (Griffith 1967, p. 16).

The Deer dancers wear the same type of rattles on their legs as the Pascola dancers (Fig. 123); the Pascola dancers often help to clear the area for the Deer dancers and keep the crowd entertained.

Entertainment-Oriented Dances.

As I have pointed out throughout the discussion of the social entertainment functions of masked dances, each dance has a component of entertainment no matter how serious the basic purpose of the dance is. But there are also some dances whose predominant theme is entertainment. These vary from comedies to dramatic presentations similar to soap operas, as in the case of "Los Manueles" (Fig. 305). Some of these, such as the Viejitos Dance of Michoacán, probably had a serious purpose at one time, but that purpose has been lost, suppressed, or forgotten. Other dances, like that of the Negritos, are comic in one region and very serious in another. Further, as the rapid acculturation of Mexican Indian groups occurs, I fully expect that many of the serious dances of today will be reduced to mere entertainment in the near future, if they survive at all. Consequently, because of the wide range of dances that can be considered to be in this category and because the purpose of this section is only to provide a basic understanding of the context in which masks are used, I will only describe the major and the more famous of these dances: those of the Devils, Muertos, Viejitos, and Negritos.

Devil Dances.   The Dance of the Devils (los Diablos) is both a dance in its own right and, at the same time, a concept, an institution that appears in almost every other dance in Mexico. In Mexico, the Devil is more than just a symbol for sin and evil; he is the clown who pulls pranks, tells vulgar jokes, makes obscene gestures, and keeps everyone generally amused. The Devil shows up in dances such as Los Concheros (one of the Conquest dances), the Pastorela Dance, the Tigre dances, etc. He provides the counterpoint to these dances, relieving the tensions that build up in some of the more combative dances and in the com-

305. Masks for "Los Manueles," a village drama. These masks were used to enact a family drama involving a village girl who is falsely betrothed to a Novio (boyfriend or bridegroom). The girl is jilted, and the rightful Novia (girlfriend or bride) wins the young man instead. The story ends happily after much squabbling among the elders of the family. It is a realistic example of the power of the family in Mexico. All of these masks are well carved and carefully painted for maximum dramatic effect. The entire set is seen here: (*a*) the Grandfather of the Novia; (*b*) the Jilted Girl; (*c*) the Mother of the Jilted Girl; (*d*) the Father of the Novia; (*e*) the Mother of the Novio; (*f*) the Novio; and (*g*) the Novia. Property of the University of Arizona. *Zoquiapan, Guerrero (Nahua); 19 cm. (approx.); wood, paint (oil), gesso, animal hair (a).* I.A.C.

307. Two dancers in Devil masks for the Pastorela Dance. *Cherán, Michoacán, 1935 (Tarascan).*

306. Devil mask, Dance of the Devils. This Devil is said to have traveled annually from Huetamo to Corovillas, Michoacán, to perform for the festival of La Purísima (December 8). It has three sets of horns, a carved devil-creature nose, and a long leather tongue. It is possible that this mask was made in Teloloápan, Guerrero, although used in Huetamo, Michoacán. *Huetamo, Michoacán (Tarascan); 60 cm., including horns; wood, paint, animal horns, leather, sheepskin, pieces of bone.* IV.B.D.

munity at large. He can talk about peoples' weaknesses and local scandals with immunity, for whatever he says will be dismissed because it comes from the Devil.

This basic tradition is also reflected in the various Devil dances themselves. One such dance is performed during the Carnival in Zaachila, Oaxaca, and takes the form of a battle between the Devils and the Priests, with the Devils winning:

> *The costumes and masks are extraordinarily imaginative. A green devil may be covered with brilliant bits of china paper, so that his costume is reminiscent of the ancient warriors. The devils present a kaleidoscope of bright solid colors which shine and alternate with the black cassocks of the priests and their white masks, pointed black hoods, and enormous rosaries.*
>
> *The devils fight with long canes, at one end of which are standards of perfect geometrical forms, painted in bright colors and adorned with shells. They jump and dance about as they attack the priests, who defend themselves with whips, sticks, and lances. The fights become heated, the combatants hurling insults at each other in Zapotec. They continue until after dark, affording a beautiful spectacle of bright colors dancing in the dim torch lights and shadows of the night.*
>
> *At intervals, the devils make prisoners of some of the priests, whom they take into the presence of the head devil to be tried publicly, with the spectators joyously applauding the sentences.*
>
> *(Toor 1947, pp. 199–200)*

The Devil masks are certainly some of the most skillfully made and interestingly designed of contemporary masks. They range from traditional European Devils, like the one on the forehead of the mask in Fig. 1, to wild, animalistic Devils from indigenous traditions (Figs. 40, 248, 307, 308). As previously noted, these animal-like Devils were probably once masks of Indian gods to which the priests added horns in order to denigrate them.

Los Muertos. Los Muertos (the Dead, or the Corpses) do not usually have a dance of their own, but, like the Devils, they can and do show up in many other dances. In all the allegorical dances, such as the Dance of the Tres Potencias and the Apache Dance, Death is constantly present as a reminder of the fate awaiting all humans. Within this context, then, it may seem somewhat paradoxical to place the Muertos in the category of entertainment, but one must realize that the concept of death sometimes contains a comic element in Mexico. This is not to say that Mexicans do not respect and fear death; they simply accept it, fraternize with it, and play with it. Mexico is one of the few countries that has the Day of the Dead (El Día de los Muertos) as an official national holiday. For weeks before the Day of the Dead (November 2), toy stores are full of skeleton presents for children and bakeries specialize in trying to outdo one another in

308. Devil mask, Devil Dance. A beautifully carved and painted Indian-type animal Devil, collected in 1931. *Tixtla, Guerrero; height: 23 cm.; width: 27 cm.; wood, paint. IV.A.D.*

309. Helmet mask, Devil Dance and Bat Dance. The Death Head side of this helmet mask is in the best Pre-Columbian tradition. The features are effectively exaggerated and reminiscent of Picasso. The ears are freely painted on, and each has a small dot on the lobe indicating a hole for an earring. The other side of this helmet mask (not shown) was used in the Bat Dance. A dark bat is superimposed over and integrated into a human face, with the bat tail, which is often used by the Indians to symbolize genitalia, making up the goatee. Property of the Smithsonian Institution. *Totozintla, Guerrero (Nahua); height: 32 cm.; circumference: 104 cm.; wood, paint.* I.B.C.

baking elaborate pastries of the dead. Almost every possible article is turned into some type of skeleton, coffin, or corpse. Nor are these tame representations like the stylized skeletons of Halloween in the United States; they are graphic depictions.

Although this is not the place to explore all the interesting aspects of the Mexicans' relationship with the Dead, it is relatively easy to see that within this general context, they are considered somewhat comic figures and function as clowns, much as the Devils do. Of course, the jokes of the Dead are more of the graveyard variety. A good selection of Death masks can be seen in Fig. 47.

Viejitos Dance. The Viejitos (Little Old Men) Dance of Michoacán is one of the best known of all the masked dances in Mexico. As noted in Chapter 5, records suggest that this dance is Pre-Conquest in origin. The dance is peculiar to the Tarascan Indians near Lake Pátzcuaro and in the Sierra around Uruapan. It basically consists of young men donning masks and costumes of old men. At first, these masked dancers mimic decrepit old men by leaning on their walking sticks, shaking, and walking slowly and unsteadily; than all of a sudden they do a series of strenuous, acrobatic steps to a quick, merry tune, which is played on the *jarana*, a small stringed instrument.

A typical Viejito costume consists of a white cotton suit with long flaring trousers that are embroidered at the bottom, a tunic with a red sash tied at the side, a wide-brimmed hat, and a handkerchief around the neck. Each dancer also carries a walking stick with an animal's head carved at the handle. The masks can be seen in Fig. 311.

Dance of the Negritos. As mentioned earlier, the Dance of the Negritos (Little Negroes) (Fig. 86) can be either comic or serious depending on where it is performed. When the dance is done seriously, it probably is used as a crop-fertility dance, as I have pointed out in the section on the serpent in Chapter 9. The comic associations of the Negritos are not restricted to this dance. Negritos pop up in a number of other dances and function most often as clowns, in much the same way that Devils and Muertos do; the Negritos tend to be involved more in burlesque sexual comedy than the other two groups. One example of this can be found in the village Carnivals in the highlands of Chiapas, where the Negritos interject a very broad sexual comedy into the ritual, much to the delight and amusement of all involved.

The following description of the Dance of the Negritos from Papautla, Veracruz, was recorded by Frances Toor and is typical of the way this dance is performed in the states of Puebla and Veracruz:

> *In 1945 when I last saw this dance, there were ten men, representing field workers and a foreman similarly clad; two clowns in old torn coats and trousers and battered hats, their faces painted with black lines, dots and little snakes; a white adult Maringuilla, whose part was enacted by a man in a woman's dress, wearing a rose-colored mask. He carried a whip in one hand and in the other a gourd vessel in which a small live snake was carefully tied with handkerchiefs. The Maringuilla with the snake is part of all the Negrito dances and others of this region.*
>
> (Toor 1947, pp. 354–355).

In some cases, this is a live but harmless snake; in others, it is a wooden snake. Generally, the Negritos' roles are those of sexual jesters, making ribald remarks and gestures. Often, they too will hold wooden snakes and/or lizards and use them to make their gestures with.

The basic plot of this variation of the Dance of the Negritos involves the workers and the clowns getting mock bites from Maringuilla's snake, only to be magically cured. Some dances of this type end with the snake temporarily escaping and all of the dancers killing it; others end with the dancers weaving and unweaving ribbons around a maypole.

310. Mask for Dance of Death. This very rare mask shows great age, hard use, and loving maintenance over many years. The irregular contours, cheek projections, and eye placement are all unusual factors and are noteworthy. *Tlapa, Guerrero (Tlapanec); 24 cm.; wood (zompantle), paint.* I.B.C.

311. Masked dancers for the Viejitos Dance.
This dance has Pre-Hispanic antecedents and
continues to be the most popular Indian dance
in Michoacán. It has inspired a very lively
interpretation in the "Ballet Folklórico" by
Amalia Hernández. *Pátzcuaro, Michoacán,
1935.* I.B.C.

CONCLUSION

312. **Devil mask, Pastorela Dance.** This Devil was made by Benjamín Campos for use during the December 25 and January 1 fiestas in Ocumichu, Michoacán. Like all the folk art from this town, it has a touch of the fantastic, with its exotic red, white, and black paint. The flap of cloth that covers the dancer's head at the rear has horsehair sewn onto it. The nose is made as a hook and is seen as such in one view, whereas from another angle, one actually sees a different face—a touch of the surreal. Property of the University of Arizona. *Ocumichu, Michoacán (Tarascan); 29 cm., including horns and tongue; wood, paint, leather, horsehair, cloth.* IV.B.C.

THE MASKS OF MEXICO are an expression of the fertile artistic imagination and skill of the Mexican people. Although these highly individualistic works are not rigidly bound by traditional styles, they reveal the past, the religious beliefs, the archetypes, and the culture of their makers. As such, these masks clearly show two basic aspects of the Mexican people: the Christian face of European tradition, and the older face of an Indian world, whose miraculous survival provides a window to the past—a survival which can only be ascribed to the strength of oral tradition in remote Indian villages.

Within this Indian world, masks were a means of magical transformation where the wearer's face, personality, and even soul were replaced by those of another. In studying the symbolism within contemporary masks, we still find the faces of the older, animalistic gods of ancient Mexico, whose basic attributes were rooted in the terrible dualism of Nature. This dualism is reflected in the design of masks, in dances where there are male and female pairs of masks, and in the basic purpose of many of the masked dances themselves, as they were efforts to control the destructive aspects of Nature (and the gods) and transform them into those of abundance and fertility. However, masks cannot be viewed only in terms of religion, for as we have found, they also functioned to maintain social control within these Indian villages. Indeed, masks are an expression of the whole Mexican Indian way of life.

Today, the art of mask-making is dying, and the hidden, fragile worlds that it reflected are disappearing. Better communication, new roads and schools, and modern systems of values are destroying the isolation that allowed this art to flourish. This book, then, is an effort to preserve the symbolism and the craft of Mexican masks and to acquaint the reader with a past that has been recorded within these works of art.

254

313. Corn Spirit mask, dance unknown.
Compare the complex symbolism and sophisticated execution of this José Rodríguez mask with a simpler one of his seen in Fig. 18. Although probably made in the general area where Rodríguez usually tended his goats, this mask has traveled far and may have been painted by a *santero* mask-maker in a large town. The symbolism is in the carver's distinct style, seen often in this book, but the bearded human face is reminiscent of the sophisticated tastes of the carvings of the Ostotitlán area of Guerrero (Fig. 32). As with many Rodríguez carvings, the head is topped by a bat or devil bat. In this double image the creature's chest is clasped by two lizards that form breasts. Highly unusual are the serpents that rise above the head in the shape of cornstalks; this is one of the few masks I have seen using plant forms. Further fertility symbolism is seen in the three large snakes at the base of the mask. The expression of the open mouth of the central human character strongly suggests the mouth of the Lord of the Animals as seen, for example, in Fig. 222. *Specific area of use not known, Guerrero; 44 cm.; wood, paint.* VII.A.C.

MAPS

Map 1. Mexico. Masks from the following states are represented in this book: Chiapas, Durango, Federal District, Guanajuato, Guerrero, Hidalgo, Jalisco, Mexico, Michoacán, Morelos, Nayarit, Oaxaca, Puebla, Querétaro, San Luis Potosí, Sonora, Tlaxcala, Veracruz, and Zacatecas.

Map 2. Mask-making area of Guerrero.

APPENDIX: A SURVEY OF MASK-MAKERS

The following questionnaire was distributed to mask-makers in the states of Chiapas, Guerrero, Hidalgo, Michoacán, Oaxaca, Puebla, Querétaro, and Zacatecas, with the assistance of María Teresa Pomar and her helpers, in 1976–1977. Completed questionnaires were returned for forty-two mask-makers. The resulting information for each mask-maker is given below. See Chapters 6 and 7 for discussion of the survey's findings.

QUESTIONNAIRE

1. Name of mask-maker
   Age
2. Town
3. State
4. Languages spoken in the town
5. Was his father also a mask-maker? [omission in entries below means answer is "no"]
6. Was his grandfather also a mask-maker? [omission means answer is "no"]
7. Woods used
8. Paints used
9. Is vegetable glue used, and from which plant is it extracted?
10. Tools used
11. Dances in which masks are used
12. When masks are used
13. Other towns to which masks are sold

Chiapas

Antonio López Hernández, age 40, Chiapa de Corzo. Language: Spanish. Wood: root of the poplar tree (*raíz de álamo*). Paint: oil paint combined with mineral paints in powder (lacquer technique). Vegetable glue not used. Tools: machete, saw, compass, gouge (*gurbia*), chisel, and polishers of various sizes. Also, the esophagus of a bull is used to smooth the paint. Dance: Parachicos. Used on January 15 (Esquipulas), 17 (San Antonio Abad), 18–20 (San Sebastián martyr), 22–23. Not sold to other towns.

Guerrero

Lengino Zuluaga, age 80, Acapetlahuaya. Language: Nahuatl. Father and grandfather also mask-makers. Woods: *clabellino*, *zumpanetet* (zompantle), *palo hediondo*, *corazón de parota* (heart of conacaste), plum, copal. Paint: extracts from leaves and tree bark. Glue: oils extracted from the chia by fire. Tools: homemade provisional tools. Dances: El Marquez, Moros Chinos, Moros Pasión, Gachupines, Danza La Gila, and others. Used on first and second Fridays of Lent, March 19, August 15, December 12, and others. Sold to various towns in Guerrero.

Baldomero Mendoza, age 66, Chapa. Language: Spanish. Father not a mask-maker but was a different type of artisan; not known whether grandfather was a mask-maker. Woods: *camaroncillo*, *aguacatillo* (avocado), *zopilote*. Paint: "oil paints that they prepare themselves." Vegetable glue extracted from *cañuela* and *ixcapante*. Tools: crude homemade tools. Dance: El Marquez. Used during religious festivals. Other towns: no reply.

Santiago Martínez, age 30, Chapa. Language: Mixtec. Father-in-law also a mask-maker. Woods: plum, *aguacatillo* (a kind of avocado), *zumpanetet* (zompantle). Paints made from mineral powders. Glue: an animal substance called *cola*. Tools: provisional homemade tools. Dances: many of the dances of the region. Used during the religious festivals of various towns. Sold to various towns of the region.

Florentino Casiano, age 67 (deceased), Ocotepec. Language: Nahuatl. Father also a mask-maker. Woods: *siringuanillo*, *clabellino*, *zumpanetet* (zompantle), plum, *corazón de parota* (heart of conacaste), and others. Paint: previously vegetable paints were used, and later mixtures with *mermeyon chino*. Glue: oil of chia and other mineral substances. Tools: homemade steel tools. Dances: Moors, Gachupines, El Marquez, and others. Used for the religious festivals of the region. Sold to a few other towns in the area.

Anastacio Benítez, age 40, San Francisco Somatlán. Language: Nahuatl. Wood: zompantle. Paint: enamel and water.

Glue: Resistol only. Tools: knife, saw. Dances: masks are made for sale. When used: no reply. Other towns: no reply.

Filiberto Jenoncio Baltazar, age 28, San Francisco Somatlán. Languages: Nahuatl, Spanish. Father also a mask-maker. Wood: zompantle. Paint: enamel. Glue: Resistol only. Tools: adz, sickle, knife. Dances: no reply. When used: no reply. Other towns: no reply.

José Antonio Gabriel and wife, ages 52 and 45, Temalacatzingo. Languages: Nahuatl, Spanish. Father (of one) also a mask-maker. Woods: colorín (zompantle), *parota*. Paint: lacquer made with tecoxtle and tolte; mineral and earth paints and oil of chia (*aceite de chia*). Glue: dirt, linseed oil, oil of chia. Tools: machete, gouge (*gurbia*), chisel, knife. Dances: Tecuani, Carnival. Used on September 28 and 29, for Fiesta of San Miguel, and during Carnival. Sold to the Fondo Nacional.

Niño Romero, age 83(?) (deceased), Totozintla. Language: Nahuatl. Father also a mask-maker. Grandfather: no reply. Woods: zompantle, *sabino*. Paint: enamel. Glue: *cola*. Tools: no reply. Dances: Tigre, Costeño, Negritos. When used: no reply. Other towns: no reply.

Efrosino Romero Angeles (son), age 45, Totozintla. Language: Nahuatl. Father and grandfather also mask-makers. Wood: zompantle. Paint: enamel. Glue: *cola*. Tools: knife, chisel. Dances: Costeño, Horos. When used: no reply. Other towns: no reply.

Hidalgo

Gilberto Alvarado Flores, age 42, El Nante. Language: Otomí. Grandfather also a mask-maker. Wood: pine. Paint: oil paints and zapolin. Glue: no reply. Tools: gouge, chisel, knife. Carnival dances. Used during Carnival (March 2). Other towns: no reply.

Rodrigo Santos, age 32, San Pablo. Language: Otomí. Wood: pine. Paint: varnish and zapolin. Glue: no reply. Tools: gouge, knife, sandpaper. Carnival dances. Used during Carnival. Other towns: no reply.

Michoacán

Eliseo Alvarez Trinidad, age 50, Acachuen. Languages: Tarascan, Spanish. Woods: *cirimo*, copal, colorín (zompantle), *jaboncillo*. Paint: oil paints. Vegetable glue not used. Tools: handsaw, rasp, knife, gouge. Dances: Devils, Hermits. Used on December 24. Occasionally sold to Uruapan.

Antonio Tomás Zalpa, age 36 or 37, Ahuiran. Languages: Tarascan, Spanish. Woods: *tepamo*, *cirimo*, pine. Paint: oil paints, plaster combined with oil and paint. Vegetable glue not used; a prepared, store-bought sealer is used. Tools: handsaw, rasp, knife, gouge (*gurbia*), brush (*angarito*), chisel. Dances: Viejitos, Devils, Negritos, Hermits, Maringuilla, Figures. Used during Christmastime and on January 6, 7, and 8. Sold to Paracho, Uruapan, and Morelia. This mask-maker is director of the Dance of the Viejitos in Ahuiran, in which sombreros made of Xararen (encino) leaves are used.

Hipolito Gutiérrez, age 40, Aranza. Language: Spanish. Woods: *cirimo*, *tepamo*, and rarely avocado. Paint: enamel and oil paints. Vegetable glue not used. Tools: handsaw, gouge, knife, chisel, rasp. Dance: Pastorela. Used on December 24. Other towns: no reply.

Esteban Gutiérrez Equihua, age 29, Aranza. Language: Spanish. Woods: *tepamo*, *cirimo*. Paint: varnish and enamel. Vegetable glue not used. Tools: handsaw, gouge. Dance: Pastorela. Used on December 24 for the celebration of Christmas Eve and the Three Kings. Rarely sold to other towns.

Salvador Gaspar Pahuamba, age 32, Cherán. Languages: Tarascan, Spanish. Woods: *tepamo*, *cirimo*. Paint: oil paints and enamel. Vegetable glue not used. Tools: handsaw, rasp, gouge, knife. Dances: Pastorela, Negritos, Devils. Used on December 25. Not sold to other towns.

Soilo Sánchez Cayetano, age 35, Huancito. Languages: Tarascan, Spanish. Woods: *cirimo*, *tepamo*. Paint: oil paints. Vegetable glue not used. Tools: handsaw, rasp, knife, gouge. Dances: Viejitos, Hermits, Maringuias. Used on December 24, New Year. Other towns: no reply.

Ramón Guerrero, age 63, Nuevo San Juan Parangarieutiro. Languages: Tarascan, Spanish. Father and grandfather also mask-makers. Wood: *tepamo*. Paint: common paint, as he can no longer obtain carnation (flesh-colored tint). Vegetable glue not used. Tools: machete, gouge (*gurbia*), knife. Dances: Cúrpites, Tataquieri, Maringuilla. Used on September 4 (Festival of San Juan Nuevo), December 25, January 8. Sold at times to Uruapan.

Elías Ponce Sánchez, age 60, Pátzcuaro. Language: Spanish. Woods: *cirimo*, pine. Paint: oil paints and enamel. Vegetable glue not used. Tools: handsaw, knife, gouge, rasp. Dances: festivals of the Zona Lacustre. When used: no reply. Other towns: no reply.

Ciriaco Cruz Mendoza, age 54, San Bartolo Cuitareo. Language: Spanish. Wood: poplar. Paint: black and red enamel. Vegetable glue not used. Tools: knife, handsaw, gouge, plane. Dance: Vasallos de la Noche Buena (Vassals of Christmas Eve). Used on December 25, January 6. Sold in Paracho.

Victoriano Gómez Lazaro, age 25, Santo Tomás. Languages: Tarascan, Spanish. Woods: copal, *cirimo*, colorín (zompantle), *jaboncillo*. Paint: oil paints and *yeso* (gesso). Vegetable glue not used. Tools: handsaw, gouge, sandpaper, knife, *escofina* (rasp). Dance: Viejitos. Used on February 2 (Candlemas). Sold rarely to Uruapan.

Clemente Valencia R., age 45, Sevina. Languages: Tarascan, Spanish. Wood: *tepamo*. Paint: oil paints. Vegetable glue not used. Tools: handsaw, rasp, gouge, knife. Dances: Viejitos. Negritos. Used on December 24, New Year. Other towns: no reply.

Rogelio Valencia Valdez, age 38, Turícuaro. Languages: Tarascan, Spanish. Wood: *tepamo*. Paint: oil paints. Vegetable glue not used. Tools: handsaw, rasp, knife, gouge. Dance: Pastorela. Used on December 24, January 6. Other towns: no reply.

Alejandro Sánchez Mercado, age 32, Zacán. Language: Spanish: Woods: *cirimillo*, copal. Paint: varnish and enamel. Vegetable glue not used. Tools: handsaw, rasp, gouge, knife, sandpaper. Dance: Pastorela. Used on December 25, February 2 (Candlemas). Not sold to other towns.

Oaxaca

Elustesio Calvo Martínez, age 52, San Martín Tilcajete. Language: Zapotec. Woods: copal, zompantle, pochote, pine. Paint: anilines. Vegetable glue extracted from mesquite. Tools: chisel, gouge, machete, knife, handsaw. Carnival dances. Used in the religious festivals during Carnival. Not sold to any other towns.

Zenén Fuentes Méndez, age 50, San Martín Tilcajete. Language: Zapotec. Father and grandfather also mask-makers. Woods: copal, pine. Paint: anilines. Vegetable glue extracted from mesquite. Tools: chisel, knife, blacksmith's plane (*suela de herrero*). Dances: Negritos, Plume, Carnival dances. Used during Carnival. Not sold to other towns.

Fabian Santiago Ortega, age 44, San Martín Tilcajete. Languages: Zapotec, Spanish. Woods: ash, copal, zompantle. Paint: *puchino*. Vegetable glue extracted from mesquite. Tools: ax, chisel, knife, gouge, machete, plane (*suela*). Carnival dances. Used during Carnival. Not sold to other towns.

Isidoro Cruz Hernández, age 41, San Martín Tilcajete. Language: Zapotec. Woods: copal, zompantle, pochote, willow, *palo mulato*. Paint: anilines. Vegetable glue extracted from mesquite. Tools: plane (*suela*), chisel, knife, gouge. Dances: Carnistolenda, Plume. Used during Carnival and Holy Week. Not sold to other towns.

Marciano Ramírez Cruz, age 34, San Martín Tilcajete. Language: Zapotec. Father also a mask-maker, "150 masks (before)." Grandfather also a mask-maker. Woods: *huamúchil*, *huaje*, *sapote*, copal, willow, *cremilín*. Paint: aniline. Vegetable glue extracted from mesquite. Tools: chisel, plane (*suela*), gouge (*gurbia*), knife, *moso de medra*. Carnival dances, dances during

Holy Week. Used during Carnival (in February) and Holy Week. Sold to other towns in Oaxaca.

Margarito Melchor Fuentes, age 26, San Martín Tilcajete. Language: Zapotec. Woods: copal, pine, zompantle, pochote. Paint: anilines. Vegetable glue extracted from mesquite. Tools: ax, chisel, gouge, knife, machete, handsaw, plane (*suela*). Carnival dances, Plume Dance. Used during Carnival. Not sold to other towns.

Augustín Buey Simón, age 24, San Martín Tilcajete. Language: Zapotec. Woods: copal, pochote, *sompan*, *huamúchil*. Paint: aniline. Vegetable glue not used; Resistol is used. Tools: chisel, knife, gouge. Carnival dances. Used in February (during Carnival). Not sold to any other towns.

Justo Huana Luís, age 22, San Martín Tilcajete. Language: Spanish. Woods: copal, zompantle, willow, pochote. Paint: aniline. Vegetable glue not used; Resistol is used. Tools: machete, gouge, chisel, knife. Carnival dances. Used during Carnival. Sold to other states.

José Luna López, age 38, Santa María Huazolotitlán. Language: Mixtec. Woods: *parota* (conacaste), *tutucunyi* (white wood). Paint: enamel. Vegetable glue not used. Tools: chisel, three types of sandpaper, *barbequi* (*serote*, or saw). Dances: Tejorones, Tigre, Dog, Bull, Old Lady, Old Man, Goat, Burro. Used on Ash Wednesday. Sold to Huaspaltepec, Mechoacán, Jamiltepec (for these towns a more commercial paint called Marlux is used).

Rosalino Sánchez Simón, age 30, Santa María Huazolotitlán. Languages: Mixtec, Spanish. Father also a mask-maker. Woods: *parota* (conacaste), *tutucunyi*. Paint: enamel. Vegetable glue not used. Tools: chisel, three types of sandpaper, *barbequi*, knife. Dances for Ash Wednesday, Carnival dances, Dance of the Tejorones. Used on Ash Wednesday and during Carnival. Sold to Huaspaltepec, Mechoacán, Jamiltepec.

Puebla

Carlos Saloma Lozano, age 39, Huejotzingo. Language: Spanish. Father and grand-

father also mask-makers. Material used: bull hide. Paint: Vinilica (vinyl). Vegetable glue not used. Tools: hammer, knife, wooden mallet, mold. Dances: Franceses, Indios Apaches Cristianos. Used on Tuesday of Carnival. Sold to Tlanicontla and Tlaltenango.

Querétaro

Francisco Licea, age 75, San Bartolomé del Pino. Language: Otomí. Father also a mask-maker. Grandfather: no reply. Wood: ash. Paint: aniline. Glue: no reply. Tool: gouge. Carnival dances. Used in February, during Carnival. Other towns: no reply.

Alcadio Chávez, age 65, San Bartolomé del Pino, municipality of Ambalco. Language: Otomí. Father and grandfather: no reply. Wood: ash. Paint: oil paints. Glue: no reply. Tool: gouge. Carnival dances. Used in February and March, during Carnival. Other towns: no reply.

Zacatecas

Jo. Jesús Cuevaz, age 36, Villa García. Language: Spanish. Wood: willow. Paint: none. Vegetable glue not used. Tools: adz, gouge (*gurbia*), chisel, knife. Dance: Indios. Used on May 3 and *subida de tejas*. Sold to the Fondo del Fomento.

J. Jesús Cuevas Candelas, age 35, Villa García. Language: Spanish. Wood: willow. Paint: local paints (vinyl), oil paints. Vegetable glue not used. Tools: knife and other improvised tools. Dance: Matachines. Used on December 12. Not sold to any other town.

Pedro Morales González, age 32, Villa García. Language: Spanish. Wood: willow. Paint: Vinilica (vinyl). Vegetable glue not used. Tool: knife. Dance: Matachines. Used for the Fiesta of the Santa Cruz Fair in Villa García in December and during the Quincenario to the Virgin of the Assumption of Aguascalientes in August. Not sold to any other towns.

WORKS CONSULTED

Acosta, El P. Joseph de. 1940. *Historia natural y moral de las Indias*. Mexico City and Buenos Aires: Fondo de Cultura Económica.

Alvarado Tezozomoc, Fernando. 1944. *Crónica mexicana*. Notes by Manuel Orozco y Berra. Mexico City: Editorial Leyenda.

Amoss, Pamela. 1967. *Anales del Instituto Nacional de Antropología e Historia, vol. 18, 1965*. Mexico City: Secretaría de Educación Pública.

———. 1970. "An Art in Its Own Right." In *Americas* 22, no. 8 (August 1970). Book review of *Art of the Americas, Ancient and Hispanic*, by Pal Kelemen. Washington, D.C.: Organization of American States.

———. 1975. "The Power of the Wolf." In *Pacific Search* (April 1975).

Anders, F., ed. 1967. *Codex Tro-Cortesianus (Codex Madrid)*. Codices Selecti, edited by Francisco Sauer and Josepho Stumvoll, vol. 8. Graz, Austria: Akademische Druck-u. Verlagsanstalt.

Anton, Ferdinand, and Frederick Dockstader. 1968. *Pre-Columbian Art and Later Indian Tribal Arts*. New York: Harry N. Abrams.

Bandi, Hans-Georg. 1969. *Eskimo Prehistory*. Translated by Ann E. Keep. College, Alaska: University of Alaska Press.

Bandi, Hans-Georg, Henri Breuil, Lilo Berger-kirchner, Henri Lhote, Erik Holm, and Andreas Lommel. 1961. *The Art of the Stone Age*. Art of the World, vol. 5. London: Methuen.

Bayley, Harold. 1952. *The Lost Language of Symbolism*. 2 vols. New York: Barnes and Noble.

Beals, Ralph L. 1943. *The Aboriginal Culture of the Cahita Indians*. Berkeley and Los Angeles: University of California Press.

———. 1945. *The Contemporary Culture of the Cahita Indians*. Smithsonian Institution Bureau of American Ethnology Bulletin 142. Washington, D.C.: United States Government Printing Office.

———. 1946. *Cherán: A Sierra Tarascan Village*. Smithsonian Institution Institute of Social Anthropology Publication No. 2. Washington, D.C.: United States Government Printing Office.

Benítez, Fernando. 1968. *En la tierra mágica del peyote*. Mexico City: Ediciones Era.

Benítez, Wendell C., and Robert M. Zingg. 1935. *The Tarahumara: An Indian Tribe of Northern Mexico*. Chicago: University of Chicago Press.

Bernal, Ignacio. 1968. *3,000 Years of Art and Life in Mexico*. Translated by Carolyn B. Czitrom. New York: Harry N. Abrams.

———. 1969. *The Olmec World*. Translated by Doris Heyden and Fernando Horcasitas. Berkeley and Los Angeles: University of California Press.

Bernal, Ignacio, and Fernando Horcasitas, eds. 1965. *Tlalocan* 5, no. 1. Mexico City: Casa de Tlaloc.

Bierhorst, John, ed. 1974. *Four Masterworks of American Indian Literature*. New York: Farrar, Strauss and Giroux.

Blaffer, Sarah C. 1972. *The Black-man of Zinacantan*. Austin: University of Texas Press.

Boas, Franz. 1955. *Primitive Art*. New York: Dover Publications, Inc.

Bonfil Batalla, Guillermo, ed. 1972. *INAH Boletín*, no. 1 (April–June); no. 2 (July–September); no. 3 (October–December). Mexico City: Instituto Nacional de Antropología e Historia.

———. 1975. *INAH Boletín* 14. Epoca II (July–September). Mexico City: Instituto Nacional de Antropología e Historia.

Breuil, Henri, and Raymond Lantier. 1965. *The Men of the Old Stone Age*. Translated by B. B. Rafter. London: George G. Harrap and Co.

Bunker, Emma C., C. Bruce Chatwin, and Ann R. Farkas. 1970. "Animal Style." In *Art from East to West*. New York: Asia Society.

Burgoa, Fray Francisco de. 1934. *Geográfi-*

ca descripción. 2 vols. Mexico City: Talleres Gráficos de la Nación.

Burland, C. A. 1967. *The Gods of Mexico*. London: Eyre and Spottiswoode.

Campos, Ruben M. 1929. *El folklore literario de México*. Mexico City: Talleres Gráficos de la Nación.

Caso, Alfonso. 1958. *The Aztecs: People of the Sun*. Norman: University of Oklahoma Press.

———. 1970. "Xolotl, no jaguar." In *INAH Boletín*, no. 39 (March): 31–33. Mexico City: Instituto Nacional de Antropología e Historia.

Castaneda, Carlos. 1968. *The Teachings of Don Juan: A Yaqui Way of Knowledge*. Berkeley and Los Angeles: University of California Press.

Cervantes de Salazar, Francisco. 1914. *Crónica de la Nueva España*. In *Papeles de Nueva España*, compiled and published by Francisco del Paso y Troncoso, 3d ser., 1. Madrid: Est. Fot. de Hauser y Menet.

———. 1936. *Crónica de la Nueva España*. Papeles de Nueva España, compiled and published by Francisco del Paso y Troncoso, 3d ser., 2, 3. Mexico City: Talleres Gráficos del Museo Nacional de Arqueología, Historia y Etnografía.

Cirlot, J. E. 1962. *A Dictionary of Symbols*. Translated by Jack Sage. London: Routledge and Kegan Paul.

Clavigero, Abbé D. Francisco. 1807. *The History of Mexico: Collected from Spanish and Mexican Historians, Manuscripts and Ancient Paintings of the Indians*. Translated from the original Italian by Charles Cullen. 2d ed. in 2 vols. London: Printed for J. Johnson, St. Paul's Churchyard, by Joyce Gold, Shoe Lane.

Codices:

———. Borbonicus. *See* Paso y Troncoso, Don Francisco del, 1952.

———. Borgia. *See* Seler, Eduard, 1963.

———. Cospi. *See* Kingsborough, Lord, 1967.

———. Fejervary-Mayer. *See* Kingsborough, Lord, 1967.

———. Florentine. *See* Sahagún, Fray Bernardino de, 1950; 1951.

———. Laud. *See* Kingsborough, Lord, 1964.

———. Magliabecchiano. *See* Nuttall, Zelia, ed., 1903.

———. Nuttall. *See* Nuttall, Zelia, ed., 1903; 1974.

———. Telleriano-Remensis. *See* Kingsborough, Lord, 1964.

———. Tro-Cortesianus (Madrid). *See* Anders, F., ed., 1967

———. Vaticano-Ríos. *See* Kingsborough, Lord, 1964.

———. Vindobonensis. *See* Kingsborough, Lord, 1967.

Coe, Michael D. 1965. *The Jaguar's Children: Pre-Classic Central Mexico*. New York: Museum of Primitive Art.

Cordry, Donald B. 1973. *Mexican Masks*. Amon Carter Museum Catalogue. Fort Worth, Texas: Amon Carter Museum.

Cordry, Donald B., and Dorothy M. Cordry. 1940. *Costumes and Textiles of the Aztec Indians of the Cuetzalan Region, Puebla, Mexico*. Southwest Museum Papers 14. Los Angeles: Southwest Museum.

———. 1941. *Costumes and Weavings of the Zoque Indians of Chiapas, Mexico*. Southwest Museum Papers 15. Los Angeles: Southwest Museum.

———. *Mexican Indian Costumes*. Austin: University of Texas Press.

Coss, Julio Antonio, n.d. *Fiestas tradicionales del Istmo de Tehuantepec, Oaxaca*. Mexico City: FONADAN.

Covarrubias, Miguel. 1954. *The Eagle, the Jaguar and the Serpent: Indian Art of the Americas*. New York: Alfred A. Knopf.

———. 1957. *Indian Art of Mexico and Central America*. New York: Alfred A. Knopf.

Cruz, Martín de la. 1964. *Libellus de Medicinalibus Indorum Herbis*. According to the Latin translation by Juan Badiano; Spanish version with commentary by various authors. Mexico City: Instituto Mexicano del Seguro Social.

Dahlgren de Jordán, Barbro. 1954. *La Mix-*

teca: Su cultura e historia prehispánicas. Mexico City: Imprenta Universitaria.

Díaz del Castillo, Bernal. 1939a. *The Discovery and Conquest of Mexico, 1517–1521*. Edited by Genaro García. Translated by Percival Maudslay. London: George Routledge and Sons.

———. 1939b. *Historia verdadera de la Conquista de la Nueva España*, vol. 2. Mexico City: Editorial Pedro Robredo.

Duby, Gertrude. 1961. *Chiapas Indígena*. Mexico City: Universidad Nacional Autónoma de México.

Durán, Fray Diego de. 1964. *The Aztecs: The History of the Indies of New Spain*. Translated by Doris Heyden and Fernando Horcasitas. New York: Orion Press.

———. 1971. *Book of the Gods and Rites and the Ancient Calendar*. Translated by Doris Heyden and Fernando Horcasitas. Norman: University of Oklahoma Press.

Easby, Elizabeth Kennedy, and John F. Scott. 1970. *Before Cortes: Sculpture of Middle America*. Catalogue. New York: Metropolitan Museum of Art.

Eliade, Mircea. 1964. *Shamanism: Archaic Techniques of Ecstasy*. Translated by Willard R. Trask. Bollingen Series, 76. New York: Bollingen Foundation.

Enciso, Jorge. 1945. *Máscaras mexicanas*. Second Exposition of the Sociedad de Arte Moderno, January 1945. Mexico City: Sociedad de Arte Moderno.

Fabila, Alfonso. 1940. *Las tribus yaquis de Sonora*. Primer Congreso Indigenista Interamericano. Mexico City: Departamento de Asuntos Indígenas.

———. 1949. *Sierra norte de Puebla*. Mexico City.

Fennell, T. A., Jr. 1956. *Orchids for Home and Garden*. New York and Toronto: Rinehard and Company.

Firth, Raymond. 1966. "The Social Framework of Primitive Art." In *The Many Faces of Primitive Art*, edited by Douglas Fraser. Englewood Cliffs, N.J.: Prentice-Hall.

FONADAN (Fondo Nacional para el Desarrollo de la Danza Popular Mexicana; dir. Josefina Lavalle). n.d. *Ceremonial de Pascua entre los indígenas mayos.* Mexico City.

Fontana, Bernard L., Edmond J. B. Faubert, and Barney T. Burn. 1977. *The Other Southwest: Indian Arts and Crafts of Northwestern Mexico.* Phoenix, Ariz.: Heard Museum.

Foster, George M. 1960. *Culture and Conquest: America's Spanish Heritage.* Viking Fund Publications in Anthropology, No. 27. New York: Wenner-Gren Foundation for Anthropological Research.

———. 1967. *Tzintzuntzan: Mexican Peasants in a Changing World.* Boston: Little, Brown and Co.

Fraser, Douglas, ed. 1966. *The Many Faces of Primitive Art: A Critical Anthology.* Englewood Cliffs, N.J.: Prentice-Hall.

———. 1968. *Early Chinese Art and the Pacific Basin: A Photographic Exhibition.* New York: Intercultural Arts Press.

Frazer, Sir James George. 1963. *The Golden Bough: A Study in Magic and Religion,* Part 1, vols. 2, 7, 8, 9, Part 6. London and New York: Macmillan Co.

Fromm, Erich. 1951. *The Forgotten Language.* New York: Grove Press.

Furst, Peter T. 1965. *West Mexican Tomb Sculpture as Evidence for Shamanism in Pre-Hispanic Mesoamerica.* Los Angeles: Latin American Center, University of California. December.

———. 1968. "The Olmec Were-Jaguar Motif in the Light of Ethnographic Reality." In *Dumbarton Oaks Conference on the Olmecs,* edited by Elizabeth P. Benson, pp. 143–174. Washington, D.C.: Dumbarton Oaks Library and Collection, Trustees for Harvard University.

———. 1972. *Flesh of the Gods: The Ritual Use of Hallucinogens.* New York: Praeger Publishers.

Gadow, Hans. 1908. *Through Southern Mexico.* London: Witherby and Co.

Gage, Thomas. 1946. *The English-American, a New Survey of the West Indies, 1648.* Edited by A. P. Newton. London: George Routledge and Sons.

Gamboa, Fernando. 1963. *Masterworks of Mexican Art.* Catalogue of Exhibition at Los Angeles County Museum of Art. Copenhagen, Denmark: S. L. Moller's Bogtrykkeri.

García Icazbalceta, Joaquín. 1971. *Colección de documentos para la historia de México,* vol. 2. Biblioteca Porrúa 48. Primera edición facsimilar. Mexico City: Editorial Porrúa.

Gerhard, Peter. 1972. *A Guide to the Historical Geography of New Spain.* Cambridge: Cambridge University Press.

Giedion, S. 1962. *The Eternal Present: The Beginnings of Art,* vol. 1. London: Oxford University Press.

Gil, Alfonso Rodríguez. 1907. *Los indios ocuiltecas actuales.* December 30, 1907. Mexico City.

Gillmor, Frances. 1942. "Spanish Texts of Three Dance Dramas from Mexican Villages." In *University of Arizona Bulletin,* Humanities Bulletin No. 4. Vol. 13 (October 1, 1942). Tucson.

———. 1943. "The Dance Dramas of Mexican Villages." In *University of Arizona Bulletin,* Humanities Bulletin no. 5. Vol. 14, no. 2 (April 1, 1943). Tucson.

Gómara, Francisco López de. 1943. *Historia de la Conquista de México,* vol. 1. Mexico City: Editorial Pedro Robredo.

———. 1965–1966. *Historia general de las Indias.* 2 vols. Barcelona: Editorial Iberia.

Grant, Michael. 1962. *Myths of the Greeks and Romans.* New York: New American Library.

Griffith, James S. 1967. *Legacy of Conquest: The Arts of Northwest Mexico.* Colorado: Taylor Museum of the Colorado Springs Fine Arts Center.

Guerra, Francisco. 1971. *The Pre-Columbian Mind.* New York: Seminar Press.

Guiteras-Holmes, C. 1961. *Perils of the Soul: The World View of a Tzotzil Indian.* New York: Free Press of Glencoe.

Harley, George W. 1950. *Masks as Agents of Social Control in Northeast Liberia.* Papers of the Peabody Museum of American Archaeology and Ethnology, Harvard University, vol. 32, no. 2. Cambridge, Mass.

Harner, Michael J., ed. 1973. *Hallucinogens and Shamanism.* New York: Oxford University Press.

Harvey, H. R., and Isabel Kelly. 1965. "The Totonacs." In *Handbook of Middle American Indians,* edited by Robert Wauchope, vol. 8, *Ethnology, Part Two,* edited by Evon Z. Vogt, pp. 638–681. Austin: University of Texas Press.

Hegner, Robert W. 1947. *College Zoology.* New York: Macmillan Company.

Hendrichs Pérez, Pedro R. 1945. *Por tierras ignotas: Viajes y observaciones en la región del Río de las Balsas,* vol. 1. Mexico City: Editorial Cultura.

Hernández, Francisco. 1959, 1960, 1966. *Obras completas,* vol. 1 (1959); vol. 2 (1960); vol. 3 (1960); vol 4 (1966). Mexico City: Universidad Nacional Autónoma de México.

Hessink, Karen, and Albert Hahn. 1961. *Die Tacana.* Stuttgart: W. Kahlhammer Verlag.

Heyden, Doris. 1976. "Caves, Gods and Myths: World View on Planning in Teotihuacán." Paper presented at symposium on "Meso-American Sites and World Views." Dumbarton Oaks, Center for Pre-Columbian Studies, Washington, D.C., October 1976. To be published.

Himmelheber, Hans. 1963. "Personality and Technique of African Sculpture." In *Technique and Personality.* New York: Museum of Primitive Art.

Horcasitas, Fernando. 1971. "El noble tigre sigue muriendo." In *Lo efímero y eterno del arte popular mexicano,* vol. 2. Mexico City: Fondo Editorial de la Plástica Mexicana.

———. 1974. *El teatro náhuatl: Epocas novohispana y moderna.* Mexico City: Universidad Nacional Autónoma de México.

Ichon, Alain. 1973. *La religión de los totonacas de la Sierra.* Mexico City: Instituto Nacional Indigenista, Secretaría de Educación Pública.

Jenkins, Katharine D. 1962, 1964. *Aje or Ni-in (The Fat of a Scale Insect) Painting Medium and Unguent.* Mexico City: XXXV Congreso Internacional de Americanistas.

Jung, C. G. 1953. *Psychology and Alchemy.* Vol. 12 of *The Collected Works of C. G. Jung,* translated by R. F. C. Hull. Bollingen Series, 20. New York: Pantheon Books.

———. 1956. "The Relations between the Ego and the Unconscious." In *Two Essays on Analytical Psychology,* translated by R. F. C. Hull, p. 160. New York: Meridian Books.

———. 1970a. *Symbols of Transformation.* Vol. 5 of *The Collected Works of C. G. Jung,* translated by R. F. C. Hull, 2d ed. 2d printing. Bollingen Series, 20. Princeton, N.J.: Princeton University Press.

———. 1970b. *Alchemical Studies.* Vol. 13 of *The Collected Works of C. G. Jung,* translated by R. F. C. Hull, 2d ed., 2d printing. Princeton, N.J.: Princeton University Press.

Kelly, Isabel T. 1939. *Southern Paiute Shamanism.* Anthropological Records, vol. 2, no. 4. Berkeley: University of California Press.

———. 1953. "The Modern Totonac." In *Huastecos, totonacas y sus vecinos. Revista Mexicana de Estudios Antropológicos* 13, nos. 2 and 3. Bernal y Hurtado. Mexico City: Sociedad Mexicana de Antropología.

Kelly, Isabel T., and Angel Palerm. 1952. *The Tajin Totonac,* Part 1. Smithsonian Institution, Institute of Social Anthropology, Publication 13. Washington D.C.: Government Printing Office.

Kingsborough, Lord. 1964, 1967. *Antigüedades de México,* vol. 1 (1964); vol. 3 (1964); vol. 4 (1967). Mexico City: Secretaría de Hacienda y Crédito Público.

Knab, Timothy. 1976. "Talocan Talmanic: Supernatural Beings of the Sierra de Puebla." Unpublished paper.

Kubler, George. 1962. *The Art and Archaeology of Ancient America.* Baltimore: Penguin.

Lantis, Margaret. 1947. *Alaskan Eskimo Ceremonialism.* Seattle and London: University of Washington Press.

Leonard, Carmen Cook de. 1965. *El México Antiguo,* vol. 10. Mexico City: Sociedad Alemana Mexicanista.

Leonard, Donald. 1955. "General Information about Anthropological Exploration of the Lacandon Jungle: Ethnology." Preliminary report. Mexico City: Centro de Investigaciones Antropológicas. Mimeographed.

Leonard, Irving A. 1959. *Baroque Times in Old Mexico.* Ann Arbor: University of Michigan Press.

León-Portilla, Miguel. 1958. *Ritos, sacerdotes y atavíos de los dioses.* Mexico City: Universidad Autónoma de México.

———. 1963. *Aztec Thought and Culture.* Translated by Jack Emory Davis. Norman: University of Oklahoma Press.

León-Portilla, Miguel, and Salvador Mateos Higuera. 1957. *Catálogo de los códices indígenas del México antiguo.* Supplement to the *Boletín Bibliográfico de la Secretaría de Hacienda.* Año 3, no. 111 (June). Mexico City: Talleres de Impresión de Estampillas y Valores.

Leopold, A. Starker. 1972. *Wildlife of Mexico: The Game Birds and Mammals.* Berkeley, Los Angeles, and London: University of California Press.

Lévi-Strauss, Claude. 1967. *Structural Anthropology.* Garden City, New York: Anchor Books, Doubleday and Co.

———. 1969. *The Raw and the Cooked.* Translated by John and Doreen Weightman. New York and Evanston: Harper and Row, Publishers.

Lhote, Henri. 1959. *The Search for the Tassili Frescoes.* New York: E. P. Dutton and Co.

Lommel, Andreas. 19__. *Prehistoric and Primitive Man.* London: Paul Hamlyn.

———. 1967. *Shamanism: The Beginnings of Art.* New York: McGraw-Hill Book Company.

———. 1972. *Masks: Their Meaning and Function.* Translated by Nadia Fowler. New York and Toronto: McGraw-Hill Book Company.

Lumholtz, Carl. 1902. *Unknown Mexico.* 2 vols. New York: Charles Scribner's Sons.

———. 1912. *New Trails in Mexico.* New York: Charles Scribner's Sons.

Mace, Carroll Edward. 1970. *Two Spanish-Quiché Dance-Dramas.* Tulane Studies in Romance Languages and Literature, no. 3. New Orleans: Tulane University.

McGee, W. J. 1898. *The Seri Indians.* Part 1 of the *Seventeenth Annual Report of the Bureau of American Ethnology to the Secretary of the Smithsonian Institution, 1895–1896.* Washington, D.C.: Government Printing Office.

Macgowan, Kenneth, and Herman Rosse. 1923. *Masks and Demons.* New York: Harcourt, Brace and Co.

Maringer, Johannes, and Hans-Georg Bandi. 1953. *Art in the Ice Age.* Translated by Robert Allen. London: George Allen and Unwin.

Martínez, Maximino. 1937. *Catálogo de nombres vulgares y científicos de plantas mexicanas.* Mexico City: Ediciones Botas.

———. 1959a. *Les plantas medicinales de México.* Mexico City: Andrés Botas.

———. 1959b. *Las plantas útiles de la flora mexicana.* Mexico City: Andrés Botas.

———. 1974. *Pegamentos, gomas y resinas en el México prehispánico.* Mexico City: SepSetentas.

Medina, Jesús, ed. 1970. *México: Leyendas—Costumbres, Trajes y Danzas.* Mexico City: Medina Hermanos.

Mendieta, Fray Gerónimo de. 1945. *Historia eclesiástica indiana,* vol. 1, Chapter 40. Mexico City: Editorial Salvador Chávez Hayhoe.

Mendieta y Núñez, Lucio. 1940. *Los tarascos.* Mexico City: Imprenta Universitaria.

Mentero, Sergio Arturo. 1967. "Restauración de las máscaras de turquesa de Coixtlahuaca y Zaachila, Oaxaca." In *INAH 29 Boletín* (September). Mexico City: Instituto Nacional de Antropología e Historia.

Miller, Roseann. 1966. "The Mask-Makers of Tocuaro." In *American Society of Mexico Bulletin* (January). Mexico City: Imprenta Moderna Pintel.

Moar Prudente, Alfonso. 1964. *Danza de los "Tejorones."* Oaxaca de Juárez: Universidad Benito Juárez de Oaxaca.

Molina, Fray Alonso de. 1944. *Vocabulario en lengua castellana y mexicana.* Colección de Incunables Americanos, vol. 4. Madrid: Ediciones Cultura Hispánica.

Morley, Sylvanus G. 1956. *The Ancient Maya.* Stanford: Stanford University Press.

Motolinía, Fray Toribio de. 1950. *History of the Indians of New Spain.* Translated and edited by Elizabeth Andros Foster. Berkeley: Cortés Society.

Moya Rubio, Victor José. 1974. *Máscaras mexicanas: Exposition of the Museo Nacional de Antropología.* Mexico City: Imprenta Madero.

Muensterberger, Warner. 1971. "Roots of Primitive Art." In *Anthropology and Art: Readings in Cross-Cultural Aesthetics,* edited by Charlotte M. Otten, pp. 106–128. American Museum Sourcebooks in Anthropology, published for the American Museum of Natural History. Garden City, N.Y.: Natural History Press.

Naranjo, Claudio. 1973. "Psychological Aspects of the Yagé Experience in an Experimental Setting." In *Hallucinogens and Shamanism,* edited by Michael J. Harner. New York: Oxford University Press.

Navarrete, Carlos. 1971. "Prohibición de la Danza del Tigre en Tamulte, Tabasco, en 1631." *Tlalocan* 6, no. 4: 374–376. Mexico City: Casa de Tlaloc.

Neumann, Erich. 1955. *The Great Mother.* London: Routledge and Kegan Paul.

Nicholson, Henry B. 1971. "Religion in Pre-Hispanic Central Mexico." In *Handbook of Middle American Indians,* edited by Robert Wauchope, vol. 10, *Archaeology of Northern Mesoamerica, Part 1,* edited by Gordon F. Ekholm and Ignacio Bernal, pp. 395–446. Austin: University of Texas Press.

Novick, Alvin, and Nina Leen. 1969. *The World of Bats.* Switzerland: Holt, Rinehart and Winston.

Nuttall, Zelia, ed. 1903. *The Book of the Life of the Ancient Mexicans.* Part 1, Introduction and Facsimile. Berkeley: University of California.

———. 1974. *Códice Nuttall.* Reproduction of the facsimile edited by the Peabody Museum of the University of Harvard. Mexico City: Imprenta Madero.

Olivera B., Mercedes. 1974. "Las danzas y fiestas de Chiapas." In *Catálogo nacional de danzas,* vol. 1. Mexico City: FONADAN.

Osborne, Lilly de Jong. 1935. *Indian Crafts of Guatemala.* Norman: University of Oklahoma Press.

Paddock, John, ed. 1966. *Ancient Oaxaca: Discoveries in Mexican Archaeology and History.* Stanford: Stanford University Press.

Park, Willard Z. 1975. *Shamanism in Western North America: A Study in Cultural Relationships.* New York: Cooper Square Publishers.

Parsons, Elsie Clews. 1936. *Mitla: Town of the Souls.* Chicago and London: University of Chicago Press.

Paso y Troncoso, Don Francisco del. 1952. *Tratado de las idolatrías, supersticiones, dioses, ritos, hechicerías y otras costumbres gentílicas de las razas aborígenes de México,* vols. 1 and 2. Mexico City: Ediciones Fuente Cultural.

Paul, Anne C. 1976. "History on a Maya Vase?" *Archaeology* 29, no. 2 (April): 121–126.

Paz, Octavio. 1970. *Posdata.* Mexico City: Siglo XXI.

Peterson, Frederick A. 1961. *Ancient Mexico: An Introduction to the Pre-Hispanic Cultures.* New York: G. P. Putnam's Sons.

Powell, T. G. E. 1966. *Prehistoric Art.* New York and Washington: Frederick A. Praeger, Publishers.

Ray, Dorothy Jean. 1967. *Eskimo Masks: Art and Ceremony.* Seattle and London: University of Washington Press.

Rea, Vargas, ed. 1953. *Datos para la historia de la farmacia pre-Cortesiana.* Mexico City: Vargas Rea Editor.

Recinos, Adrián, trans. 1950. *Popol Vuh: The Sacred Book of the Ancient Quiché Maya.* English version by Delia Goetz and Sylvanus G. Morley. Civilization of the American Indian Series, vol. 29. Norman: University of Oklahoma Press.

Redfield, Robert. 1930. *Tepoztlán: A Mexican Village.* Chicago: University of Chicago Press.

Redfield, Robert, Melville J. Herskovits, and Gordon F. Ekholm. 1959. *Aspects of Primitive Art.* New York: Museum of Primitive Art.

Reichel-Dolmatoff, Gerardo. 1971. *Amazonian Cosmos: The Sexual and Religious Symbolism of the Tukano Indians.* Chicago and London: University of Chicago Press.

Reko, Blas Pablo. 1945. *Mitobotánica zapoteca.* Tacubaya, D.F.

Robelo, Cecilio A. 1904. *Diccionario de aztequismos.* Cuernavaca: published by author.

———. 1911. *Diccionario de mitología náhuatl.* Mexico City: Museo Nacional de Arqueología y Etnología.

———. 1951. *Diccionario de mitología náhuatl.* Mexico City: Ediciones Fuente Cultural.

Roediger, Virginia More. 1961. *Ceremonial Costumes of the Pueblo Indians.* Berkeley and Los Angeles: University of California Press.

Romero de Terreros y Vinent, Manuel. 1923. *Les artes industriales en la Nueva España.* Barcelona: J. Horta, printer.

Rothenberg, Jerome, ed. 1972. *Shaking the Pumpkin: Traditional Poetry of the Indian North Americas.* New York: Doubleday and Company.

Roys, Ralph L. 1965. *Ritual of the Bacabs.* Norman: University of Oklahoma Press.

———. 1967. *The Book of Chilam Balam of Chumayel.* Norman: University of Oklahoma Press.

Runes, Dagobert D., and Harry G. Schrickel, eds. 1946. *Encyclopedia of the Arts.* New York: Philosophical Library.

Sahagún, Fray Bernardino de. 1950, 1951, 1953. *General History of the Things of New Spain,* Book 1, Part 2 (1950); Book 2, Part 3 (1951); Book 7 (1953). Translated by Arthur J. Anderson and Charles E. Dibble. Santa Fe: School of American Research and University of Utah.

Salvat, Juan, director. 1974. *Historia de México,* vol. 1, fascicles 4, 6, 7, 9, and 13. Mexico City: Salvat Editores de México.

Santamaría, Francisco J. 1942. *Diccionario general de americanismos.* 3 vols. Mexico City: Editorial Pedro Robredo.

———. 1959. *Diccionario de mejicanismos.* Mexico City: Editorial Porrua.

Séjourné, Laurette. 1956. *Burning Water: Thought and Religion in Ancient Mexico.* London and New York: Thames and Hudson.

———. 1962. *El universo de Quetzalcóatl.* Mexico City: Fondo de Cultura Económica.

Seler, Eduard. 1963. *Comentarios al Códice Borgia.* 2 vols. and facsimile. Translated by Mariana Frenk. Mexico City: Fondo de Cultura Económica.

———. n.d. *Collected Works of Eduard Seler,* 4 vols. Anonymous translation. Mimeographed.

Smith, Mary Elizabeth. 1973. *Picture Writing from Ancient Southern Mexico.* Norman: University of Oklahoma Press.

Sorell, Walter. 1973. *The Other Face: The Mask in the Arts.* New York: Bobbs-Merrill Co.

Soustelle, Jacques. 1959. *Pensamiento cosmológico de las antiguos mexicanos.* Puebla: Talleres de Linotipografía Económica.

———. 1961. *Daily Life of the Aztecs.* Translated by Patrick O'Brian. London: George Weidenfeld and Nicolson.

Spence, Lewis. 1923. *The Gods of Mexico.* New York: Frederick A. Stokes Co.

———. n.d. *The Magic and Mysteries of Mexico.* London: Rider and Co.

Spencer, H. 1873–1910. *Descriptive Sociology.* London.

Spranz, Bodo. 1973. *Los dioses en los códices mexicanos del grupo Borgia.* Mexico City: Fondo de Cultura Económica.

Standley, Paul C. 1926. *Trees and Shrubs of Mexico.* Contributions from the United States Herbarium, vol. 23. Washington, D.C.: Smithsonian Institution.

Starr, Frederick. 1901. "Notes upon the Ethnography of Southern Mexico." In *Proceedings of the Davenport Academy of Natural Sciences,* vol. 8. Davenport, Iowa: Putnam Memorial Fund.

———. 1902. *The Physical Characteristics of the Indians of Southern Mexico.* Decennial Publications, University of Chicago.

———. 1908. *In Indian Mexico.* Chicago: Forbes and Company.

Steward, Julian H., ed. 1963. *Handbook of South American Indians.* 7 vols.

New York: Cooper Square Publishers.

Tapia, Andrés de. 1971. "Relación hecha por el señor Andrés de Tápia, sobre la conquista de Mexico." In García Icazbalceta 1971, 2: 554–594.

Thomas, Cyrus. 1882. *A Study of the Manuscript Troano.* Washington, D.C.: Government Printing Office.

Thompson, J. Eric S. 1933. *Mexico before Cortéz.* New York: Charles Scribner's Sons.

———. 1954. *The Rise and Fall of Maya Civilization.* Norman: University of Oklahoma Press.

———. 1962. *A Catalog of Maya Hieroglyphs.* Norman: University of Oklahoma Press.

———. 1970. *Maya History and Religion.* Norman: University of Oklahoma Press.

Tibon, Carletto. n.d. Unpublished Cora notes.

Toor, Frances, ed. 1925–1937. *Mexican Folkways,* vols. 1–9. Mexico City.

———. 1947. *A Treasury of Mexican Folkways.* New York: Crown Publishers.

Torquemada, Fray Juan de. 1943. *Grijalva Expedition: Mouth of Río Grijalva,* vol. 1. From the files of Isabel Kelly.

———. 1969. *Monarquía indiana.* 2 vols. Mexico City: Editorial Porrua.

Tozzer, Alfred M. 1907. *A Comparative Study of the Mayas and the Lacandones.* New York: Macmillan Company.

Tozzer, Alfred M., and Glover M. Allen. 1910. *Animal Figures in the Maya Codices.* Cambridge, Mass.: Peabody Museum of American Archaeology and Ethnology. Harvard University.

Trowell, Margaret, and Hans Nevermann. n.d. *African and Oceanic Art.* New York: Harry N. Abrams.

Turner, Victor. 1967. *The Forest of Symbols: Aspects of Ndembu Ritual.* Ithaca, N.Y., and London: Cornell University Press.

Vaillant, George C. 1935. *Artists and Craftsmen in Ancient Central Amer-*

ica. Guide Leaflet Series, no. 88. New York: American Museum of Natural History.

———. 1941. *Aztecs of Mexico.* Garden City, N.Y.: Doubleday, Doran and Co.

Vogt, Evon Z. 1976. *Tortillas for the Gods.* Cambridge, Mass.: Harvard University Press.

Warman Gryj, Arturo. 1972. *La Danza de Moros y Cristianos.* Mexico City: Secretaría de Educación Pública.

Warman Gryj, Arturo, and Irene Warman. 1971. "Danzas." In "Notas Generales." In *Lo efímero y eterno del arte popular mexicano,* 2: 742–755. Mexico City: Fondo Editorial de la Plástica Mexicana.

Wauchope, Robert, gen. ed. 1967, 1969. *Handbook of Middle American Indians,* vol. 6, *Social Anthropology,* edited by Manning Nash (1967); vol. 7, *Ethnology, Part One,* edited by Evon Z. Vogt (1969). Austin: University of Texas Press.

Weaver, Muriel Porter. 1972. *The Aztecs, Maya, and Their Predecessors.* New York and London: Seminar Press.

Weitlaner, Ing. Roberto J. 1941. "Chilacachapa y Tetelcingo." In *El México Antiguo* 5, nos. 7–10 (June). Mexico City: Sociedad Alemana Mexicanista.

Weitlaner, Ing. Roberto J., and Irmgard Weitlaner de Johnson. 1943. "Acatlán y Hueycantenango, Guerrero." In *El México Antiguo* 6, nos. 4–6 (February): 140–202. Mexico City: El México Antiguo.

Westheim, Paul. 1965. *The Art of Ancient Mexico.* Garden City, N.Y.: Doubleday and Company.

Whiteford, Andrew Hunter. 1972. "Enriching Daily Life: The Artist and Artisan." In *American Indian Art: Form and Tradition.* Minneapolis: Walker Art Center and the Minneapolis Institute of Art.

Williams García, Roberto. 1960. *Los Tepehuas.* Xalapa: Universidad Veracruzana.

———. n.d. *Fiestas de la Santa Cruz en Zitlala.* Mexico City: FONADAN.

Wingert, Paul S. 1962. *Primitive Art: Its Traditions and Styles.* New York: Oxford University Press.

Winick, Charles. 1956. *Dictionary of Anthropology.* New York: Philosophical Library.

Zehnder, Wiltraud, coordinator. 1973. *La dualidad en el mundo prehispánico. Artes de México,* no. 173, Año 20. Mexico City: Lito Ediciones Olimpia.

Zingg, Robert Mowry. 1938. *The Huichols: Primitive Artists.* Report of the Mr. and Mrs. Henry Pfeiffer Expedition for Huichol Ethnography. Printed in Germany.

INDEX

Boldface numbers refer to figures or their captions.

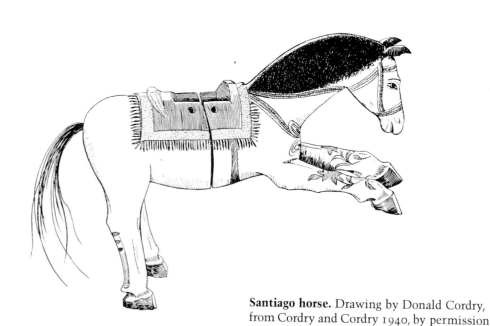

Santiago horse. Drawing by Donald Cordry, from Cordry and Cordry 1940, by permission of the Southwest Museum, Los Angeles.